MOTIVATIC
IN THE WORKPLACE

Learners are always motivated; they just may not be motivated to learn the things you are wanting them to learn. Motivational Immediacy refers to the moment-by-moment motivation of learners during a learning event. This is in contrast to typical global views of motivation, and while casting a much heavier burden on the instructor, brings with it more deep, meaningful, and permanent learning.

Motivational Immediacy in the Workplace focuses not only on fostering learner engagement with a primary emphasis on the role of the instructor, but also addresses the work and concerns of curriculum writers and training directors. The author defines Motivational Immediacy as both a phenomenon and a practice and provides concrete steps for practical action. Motivational Immediacy, as a construct, refers to a moment-by-moment feeling of motivation on the part of the learner to engage in the learning opportunity directly at hand. As a practice, it is the instructor's process of working to stay connected with individual learners and foster engagement consistently at every moment of the teaching activity. The author addresses this idea from a learner-centered orientation, making the case that understanding and empathizing with the learner's perceptions is the most effective way to promote efficient, meaningful learning.

The book will provide a comprehensive conceptualization of learning engagement and learning resistance. It begins with a substantial theoretical framework and then shifts to direct applications to practice in the workplace. Motivational Immediacy is multidisciplinary and draws from fields such as Adult Education, Workplace and Training Development, Psychology, Educational Psychology, Sociology, Cultural Anthropology, and Communications.

Jonathan E. Taylor is an Associate Professor at Auburn University (USA). He holds a Ph.D. in Educational Psychology and Research from the University of Tennessee. Prior to his academic career, he spent over a decade as a training coordinator and an instructor in workplace contexts. His areas of interest and scholarship are applied philosophy, conceptual change, and learning resistance and engagement in workplace contexts.

MOTIVATIONAL IMMEDIACY IN THE WORKPLACE

FACILITATING LEARNER ENGAGEMENT IN TRAINING ENVIRONMENTS

Jonathan E. Taylor

Routledge
Taylor & Francis Group

NEW YORK AND LONDON

Cover image: © Ekely / Getty Images

First published 2022
by Routledge
605 Third Avenue, New York, NY 10158

and by Routledge
4 Park Square, Milton Park, Abingdon, Oxon, OX14 4RN

Routledge is an imprint of the Taylor & Francis Group, an informa business

© 2022 Jonathan E. Taylor

Library of Congress Cataloging-in-Publication Data
Names: Taylor, Jonathan E., 1972- author.
Title: Motivational immediacy in the workplace : facilitating learner engagement in training environments / Jonathan E. Taylor.
Description: 1 Edition. | New York, NY : Routledge, 2022. |
Includes bibliographical references and index.
Identifiers: LCCN 2021053016 (print) | LCCN 2021053017 (ebook) |
ISBN 9780367699864 (hardback) | ISBN 9780367699857 (paperback) |
ISBN 9781003144137 (ebook)
Subjects: LCSH: Organizational learning. | Employees–Training of. |
Employee motivation. | Educational psychology. |
Teaching–Aids and devices.
Classification: LCC HD58.82 .T395 2022 (print) | LCC HD58.82 (ebook) |
DDC 658.3/124–dc23/eng/20211220
LC record available at https://lccn.loc.gov/2021053016
LC ebook record available at https://lccn.loc.gov/2021053017

ISBN: 978-0-367-69986-4 (hbk)
ISBN: 978-0-367-69985-7 (pbk)
ISBN: 978-1-003-14413-7 (ebk)

DOI: 10.4324/9781003144137

Typeset in ITC New Baskerville Std
by KnowledgeWorks Global Ltd.

Contents

**Section I: Motivational Immediacy: Changing
the Way We Think**   1

1 Something or Someone   3

2 Learning Engagement and Learning Resistance   16

3 Motivational Immediacy   35

4 From Learning Resistance to Efficient and Effectual Learning   53

5 Zones of Engagement   63

6 Training Through Conceptual Change Frameworks   80

**Section II: Motivational Immediacy: Changing
the Way We Practice**   **99**

7 Instructional Methods and Lesson Plans   101

8 Motivational Immediacy in the Classroom   120

9 Curriculum and Instructional Systems Design   137

10 Measuring Effectual Learning   158

11 Motivational Immediacy, Ethical Dilemmas,
and Facilitator as Mediator   171

12 Learning as Connection   183

References   194
Index   209

MOTIVATIONAL IMMEDIACY: CHANGING THE WAY WE THINK

Chapter 1

Something or Someone

In every field of practice, there are certain basic truths that can be ignored without consequence, and others that cannot. Most of what follows in this book rests squarely upon a single premise of the latter sort. Although it does not get chief billing in title or chapter, the foundation of much of what I will share in the following pages rests on this premise: knowing something is about knowing and understanding *something*. Teaching something is about knowing and understanding *people*. That is, knowing how to do something is about the *something* while training someone how to do something is about the *someone*. However, trite the statement might sound, and, however, narrow the distinction might be, there is no compromising this basic reality, and the failure to fully grasp it in an authentic way will create an almost perpetual series of near misses when it comes to obtaining peak efficiency and return on investment (ROI) in workplace training programs.

This is the first of a number of significant premises that serve as the foundation for motivational immediacy, both as a concept and as a practice. As you read this book, you will see that motivational immediacy is not merely about some new ways by which to motivate learners, but about some new ways to think about motivation in the first place. The conceptual frameworks that are introduced and the related practical methods that are discussed are all predicated on the following five premises.

THE PREMISES OF THIS BOOK

Over the years, a great many books have been written on the subject of workplace training and development (e.g., Brown, 2018; Holly & Rainbird, 2000; Mitchell, 1988; Ward, 1998). The titles, structure, and content of the

DOI: 10.4324/9781003144137-2

books are like the rings of a tree in some ways, marking out the eras in which they were written. Many, if not most, cover all aspects of the training world, and by doing so they tend to either be very long, or to cover broadly at the expense of deeply. It should be clear at the outset that this book is focused deeply at the expense of broadly. It is a book about training and developing people, not about all of the many important aspects of the human resource enterprise, or even about business at large. It is, however, written with an awareness of the constraints of the business world in which the training and development take place. There is a bit of idealism in the following pages, but also the realistic acknowledgement of the limitations and boundaries that influence just how well we, as trainers, are able to do our jobs.

Training is About Knowing People

In a book on high-risk training, Ward (1988) began by claiming that "you need to know only three things to develop and manage training programs…" and those three things were:

- How to develop curriculum, staff, procedures, and records;
- How to utilize curriculum, staff, procedures, and records; and
- How to evaluate curriculum, staff, procedures, and records (p. xx).

A full reading of Ward's work would reveal that he did express an understanding of the need to be aware of the learner overall, but his point of departure, not at all unusual for workplace training books, is the reason that I have started right at the outset in my own training book by sharing the first of five premises that the concepts in this book are based upon. In fact, of the five, it is this first premise that serves as the foundation for the other four.

Ward's work started by pointing out the importance of knowing about stuff; I wish to start by pointing out the importance of knowing about people. It is true, of course, that one must know both stuff and people, and my reference to Ward's opening is not an indictment of his work, but a contextual reason for my own. Ten years later, Mitchell (1998) started with the considerations of the learner as his stepping-off point, going so far as to discuss the reasons that learners may not actually want to learn and some proposed methods for working with learners to change this situation. More will be said about this later on, but for now, it will suffice to say that this book, like Mitchell's, also starts with the learner as the focus. Knowing something is about knowing and understanding *something*. Teaching something is about knowing and understanding *people*.

learner during a learning event, then it is moment-by-moment motivation we must foster. The act of doing so – motivational immediacy – is a difficult task, but a necessary part of any truly effective teaching.

Just because adults are "motivated" to get a degree, earn a certificate, or even learn something from a specific course, does not mean that they are motivated in any given instant to learn a particular thing, at that particular moment, on a particular night, etc. Therefore, the instructor/trainer must work to make every moment an engaging moment and simply cannot "clump" the learner's motivation around more global concepts such as "I want to have a degree," or "I want to be an officer in the USAF," or "I want to be able to apply for that new position."

We are Training the Wrong Sort of Thing

Going back a moment, to the three groups of learners, it is important to point out that thinking in terms of these three groups of learners may be helpful but also creates its own problem, as do nearly all attempts to snap things into rigid taxonomies. All approaches to both thought and action rely upon assumptions – it is impossible to progress in either thought or action without first setting parameters by way of assumptions. In this case, the three-types-of-learners framework carries with it the assumption that when we consider whether or not someone learns or learns well, we are assuming that they are learning what we intended them to learn; the word learning is meant to mean learning the right thing. However, there is little cause to consider this a valid assumption. In fact, literature points out that learners quite often learn something different than what the teacher or instructor intended (Illeris, 2017). Jarvis (1992) referred to this as mislearning, This, however, leads to another pressing issue to work out prior to digging into the following pages.

There are books about teaching and training, and there are books about learning. Most are about some mixture of both, knowing that teaching expertise should involve an expertise of human learning. It can become difficult at times, to remain clear when reading, about which one is being discussed. They are related but distinct. How someone learns has a direct bearing on how one might effectively teach them, but when thinking about a given learning dynamic, it is easy to get confused.

There is a different message for the reader who is reading as a student and the reader who is reading as a trainer. If this book is a training book, intended to help us be better trainers, then it would seem odd to be using terms like "mislearning" when it is probably a more accurate statement to use the word "misteaching" instead.

This is another major premise that I will write about – *we are not simply teaching less sufficiently than we might, we are very often teaching the wrong sort of thing altogether.* Training must require efforts to foster not just the acquisition of content, but also the *acceptance* of content. The combination of these two, referred to as *effectual learning* in this book, result in a different sort of learning than that which is most often discussed and fostered.

Training Beliefs Should Drive Measurement Practices

These four premises are connected to the fifth, and it is likely that it is chronic confusion about this fifth premise that has led to the prevalent confusion so often seen in the other four. *Measurement beliefs should not drive teaching practices; teaching beliefs should drive measurement practices.* The fundamental problem here is that the rules that one sets up for measuring training outcomes go far beyond measuring the outcome – they shape the very notion of training from the ground up (Taylor, 2020). Rather than serving to measure our educational success, they drive our educational practice. Using even the best tools outside the parameters for which they were designed is most always bad for both the tool and the hardware.

Learners Who Argue the Most May Be the Most Engaged

Learners who argue the most with you in class may be the learners who are the most engaged, rather than the least engaged. While persistent, inappropriate, and disruptive arguing can certainly be an indicator of learning resistance, persistent argument from an employee learner may often be a sign of true engagement rather than resistance. Resistance is a failure to engage (not a failure to accept, per se), and a well-reasoned argument over content is typically a sign of active engagement with the learning experience. This distinction and how to parse it from resistance and use it for the benefit of the teacher and learner is a vital skill for the practitioner.

If You Don't Think It is Important, the Learner Won't Either

If you are not truly interested in the class/content you are teaching and don't think it is authentically important for your students, they will not think it as interesting and important either. In talking to teachers and trainers throughout the years, it is very often the case that the teacher is stuck teaching a class that even he or she sees as a "waste of time" or "not that important." In these cases, the teacher who wishes to be highly effective absolutely must first find a way to find value in what is being taught him or herself. Failure to do this will, at best, result in an inefficient motivational context and at worst be evident to the learner. The very best way to motivate students is to be authentically motivated as a teacher first, and then work with learners to find the common ground.

An Instructor Only Ever Teaches Individuals, Never Groups

An instructor/trainer never teaches groups. An instructor/trainer only and always teaches individual learners who may sometimes be clustered together in groups. Concepts of group and organizational learning will not be contradicted in a theoretical sense in the book, but in a practical sense, practitioners will be challenged to understand that "speaking to the middle" or "teaching to the center" is not an effective tool for those who wish to rise over and above average and be highly meaningful teachers. Mitchell (1998) stresses the importance of working with the individual learners when training complex matters despite the effort it requires. He writes, "it is the most time-consuming and, therefore, the most inefficient. It is, however, the most effective way to learn, which is why so much training in American takes place on the job" (p. 17). Illeris (2011) also has pointed out that Argyris and Schon (1996, p. 16), while writing so heavily about learning at the organizational level, still maintained that learning takes place on an individual level, even with a more global context.

Paying Attention to Learner Resistance Is a Learner-Centered Approach

Understanding and paying attention to learning resistance is a very learner-centered approach to teaching. Understanding and analyzing the learning resistance dynamics at play in any given educational experience is one of the more learner-focused approaches to teaching. An approach to teaching that takes learning resistance into account is a learner-centered approach that: (a) meets the learner where they are, (b) empathizes with the learner, (c) collaborates with the learner to address the learner's conceptions, perceptions, and positionality, and (d) takes the learning journey with the learner.

Effective Instructors and Trainers Must Take an Interdisciplinary Approach

In order to understand adult learners fully and to bring the most comprehensive theory-base to bear on fostering learning engagement, practitioners must expose themselves to an interdisciplinary, cross-theoretical body of literature and research. Adult Education, as a field, has often been self-limiting in theoretical scope, particularly with respect to the motivational theory and science of mainstream educational psychology. Fields of study more tightly and directly aligned with workplace learning have done much the same by focusing on training-related research to a much greater extent than general learning research. All practitioners who deal with learners of any age absolutely must be "well-read" and "wide-read," and this book will provide the framework for that necessary exposure. More is said about this below in the discussion about the employee learner.

Learners Resist in a Few Simple Ways but for Many Reasons

Learners resist for many different reasons but the behavior manifests itself in many of the same ways despite being the outworking of different causes. Because resistance behaviors and cognitions are often manifested the same ways despite having different precipitating causes, practitioners must work to understand the complicated reasons why students may be resisting so that they do not apply a "one size fits all" remedy.

EMPLOYEE, TRAINEE, LEARNER

The words we use matter. When writing about workplace training in books and articles, learners are most often referred to as employees, workers, staff (Craig, 1996; Odiorne & Rummler, 1988; Quinones & Ehrenstein, 1997), and trainees (Brown, 2018; Mitchell, 1998; Ward, 1988). Interestingly, it is quite difficult to find the learner referred to directly at all in some cases. The word *learner* is not often used (Brown, 2018, although an edited book, is one of a few examples where it is regularly used).

There is nothing inaccurate or inherently wrong about using such terms as employee or trainee, but the terms do carry nuanced meaning with them and can set up conceptual lenses that cause us to view things in confining ways. When we refer to the learners as employees, or personnel, we are referring to the domain in which they are learning, and this can lead to an assumption that this special sort of learners are not bound by all of the natural processes that are experienced by all learners everywhere. Additionally, it can lead to a focus that is misplaced on the context surrounding the learner, rather than the learner surrounded by the context.

In this book, I will likely use all of these terms, but most often I will refer to those who are in workplace training classes as *learners*. And, because they are learners, the theory and learning science woven together in the following pages is drawn from all disciplines and contexts, so long as the information obtained is about human learners and can be used to help improve workplace learning for both the trainer and the learner. Training transfer is, despite all of the many mediating factors, a human phenomenon and there is a "critical assumption" based on cognitive research on transfer, that learning cannot be separated from the psychological processes of the learner (Smith et al., 1997, p. 91).

Odiorne and Rummler (1988) listed ten characteristics of students in formal schooling that are not present in adult training and development. Among those characteristics listed were a few that bear particular mention here. Number 3 on the list was that "high compliance is related to success in schooling" (p. 14). This is interesting for two reasons, the first being that it is not, in fact, a characteristic of the learner, but of the context. The importance of this first reason is that it leads to the second, which is that success in the educational context of the workplace is not a great deal less about compliance than it is for children in school. This matters whenever we attempt to rely on some list of adult learning principles (i.e., Knowles, 1980), which carry with them assumptions about the context which do not fit the environment that is being discussed.

Simply put, learning environments that require a high degree of compliance result in learners who are conditioned to be compliant, and when compliance is not an option (or desire), that resistance be taken underground. Underground resistance coupled with ostensible compliance looks a lot like the statistics available on workplace learning addressed in nearly every book and paper on training transfer – overall there is not as much of it happening as there should be. Over 20 years ago, Mitchell (1988) referred to a study that reported, "on average only 10 percent to 20 percent of training transfers to the job so that the performance of the employee has been enhanced and changed" (p. 425). Assessments are passed, employee learners are graduated in some form, and training is not transferred to the shop floor.

Fifth on Odiorne and Rummler's list is, "Learning motives center around retention and grades" (referring to children in school) (p. 14). Again, though, we are led to believe that there is more of difference than there really is between a sixth grader passing a math test to graduate to the next level, or keep parents and teachers happy, and an employee passing a workplace learning in-service requirement to remain in good standing at work and to make families and supervisors happy.

The last of these "differences" is number seven, which is that they "Come from mixed social and cultural backgrounds" (p. 14). This one needs little discussion other than to point out that at the present time, cultural diversity is indeed a significant factor in the workplace.

Continuing forward from this, Odiorne and Rummler (1988) also noted what they considered to be characteristics of formal schooling that are not present in adult education. First on their list is that "mandatory attendance by law to age 16" (p. 13). While the age cap is different, the essence of this statement seems to assume that workplace learning is not mandatory. Certainly, it is not always mandatory, but very often and perhaps most often it is. Others on the list include curricular control by those in charge, control of learner behavior, teacher-paced learning, and tests are used to measure learning (p. 13). Like the first one on the list, these others are not as domain-specific as one might like to think.

All of these together emphasize the reasons that theory and research on workplace learning must come from all fields that examine and discuss human learning, no matter what the age. Adult learners in the workplace may not participate more eagerly to earn a lollipop, but they will generally go to great lengths to get out of the class even 15 minutes early before lunch or at the end of the day. The *mechanism* of motivation should not be confused with the object of motivation. Likewise, the age of the learner should not be confused with the context of the learning. This book is about learners who are learning in a particular context, and as such is focused on the learner within the context, rather than the context itself.

Finally, this is ultimately a book about people and how they learn in relation to long-term training transfer. Smith et al. (1997) pointed out that "Few attempts have been made to understand transfer from what it means to learn" (p. 91), and the following chapters address this directly.

THE STRUCTURE OF THIS BOOK

This book is about motivational immediacy and how it can be applied to workplace training contexts. It is based on the book *Motivational Immediacy: Facilitating Engagement in Adult Learners*, which I wrote previously (2022), and which has been published by Stylus Publishing. That original book is focused on motivational immediacy and higher education. Most of the chapters of this present book are either entirely new or contain only very insignificant amounts of overlap from the previous book, but it is important to note that the core theoretical foundation of motivational immediacy is not new and was, in fact, presented first in that seminal work. Chapters two, three, four, and ten are, with the exception of citation updates, language and terminology updates, and more relevant anecdotes, all very nearly the same as those contained in the original work and have been included with permission.

Section I contains the theoretical backbone of the book and is the foundation for the later sections in the book. It is essential that this should be understood for a couple of reasons. First, the first section is rather heavily theoretical and might require some patience for those wanting to immediately see practical applications. Second, all of the many practical applications in the second section will not really make sense without carefully reading through the first section. This is because the very best applications of the concepts covered in this first section do not so much require a new set of methods, but that we think in an entirely different way about many of the applications we have already been using.

Chapter 2 will explore the relationship between learning engagement and learning resistance and develop a solid case for why focusing on learner resistance is the key to facilitating learner engagement in workplace training. Chapter 3 will address the book's driving principle, *Motivational Immediacy*. The concept of motivational immediacy is the core of the book and refers to the tightness of the connection between the learning content the instructor is trying to facilitate and the in-the-moment interest and motivation of the learner. This is distinct from the more globally oriented motivation traditionally addressed in the literature.

Central to this chapter is the reality that a learner's motivation to obtain a certification, promotion, new position, or any other outcome is not the same thing as being motivated in any given moment, to engage and learn specific content. The instructor's true concern is not whether the learner is interested in becoming certified, or credentialed, but in whether the learner is motivated to learn, for instance, at 1:00 pm, in room 334, the fourth Wednesday in August.

Chapter 4 will integrate the concepts discussed in the first several chapters and introduce the idea of *effectual learning*. Effectual learning refers to learning that includes not only the acquisition of information but also the acceptance of information. Information that is acquired and accepted will last longer, be remembered more accurately, and transferred to practice more effectively.

Chapter 5 discusses zones of intervention and motivation within the workplace. This chapter uses social learning theory, situated learning, and communities of practice to identify four distinct but overlapping zones of intervention in the workplace. It points out that all workplace acts are teaching acts in some form and therefore all spaces are learning spaces. Motivational immediacy can then be applied to each of these four zones.

Chapter 6 introduces conceptual change theory in the form of *framework theories*. It discusses the literature on conceptual change theory and how that line of study can inform the training process. Learners hear content through a set of filters that are derived in part from the cognitive conceptual frameworks that they have developed over time. This chapter presents both theory and research and presents some guidelines for practice as the book transitions to the more practice-based second section.

Section II shifts strongly toward practice and addresses Motivational immediacy in light of specific domains of practice within the workplace, such as classroom strategies, lesson plan methods, and curriculum and instructional design factors and practices. The second half of the book is devoted to practice-based realities, applications, and complications related to motivational immediacy.

Chapter 7 will provide a comprehensive overview of mitigation strategies for working with resistant learners and fostering engagement. This chapter provides a concrete method for approaching workplace instruction. The acronym CONNECT is used to refer to a set of steps that can be actively used in all teaching situations, and a Cognitive-Affective-Social (CAS) worksheet is provided for use, both in planning lessons and in the classroom.

Chapter 8 offers an in-depth analysis of different learning and teaching spaces and provides detailed, concrete methods for both face-to-face and distance learning contexts for fostering learner engagement and Motivational immediacy. There are strengths and weaknesses for each of these contexts, and this chapter provides a clear set of factors to consider when determining which type of instruction will be provided for any given topic and purpose, and which methods to use in each.

Chapter 9 focuses on curriculum design and Instructional Systems Design (ISD) practices, with regard to motivational immediacy. Some commonplace attitudes and practices are challenged in this chapter, and the implications of common practices are called into question. Taking the theoretical and practical concepts introduced in the first eight chapters of the book, recommendations are made for more meaningful and fruitful ISD practices in the workplace.

Chapter 10 contains a potential way forward in addressing one of the most significant complications for those wishing to use the concepts in this book – the difficulty of measuring the often-qualitative benefits of increasing engagement and reducing resistance. One of the primary claims of this book is that often less measurable but mostly more important aspects, such as engaging students emotively, should be the focus, in terms of priority, for instructors. The set of terms in this chapter, and the metric introduced in formulaic format, provides one potential means to measure the efficacy and success of engaging employee-learners using the methods and strategies discussed in this book.

Chapter 11 will highlight the ethical implications of attempting to mitigate learning resistance. This chapter will take into account multiple ethical frameworks in the evaluation of whether or not it is ethical to try to reduce or work around an individual learner's resistance to a given content or learning experience. This chapter will present a number of different common dilemmas that training professionals might face in the workplace, and it provides a facilitator-as-mediator (FAM) concept for working through these dilemmas.

Chapter 12 will draw upon the concepts together into a comprehensive whole and provide a set of goals for those hoping to become more and more influential and effective as training coordinators, curriculum designers, and trainers in the workplace. It presents training as a connection and in so doing, brings together all of the concepts in the book into a comprehensive summary.

KNOWING WHAT YOU WANT FROM THIS BOOK

What is taken away from reading an article or book is always a confluence of the author's purpose in writing it, and the reader's purpose in reading it. In an ideal world, the two might match, but what we know of human learning shows that they quite often do not. The reader then must be aware of both, before pressing on. I can share my own intentions and have done so clearly here in the preceding pages, but the reader must be critically self-reflective before, during, and after reading. The following questions are for you to answer:

1. What is my primary purpose in reading this? What type of learner or learning situation am I actually thinking of when I sit down with this?
2. What do I want to learn by reading this?
3. What assumptions do I already have about training and learning?
4. How are these assumptions likely to affect how I think about what I read?
5. And, perhaps most importantly – Am I willing to have those assumptions challenged?

Chapter 2

Learning Engagement and Learning Resistance

While there is little dispute that learning is vital to any human enterprise, and perhaps even especially so in the workplace, it is also "perplexingly sticky" (Brown, 2018). Although a natural and libidinal human activity, learning is not at all straightforward. In addition to all of the learning that does occur in the workplace, training environments are also fraught with "non-learning" (Illeris, 2011) and "mislearning" (Jarvis, 1992). Nearly 25 years ago, Quinones and Ehrenstein (1997) pointed out that, "in order to develop efficient and effective training activities, we need a better understanding of fundamental psychological principles of skill acquisition" (p. 6). Since that time, great effort has been made to also acknowledge and address the social process of learning, and to recognize the dynamic interplay between the two (Illeris, 2011; Wenger, 1998).

Training transfer, specifically, has long been a topic of concern in the workplace training literature. It has been conceptualized as the process in which knowledge, skills, and attitudes employees learn in training are used in a practical way on the job (Salas, Tannenbaum, Kraiger, & Smith-Jentsch, 2012; Smith et al., 1997). As might be expected for such a broad concept, training transfer has been the subject of many theoretical models and associated empirical studies (see, e.g., Baldwin & Ford, 1988; Burke & Hutchins, 2008; Nijman et al., 2006; Pham, Segers, & Gijselaers, 2012; Richey, 1992). While there are many suggested causes of suboptimal training transfer, the transfer process itself has traditionally been identified as encompassing three components – training inputs, training outputs, and conditions of transfer (Baldwin & Ford, 1998). This chapter, and really, the book as a whole, is concerned with the latter component – conditions of transfer.

As noted by Hutchins and Burke (2007), this *conditions of transfer* component has, itself, been broken into three areas of study: personal

DOI: 10.4324/9781003144137-3

characteristics of the trainees (Colquitt, LePine, & Noe, 2000), training intervention designs (Machin & Fogarty, 2004), and the role of work environments (Holton et al., 2000; Lim & Johnson, 2002; Tracey et al., 1995). Since all three of these areas converge in workplace learning dynamics, all three are important. Rainbird (2000) situates "both formal training and development and informal learning in the context of complex organizational process and the conflict embedded in the employment relationship" (p. 14). But, given the focus on the personal nature of learning, it is a natural starting place to consider the third of these three – trainee characteristics.

Colquitt, LePine, and Noe (2000) provide an overview of personal characteristics as they relate to transfer and distinguish between broad personological factors – such as cognitive ability and self-efficacy – and situational characteristics, which take into account environmental and contextual factors that affect learners during the learning process. One of the most important personal factors which can impede the learning process is learning resistance, and learning resistance often resides at the intersection of the personal and the environmental. It is for this reason that this first chapter that addresses workplace learner motivation, addresses all of the reasons that learners are regularly motivated to *not* learn in the workplace.

Because of its history, learning resistance is a term that can only be used effectively after pains are taken to clearly specify the meaning that is intended. The adage about words having usage rather than definitions is particularly apt here. Throughout this book, I am using learning resistance to refer to *a lack of engagement on the part of the learner.* It is a lack of openness to learning in a given situation. When situated in contrast to engagement, it can be generally viewed as a negative phenomenon. Importantly, being engaged doesn't mean that the learner gullibly accepts any given thing they hear, blindly adopts new ways of seeing things, or allows themselves to be manipulated by the training instructor in ways that diminish their own individuality and agency. But, it does mean that the learner is open to learning, engaged in the experience, and attentive to the exchanges and dynamics involved in the classroom.

LEARNING ENGAGEMENT AS DISTINCT FROM MOTIVATION

Learning engagement has been viewed many different ways. Some have tended toward clumping engagement loosely with motivation. One can see this by looking at some of the definitions used for these terms. Merriam & Bierma (2014) write that, "motivation can also be described as educational engagement" (p. 147) and then go on to cite Kuh (2003) in support. Wlodkowski and Ginsberg (2017) point out that engagement research tends to focus on engagement as, "observable interaction" (p. 6), which is more in-line with how it is used in this book, but they also define motivation itself in part as, "to try to make sense of the information available, relate this information to prior knowledge, and attempt to gain the knowledge," (p. 5) something they draw from Brophy (2004). The actions contained in that definition of motivation necessarily tilt it toward entanglement with engagement. Wlodkowski and Ginsberg (2017) refer to engagement as a "motivational construct" (p. 6), which is an indicator of how it was used in their book. Coming from the other direction, in the third edition of the *Handbook of Educational Psychology*, Linnenbrink-Garcia and Patall (2016) define motivation as "initiating and sustaining behavior" (p. 91), which tends to close the gap between the two constructs.

My point in referring to the way in which these authors talk about engagement is not to claim that they are in error. In all of the cases cited here, the definitions were either purposefully set for the context of the writing it was found within (i.e., Linnenbrink-Garcia & Patall, 2016) or was only a small part of a much larger work (i.e., Wlodkowski & Ginsberg, 2017). The point is rather that there are implications of using motivation and engagement in a more or less interchangeable way. In none of the cases referred to here, were they detrimental to the point the respective authors were intending to make. However, one of the significant points being put forward in this book is that motivation and engagement are meaningfully distinct, and as such, there is value in using them in two very different ways.

Renniger et al. (2018) make a point of teasing apart the constructs of motivation, engagement, and interest, and define engagement as, "how invested people are in a given task, their conscientiousness and willingness to exert effort in order to master challenging content and difficult skills" (p. 119). They, like those above, acknowledge that engagement is related to motivation, but they also parse out engagement as a series of participatory responses to motivation, and therefore provide a way for the reader to see it as distinct.

In this book, and especially in this chapter, *learning engagement* is used to refer to "a psychological process, specifically, the attention, interest, investment, and effort students expend in the work of learning" (Marks, 2000, pp. 154–155). It includes both cognitive investment (Fredricks et al., 2004) and psychic energy (Csikszentmihalyi, 1990), and it implies a learner's openness to learning in a given context (for a brief discussion of the relationship between openness and resistance, see Taylor, 2010; Taylor & Lounsbury, 2016). Learning requires a degree of willingness to mobilize the necessary energies (i.e., physical, emotional, and psychological), and learners who are willing to commit to this in any given learning context can be said to be engaged.

Walberg (1995) defines engagement as the "extent to which students actively and persistently participate in learning" (p. 56). Tyler (1949) referred to this, without using the word, when he wrote, "Education is an active process [and] it involves the active efforts of the learner..." (p. 11).

Engagement is another of the many constructs that has tended to be co-opted by other constructs in a way that has caused important aspects of learning to be overlooked. Gagne' (1965) referred to the "first event of instruction" as gaining learner attention. That is, Gagne' recognized that instruction cannot occur unless the trainer first has the attention of the learner, who then becomes engaged in the process (also in Kraiger & Mattingly, 2018, p. 17). This may be true in some cases, but the assumption that attention necessarily leads to engagement is unfounded.

A fuller treatment of motivation and engagement will be provided in Chapter 3. In the meantime, those concepts are being addressed here in a limited way to the extent that they provide structure to the discussion on learning resistance.

FROM LEARNING RESISTANCE TO ENGAGEMENT

Learning engagement and learning resistance can be seen as two end points on a continuum, and while it is conceivable that a learner might be completely neutral in a given learning situation, this tends to be a more theoretical than practical consideration largely because the point of intersection between passive engagement and passive resistance would be very difficult to detect. Using engagement as a starting point is consistent with positive psychology but can result in the learner's difficulties being marginalized or even ignored. When trying to improve something, it is always a good idea to find the cause of the problem, and Odiorne and Rummler (1988) make mention of this in their own book on workplace training.

It is because of this that learner engagement is used here as the desired learner characteristic but is addressed through its opposite pole, learner resistance. There may be some debate as to the efficacy of focusing on the more negative end of the spectrum in order to achieve the more positive end, but there are solid grounds for doing so and they are addressed in Chapters 3 and 11. In the meantime, it will suffice to know that I share the view of White et al. (2010) when, speaking of active-learning situations, they write "Understanding [learner] resistance...provides a framework for developing strategies more likely to help [learners] succeed..." (p. 127). Simlarly, Ghodsian, Bjork, and Benjamin (1987) point out the importance in the workplace of taking the learner's point of view into consideration, and this seems wise in light of the fact that employers and employee learners are quite often not "on the same page" and that it is an "illusion" to believe otherwise (Rainbird, 2000, p. 1).

One of the chief difficulties in studying learning resistance is getting past the unnecessary dichotomies that mire it within the literature of educational psychology, sociology, anthropology, workplace education, and the many other fields from which it is addressed. Atherton (1999) expresses this well in saying, "to speak of 'resistance to learning' is in some measure to beg the question" (p. 77). An examination reveals a construct so varied in meaning and inconsistent in use that it is difficult to determine how to clarify the term and integrate its various lines of scholarship into a coherent whole. The terms resistance (Applebaum, 2016; Baker & Hill, 2017; Brookfield, 2006; Illeris, 2011, 2017; Layte, 2017), mislearning (Jarvis, 1992), defense (Illeris, 2011, 2017), blocking (Illeris, 2011, 2017), and turn-off (Jensen, 1969) have all been used in slightly different ways to talk about some of the same things. Resistance to learning has been addressed in many contexts. Table 2.1 provides a quick rundown of some of these.

DEFINING LEARNING RESISTANCE

Learning resistance as a construct is very "slippery" and does not seem to "sit still in the analytic categories we develop" (Field & Olafson, 1999, p. 4). There are likely many reasons this is the case, but certainly one of the more noteworthy potential reasons is the different types of value that have been assigned to resistance. In this section, a broad array of perspectives will be examined culminating in a concise and somewhat simple working definition for the purposes of the analysis offered here. Table 2.1 provides a list of many of the domains in which learning resistance has been addressed in the literature.

Resistance as a Negative Construct

A more traditional view of learning resistance, framed largely upon psychological and cognitive perspectives, is that resistance to learning is a negative force in learning contexts. Early examples of such perspectives are Caplin's (1969) reference to the resistant student as "one who fails to apply himself to the learning tasks of the school" (p. 36), and Kidd's (1959) use of the term "defensive behavior" (p. 96). Using the term turn-off, Jensen (1969) refers to it as "increasing inhibition of the very behaviors that promote learning" (p. 10). This view has continued to be expressed, though to a lesser extent. Long (1994, p. 14) referred to it as a "force that opposes or retards," McFarland (2001) referred to it as an "endemic problem" (p. 612) and used words, such as "disruptions" and "defiance" (p. 614). In fact, in McFarland's

Table 2.1 *Learning Resistance Scholarship by Domain*

Context	Authors
US Board of Education's Interaction with the Native Alaska Inupiats	Wexler, 2006
Communicative Language Teacher	Little & Sanders, 1990
Workplace Training Skills	Illeris, 2003; Mitchell, 1998
Mandatory Workplace Training Contexts	Cutcher, 2009
	Jarvensivu & Koski, 2012
	Rainbird, 2000. Taylor, 2010, 2017. Taylor & Lounsbury, 2016. Taylor, 2022
Science Education	Moscovici, 2003
	Seiler et al., 2003
Library Instruction	Antonelli et al., 2000
ESL Education	Alatis, 1974
Reading Education	Boldt, 2006
Healthcare Education	Wells et al., 2014
Educational Administration	Janas & Boudreaux, 1997
Adult Education (Broadly)	Brockett, 2015
	Brookfield, 2006
	Illeris, 2011
Literacy	Quigley, 1997
Learner Self-Direction	Hiemstra & Brockett, 1994
Motivation	Taylor, 2020
	Wlodkowski & Ginsberg, 2017
Critical Pedagogy	Giroux, 2001
Communications	Burroughs, 2007
	Burroughs et al., 1989
	Goodboy & Bolkan, 2009
	McLaughlin et al., 1980
	Zhang, 2007

long article, some form of the word "disrupt" appears nearly 100 times. Later, he also referred to it as an "oppositional form of nonconformity" (p. 1253). Also, in keeping with the traditional classroom view of resistance is Henson and Gilles's (2003) description of students who have "inhibiting beliefs" and therefore "opt out of learning opportunities by removing themselves or sabotaging instruction" (p. 260). Writing from the communications field, Burroughs et al. (1989) consider resistance to be all "off-task" behavior in a classroom. Tolman et al. (2016) defined learner resistance as "…a motivational state in which students reject learning opportunities due to systemic factors." (p. 3). This is a good definition because it clearly sees motivation as a bidirectional construct (learner's can be motivated to resist *or* to learn) and also because it takes into account systemic factors.

Going way back, Kurt Lewin (2013/1935) referred to behavior he called "going-out-of-the-field," by which he meant leaving the learning situation either physically or psychologically. Even Brookfield (2006), who later addresses resistance in a different light from a critical theory orientation, presented learning resistance as something that often should be mitigated through teaching strategies.

Resistance as a Positive Construct

Approaching from an almost opposite perspective, others have viewed learning resistance as a positive and necessary phenomenon, and something that should, at least within certain contexts, be encouraged by the teacher. Giroux (1983, 2001) is probably the most widely known in adult education circles, but others take this view as well (e.g., Moore, 2007). Resistance in these instances involves learner resistance to the status quo and social norms of those in power. Education can be a "technology of power" (Foucault, 2001, p. 125), and as such, educational efforts should not be faced with indiscriminate acceptance.

Approaching from this direction, resistance is rooted in a battle between those who are dominant and those who are dominated (Cowles, 2001; Field & Olafson, 1999; Giroux, 1983, 2001; Moore, 2007; Quigley, 1997). It should not escape notice, however, that many of those writing of resistance as a positive dynamic for the learner (i.e., resisting the status quo) have also written about the "negative" effects of learners resisting critical aspects of learning, in effect, agreeing that while resisting the status quo is a good thing, being resistant to being taught to resist the status quo might be best avoided (e.g., Brookfield, 2005). This perspective is not often discussed in the workplace literature training, but does appear in Rainbird's (2000) work.

Resistance as Both a Positive and Negative Construct

There have been a relative few who have attempted to address resistance as a more neutral term. Canagarajah (1993) distinguished between opposition and resistance, where resistance is more radical and political in nature and opposition as a more unclear and ambiguous phenomenon. Jing (2006) used Canagarajah's definition of resistance as "ambivalent student opposition" in her research in an effort to "broaden the sense of resistance as a relatively neutral oppositional force" (p. 97). Both Illeris (2017) and Jarvis (1992) used differentiated terms under a broader conceptual umbrella, and more recent work by Taylor (2010, 2014, 2022 and Taylor and Lounsbury (2016) has also attempted to cast a broader net. Illeris (2017) used the term resistance potential in a more positive way, while using the terms blocking, and defense to represent different facets of the more "negative" side of resistance

Resistance as a Unified Negative Concept

Both sides of this coin have been examined here because they are, in many ways, a related concept. Taking into account the multiple views of learning resistance while at the same time recognizing that there is indeed significant overlap in the various conceptions, the definition provided here casts the net broadly enough to provide for the overlap without losing practical efficacy. At the most basic level, *learning resistance can be considered a state in which a learner is not open to learning in a specific learning situation as demonstrated through either active rejection or passive disengagement* (Taylor, 2014, p. 60). Figure 2.1 depicts learner resistance on the opposite pole from learner engagement.

As I mentioned at the beginning of this chapter, learning resistance is a situation in which the learner is not open to learning and is not related directly to whether or not a learner, after careful consideration, fails to

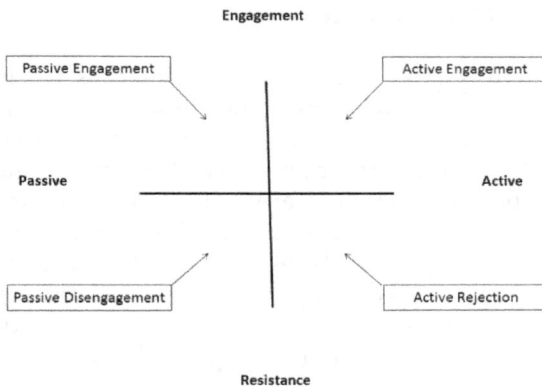

Engagement

| Passive Engagement | | Active Engagement |

Passive — Active

| Passive Disengagement | | Active Rejection |

Resistance

1. **Passive Engagement** – The learner is not resistant to the class or the content but is not actively mobilizing energy for learning in the learning context.
2. **Active Engagement** – The learner is purposefully mobilizing energy toward learning in the learning context.
3. **Passive Disengagement** – The learner is purposefully resisting and emotionally/psychologically closed to the learning activity (course or content), but is not actively mobilizing energy toward that resistance in the learning context. Resistant behaviors and cognitions are present but behaviors are typically not overt.
4. **Active Rejection** – The learner is purposefully mobilizing energy for resistance in the learning context. Resistant behaviors and cognitions are present but behaviors are typically overt.

Figure 2.1 Learning engagement-resistance continuum.

Source: Taylor (2014). Reprinted with permission.

agree with the instructor about a given matter. The training instructor then, who is attempting to facilitate engagement in learners, is not so much trying to get learners to be bamboozled into accepting everything that is taught in class, but rather, the effective instructor is working to create a situation in which their learners end up becoming and remaining interested in the learning situation, and openly engage in thought.

This definition is flawed in much the same way as the proposed typology in that in attempting to be comprehensive, some of the useful nuances may have been sacrificed and, going back to Atherton's sentiment, it may "beg" a new set of questions. Despite this weakness, this broader conception of learning resistance permits a researcher to assimilate and integrate a much broader and richer array of academic and professional literature on the topic, and, perhaps more importantly, reconcile an extensive range of knowledge and apply it toward very specific ends.

LEARNING RESISTANCE EXPRESSIONS

Hultman (1995) warns of mistaking symptoms and causes of resistance. In the section following this one, the typology of learning resistance uses a similar convention that others have used before. The basis of the types are causes (potential/hypothesized) rather than behaviors. This is because behavior is a very poor predictor of learning resistance overall. The learner in the class who argues the longest and loudest might just be the only learner actually paying attention. Wells et al. (2014) provide some ways to identify the difference between engaged arguing and resistance arguing. They point out, for instance, that those who are resisting tend to have less content-related arguments and more personally-related arguments, focused on the competence and knowledge of the instructor and efficacy of the learning environment. Still, an engaged learner might be the most likely to argue over content, when compared to someone who is not actually paying attention or trying to "get" the lesson.

On the other hand, the leaner sitting silently in the back smiling and nodding might not be paying the least bit of attention and might even be planning your demise via the upcoming instructor evaluation, like Dickens's Madame Defarge quietly knitting her secret signs into an afghan, waiting for the right time. But of course, the exact opposite dynamic could be afoot. The arguing learner might be entirely closed off to learning and wishing only to play "stump the chump" while the quiet, smiling learner is engaged in a bit of deep, authentic, albeit introverted learning.

Despite this sketchy sort of dynamic, one can be assured that learning resistance will be expressed in behavior, cognitions, or some interaction of both. While I have defined learning resistance as an internal state of being closed off and not engaging in learning. this state is evidenced in the behaviors and cognitions of the individual learner (Taylor, 2010, 2014, 2017; Taylor & Lounsbury, 2016). The term *behaviors* refer to physical behaviors, such as leaving the room, heckling the instructor, or engaging in some other activity instead of actively listening. *Cognitions* refers to the thoughts the learner has about not learning such as "this is a waste of my time" or "I have better things to do than this."

With regards to the manner in which learning resistance plays out in a given learning space, McFarland (2004) refutes what he considers the common notion that resistance is a "discrete event" and, instead, provides a learning resistance process that includes a progression from a *breach*, to a *crisis*, to a *redress*, and ending with *reintegration* (p. 1255). This way of understanding resistance portrays a long, soaking sort of process during which the process takes on a social nature rather than just an individual nature. The initial moment of disconnect between the instructor and the learner (breach) often grows into a more widespread problem as learners talk among themselves.

This growing social dissent in the classroom (crisis) must be addressed by one party or the other – typically both – before the reintegration process can begin. There are at least three important implications of this dynamic. First, small problems between a single instructor and a single learner can easily grow into group problems that are more difficult to mitigate and affect learners across the classroom. Second, the longer the initial breach is allowed to go unaddressed, the more likely the problem will expand and become more broadly problematic. Third, any such breach must be addressed, or, rather, redressed, in order to restore (reintegrate) the leaner's into the learning space.

LEARNING RESISTANCE CATEGORIZED

One of the few coherent attempts to bring order to the conceptions of resistance is the typology provided by Atherton (1999) and comes straight from workplace in-service training. Atherton grouped learning resistance into two types – situational and ulterior. Situational resistance refers to the more localized and contextualized factors that may cause a learner to resist, (i.e., classroom distractions) while ulterior resistance refers to the type of resistance brought about when an individual learner is prompted to change his or her schema about a given aspect of life. Atherton uses the word supplantive to describe learning that requires a significant change of viewpoint (p. 78), but this type of learning is similar to Piaget's (1951) accommodative learning, and on a grander scale, similar to the paradigm shift central to transformational learning theories.

This typology provides a great service to those who wish to study learning resistance because it provides a framework for connecting the volumes of work directly or indirectly addressing resistance. Despite its usefulness, it fails to adequately cover all of the different angles from which resistance has been addressed in the literature.

Quigley (1997) likewise made a strong contribution to resistance scholarship when he described three types of resistance derived from his research. He wrote of three different causes of resistance – those who resist because of teachers, those who resist because of the school system, and those who resist because of boredom. A noteworthy strength of Quigley's accounting is that it was empirically rather than theoretically derived, but a limitation of his research-based typology is that it reflected a highly specific learning and learner context (literacy). Thus, while Quigley's typology also contributed to an understanding of resistance, it had a failing similar to Atherton's in that it did not account for the broad range of perspectives from which resistance has been studied.

By closely examining an extensive volume of scholarship from multiple fields addressing learning resistance, and then attempting to make sense of it as a whole, I have come to see such an attempt at ordering the concept as the single, most effective tool for clearly understanding what has been learned about resistance. This categorization is presented here to the reader, not as an airtight conception, but as a useful frame upon which to understand what has been learned about resistance and what more might be learned.

The interdisciplinary literature provides a detailed accounting of learning resistance that can be arranged into four very broad, and potentially overlapping, categories – Environmental, Cognitive-Psychological, Sociocultural, and Epistemological resistance. These categories are based upon the general correlates (potential antecedents) of such resistance rather than the form the resistance happens to take in a given instance. This is an important distinction because resistance manifested in any particular way, in terms of behavioral and learning outcomes, could be the result of very different factors. This particular quality is shared by both Atherton's and Quigley's categories.

Caplin (1969) writes that an "adequate understanding of resistance demands careful analysis of causes" (p. 37). Mitchell, who seems to have spent more time talking about learning resistance in the workplace than most, wrote:

> "… little or no positive learning takes place without a readiness to learn. In fact, the learner merely learns how to resist more effectively, and the training becomes confrontational and ineffective. The first step in responding to resistance is to ventilate it; encourage the trainees to express their resistance. Once you know what form their resistance is taking, you can respond to it" (Mitchell, 1988, p. 7).

The following break-down of resistance allows for a better understanding of it in the workplace as well as a language to speak about it.

Environmental Resistance

Environmental resistance is resistance that is brought about because of factors in the environment of the learner during or near the specific learning event (localized). Examples of this would be loud and distracting classrooms or classrooms with poorly controlled temperatures. The word localized is used here to mean relative to the time of the learning situation. Long-term, systemic problems with the learning environment fall under the other types of learning resistance. While environmental concerns in this context would often have to do with the settings of learning, it could also include immediate life circumstances of the learner, located in close proximity to the learning situation (i.e., an argument with one's spouse just prior to the class). Garber (2002) discusses family problems and their effects on learners in the classroom. Environmental aspects of resistance are also addressed, at least in part, by Atherton (1999) and Brookfield (2006).

Many years ago while providing a company-wide training program for all employees, a group of about 15 employees and I found ourselves in the middle of an HVAC/Air Handler room with an extremely large machine hulking over us, cycling on and off. We were using a laptop, and a portable projector and screen. In this context both the sounds of the machine running and its sudden silence were almost equally deafening. More than one learner in that class expresses a deep frustration with, not only their own terrible learning environment, but the very much better conditions that many of their colleagues had for their own. The employees in my class believed that they were in the HVAC room because they were blue collar workers, while the higher paid employees were in the upscale training room at headquarters.

The truth of the matter was that those in the HVAC room were *more vital* to day-to-day operations and that was why the decision was made to keep them in the field. Optics, however, are perceived reality. When based in the workplace physical environment rather than outside of work (i.e., family problems) environmental resistance has the distinction of the being the easiest to identify and respond to in the classroom, but given many of the training rooms in many of the workplaces across the country, it should not be overlooked.

Cognitive-Psychological Resistance

Cognitive-Psychological resistance is characterized by largely internal factors. It should be noted that the vital influence of the social aspects is not denied in this category; rather it is acknowledged and/or assumed, but not focused upon. Cognitive and/or psychological resistance is related to issues of self-efficacy (Bandura, 1986; Schunk, 1995), learned helplessness (Maier & Seligman, 1976), disinterest/boredom (e.g., via discussions of interest; Schraw et al., 2001; Schraw & Lehman, 2001; Shaw et al., 1996), identity (Illeris, 2007, 2011; Torrance, 1949), and overconfidence or presumption (Jarvis, 1992; Taylor, 2010, respectively).

Easy examples of this can be taken from Mitchell's (1988) list of seven causes of workplace resistance. These include "parochial self-interest," "lack of trust," "low tolerance for change," and "mistaken first impressions" (pp. 8–9). Illeris's (2007, 2011) discussion of learner identity and its role in providing a reason for the learner to resist workplace training is important because it points out that while the trainer thinks they are trying to get the learner to simply learn something new, the learner is believing that they are being asked to be somebody different.

Jensen (1969) connects learner "turn-off" to a lack of readiness, which he defined in terms of both growth readiness and cumulative learning theories (Gagne, 1965, 1968). These terms and the related theories attached to them center on early childhood and are therefore somewhat limited in scope, when looking at learning in the workplace. However, it might be useful to think of a psychological or emotional readiness rather than a developmental readiness, when considering adult learners. The author views psychological and emotional readiness as the psychological and emotional ability to be open to learning. There are many reasons why a learner might not be psychologically and emotionally open to learning, such as feelings of vulnerability, low self-efficacy, anger, anxiety, and other common emotions.

Sociocultural Resistance

Sociocultural resistance – to borrow a term popularly attributed to Vygotskian ideas (Vygotsky, 1978) – refers to learning resistance that has as its source, social or cultural dynamics. Although the theoretical framework for critical theory is drawn from the work of philosophers, such as Althusser (1969), Bernstein (1977), Bourdieu (1977), Bowles and Gintis (1976), Foucault (2001), Giddens (1984), and Habermas (2003), one of the more widely-read educational proponents of learning resistance as a vehicle of social change is Giroux (1983,2001). Giroux's call for radical pedagogy continues to echo through the halls of the discipline. Going back much further, those such as Myles Horton (1998) and Paulo Freire (1996) left a strong heritage for those wishing for a more democratic society and more freedom in and through learning. Quigley's (1997) work mentioned earlier also falls mostly under this category, as does much of Brookfield's (2005) more recent work, and, in its own way, the work of those writing of transformative learning (i.e., Mezirow & Associates, 2000).

All of this might seem far removed from the workplace, but going back to Rainbird's (2000) claim that employers and employees are regularly not seeing eye-to-eye on things, this aligns itself particularly well to a learning context in which profit is a key factor. Organizational and contextual factors can constrain practice (Holly and Rainbird, 2000), and one must, "recognize explicitly that the workplace is a site of conflict between labor and management, and that the procedures, resources, and outcomes of formal and informal learning opportunities must be analyzed in this context." (Rainbird, 2000, p. 9).

Not only do learners in the workplace have to contend with the social dynamics of the workplace on the organizational level (Illeris, 2011), they must also face interpersonal dynamics that can affect their learning. Mitchell (1988) while listing seven causes of learning resistance in the workplace, included peer-group pressure and the drive to save face, which, of course, fits under other of the four categories as well, but the organizational culture in which the learner finds themselves situated has a great deal to do with how much pressure is present and the tone of that pressure.

Epistemological Resistance

Epistemological resistance refers to learning resistance caused by a disconnect or mismatch between the learner's and instructor's conception or understanding of: (a) what learning is and/or (b) what criteria should be used to evaluate truth claims. Mitchell (1998) again, includes an example of this on his list when he mentions that learners may resist due to having different assessments of information from those who are in the instructional role.

One of the earlier mentions of frameworks and paradigms with respect to learning resistance came from Goisman (1988). Goisman discusses professional learners' resistance to learning about a particular form of therapy (behavior therapy). He speaks of "model conflicts" and the need to address these foundational, conceptual disconnects (p. 68). White et al. (2010) examine learner resistance to changes in pedagogical practices because they are defining their own learning according to paradigms related to the previous form of pedagogy.

This type of resistance exists in the workplace in cases in which the employees are using quite different criteria for evaluating truth claims than their employers and, by extension, their instructors and trainers (Salaman &

Butler, 1990). If, for example, an individual believes that learning is about obtaining a physical skill, the ability to do something, and that individual is placed in a leadership class in which her or she is subjected to a lengthy instructional sequence on some form of leadership competency, the mismatch between the understanding of knowledge between the employee and employer could have significantly negative effects in terms of training efficacy.

In a large-scale qualitative study conducted by Paulus et al. (2009) undergraduate university learners indicated both a confusion about what exactly learning was, and also a variety of impressions about who one should use as a source of authority in competing knowledge claims. On multiple occasions learners wrote in blogs that they did not learn anything new and then, almost immediately, moved on to document, in detail, a number of things they learned that they had not previously known. There was also a prevalent theme of disregarding the content the professor had provided in exchange for different information they had been provided from parents, friends, and personal experience.

The workplace equivalent of this can easily be seen in situations in which the policies and rules laid out in an orientation training are almost immediately disregarded in the face of conflicting narratives from more senior employees who take the new employee learner under their wing and show them "how it is really done."

General Causes

The literature is replete with hypothesized causes of learning resistance. While many of these have been included under the specific types as provided above, a general list of those most commonly found in the literature are listed in Table 2.2. There is some overlap in the proposed causes listed below, and a closer examination of the literature from which they were culled leads one to suspect that different learning contexts breed different causes of resistance.

RANGE AND INTENSITY OF LEARNING RESISTANCE

Given all of the types of learning resistance, and their correlates, one can begin to see the underlying dynamics that give rise to learning resistance, and, more specifically, what determines how prominent and intense learner resistance might be. There are, of course, many ways to conceptualize this, but using Gold's (2005) discussion on learning resistance and what he referred to as "emotionally disrupted" states, an explanatory two-dimensional plot can provide a visual aid (Figure 2.2).

Table 2.2 *Suggested causes of learning resistance*

Cause	Author
Resistance to dominant culture	Giroux, 1983, 2001; Hughes, 2005; Jarvensivu & Koski, 2012;McNamee et al., 2002; Moore, 2007; Ogbu, 1991
Conflict between old and new learning	Salaman & Butler, 1990; Mitchell, 1998
Discomfort due to accommodative learning (transformative/conceptual change)	Atherton, 1999; Brady, 1975
Cultural mismatch	Cohen, 2018; Cutcher, 2009; Seiler et al., 2001
Immersion in the learning experience	Moscovici, 2003
Disliking courses, administration, and/or educational system/school environment/initiatives	Atherton, 1999; Baker & Hill, 2017; Garber, 2002; Holly & Rainbird, 2000; Hultman, 1995; Quigley, 1997; Rainbird, 2000;
Lack of interest, disinterest, and boredom	Kruglanski et al., 2018; Mitchell, 1998; Quigley, 1997; Sun, 1995
Low self-esteem; fear of the unknown/anxiety; dislike of the teacher; irrelevancy of the material; inappropriate level of required learning	Brookfield, 2006; Kunst, 1959; Mitchell, 1998; Quigley,1997; Reyes, 2002; Smith, 2005
Development of the personal will; differentiation from others; successful development of personal identity; role confusion	Caplin, 1969; Cutcher, 2009; Goisman, 1988; Illeris, 2011; Kidd, 1959; Lecky, 1945; Rank, 1945
Examination culture in school/workplace; mismatch of teacher and learner goals	Jing, 2006; Holly & Rainbird, 2000; Rainbird, 2000
Mismatch between learner's life experience and formal education	Hultman, 1995; Quigley, 1997
Resistance to change study methods and habits	Dembo & Seli, 2004; White et al., 2010
Failure to "buy in" to learning objectives	Illeris, 2003
Teacher immediacy	Burroughs et al., 1989; Burroughs, 2007
Brand loyalty – "Tribal Affiliation" and "Hero Worship"	Gold, 2005
Family issues and other external factors	Garber, 2002; Layte, 2017
Dislike of the teacher	Garber, 2002
Fear of failure	Mitchell, 1998
Peer-group pressure	Mitchell, 1998

In the diagram, the type of learning fostered in a given situation ranges from simple rote memorization on the bottom, to highly complex conceptual change and transformation on the top. The state of the learner is depicted on the other axis, with low emotional disruption on the left, and high emotional disruption on the right. Since resistance is such a complex

Conceptual Change

Most Resistant

Low Emotional Disruption ———————————————— High Emotional Disruption

Least Resistant

Rote Memory/ Procedural Skill

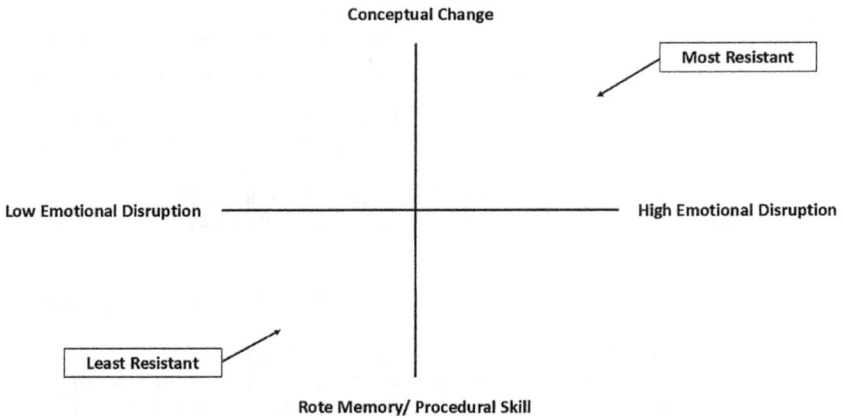

Figure 2.2 Range and strength of learning resistance.

Source: Adapted from Gold (2005)

interaction of internal and external factors, it is impossible to characterize to a high degree, much less predict, a given level of learning resistance, but as a general rule, one would expect that more complex forms of learning, such as conceptual change, and more emotional disruption in the learner would both result in a greater degree of learning resistance.

The reason I have put these on two dimensions rather than one, is to allow for a learning situation that might be simple and nonthreatening, but to which the learner comes in a state of incidental emotional disruption. For instance, a learner might enter a classroom after having had a very bad morning that started with a domestic argument and ended with not being able to find a parking space. In this case, the emotional disruption is high, and even if the learning is simple, that is, rote memorization of facts, it is likely the learner will be resistant. Likewise, in cases of very complex and normally stressful forms of learning, such as conceptual change, certain learners may be in a good place in their personal lives and/or have a personality that is conducive to handling such tasks. This situation would represent an intersection of situational and dispositional factors but could result in stressful learning that does not disrupt the emotions of the learner to a significant degree.

Those exceptions given as a general rule more complex forms of learning such as conceptual change and transformational change typically result in the learner experiencing more emotional stress, anxiety, and disruption, and because of this, as learning shifts upward from simple to complex learning, more learners would tend to experience a greater degree of naturally occurring emotional disruption, shifting into the upper right quadrant.

Finally, looking at the diagram as a whole, the strongest resistance behaviors and cognitions would indicate in the upper right quadrant, and the bottom left quadrant would represent the area with the least or weakest resistance. The dimensional diagram is certainly limited, but it does provide a simple way to view one's teaching situation in terms of what learners are being generally exposed to and asked to experience.

CONCLUSION

Returning briefly to Figure 2.1, a question arises. If there are Active and Passive Resisters, which group is of most concern to the instructor? I ask this question quite frequently in groups that I speak to and receive mixed answers. It depends, really, on which perspective one uses to answer the question. Training is difficult and we are human beings after all, and subject to the same sort of self-esteem needs as the learners, so when thinking that way, the active rejecters (Active Resistance) are the most to be feared.

They are, after all, the learners who are most likely to actually verbally attack you in class, pick apart your lectures, study only so they can catch you publicly in an error, and other such terrifying actions. If, however, we get past thinking of our own self-esteems, which all good instructors try to do most of the time, then the group that should be of most concern to us, of most educational threat, those we may not actually reach, it is the passive resistors. Why? For several reasons.

First, in the typical classroom, this is the largest group of learning resistant learners. Grumbling aside, typically, those who are overtly rude and resistant do not dominate the training classroom. Second, this is the group you can't easily see. The active rejectors, by definition sort of put themselves out there. Maybe they are unreachable, or, maybe you can dedicate your energy to changing their perspective. In the former case, you can remove them or ignore them, and in the latter, at least you know who they are and what they are thinking.

But the passive resistors make up a significant portion of everyday learners (you have been one yourself, many times, as have I). They are bound by generally good social manners and therefore go through the motions while they cognitively check into the Disney resort. This is the large group that could be reached but might not simply because they don't seem like they need to be reached. They are the complacency drivers for the instructor, not the actively engaged. Highly engaged learners generally foster energy in the instructor, not complacency. It is the middle group, the pleasant faces, with smiles and with somewhat glazed eyes. Here is where all of this leads – the passive resistors are the unengaged that we all speak about. When trying to figure out how to facilitate learner engagement, one must study learner resistance.

FROM LEARNING RESISTANCE TO MOTIVATIONAL IMMEDIACY

Where do we go from here? The literature on learning resistance reveals that learning resistance is a concern we should all share in any contexts, and particularly in mandatory contexts which are so much a part of the working world. We should know that learners are making choices in our classrooms that inhibit learning, and that an effective instructor must be aware of this because even passive resistance is nonengagement. That is, those who are engaged in passive resistance make up the lion's share of the group that we routinely call disengaged. motivational immediacy, as introduced in the next chapter, is both the *noun* and the *verb* that rises from this analysis. One must be aware of the idea of Immediate Motivation and must practice motivational immediacy.

Chapter 3

Motivational Immediacy

Jamal sat in the training room staring at the fake woodgrain on the desk in front of him. The murmur of the instructor at the front of the room and the rustle of those around him had long since faded from his conscious attention. Jamal felt a twitch and focused his attention on his little finger on his left hand. It was moving back and forth, seemingly with a mind of its own. He tried to shift his attention away from the finger. Thinking about it or any of his other physical symptoms wouldn't do any good. The test results wouldn't be back for a couple of days at the soonest and nothing good came from dwelling on all the various things that could be wrong with him. The specialist just told him with what seemed like true confidence a few hours ago that it seemed like the problem was benign and there were no serious neurological issues to deal with. But, of course, there should be a few more tests, which, Jamal, assumed, meant they were still concerned. And if they were concerned, shouldn't he be?

Something the instructor said up front caught his attention and he looked up and focused on what was going on. The instructor made eye contact and smiled as she talked about the video on the screen in front that she was about to start.

To give you some background, Jamal was sitting in a personal protective equipment (PPE) class and although he was deeply motivated to work his way up through the organization, and his various certificates and badges provided evidence of his long-term motivation, there was simply nothing in the two-hour class on wearing gloves, a helmet, and eyeglasses that could motivate him to gather his mental energy and engage on this particular day.

Except something about blacksmithing. He had shared, at the beginning of the course that he was a blacksmith hobbyist, demonstrated the art at country fairs, and was deeply interested in all things pertaining to it.

DOI: 10.4324/9781003144137-4

Each of his fellow employees had shared some basic details about themselves and the instructor actually took note of them and over the past hour of the course had been routinely finding ways to connect the training content to the individual interests of the specific, individual learners in the Monday afternoon class.

Jamal tuned into what the instructor was saying. "I found this video online called should you use safety gear while blacksmithing. Watch closely."

Jamal watched closely. His twitching finger was momentarily forgotten, and he was once more, engaged in the immediate activity of the classroom.

Samantha, or Sam, as her classmates call her, sat in her HR orientation class and tried to pay attention. She was an accountant and had been for almost 19 years. She was excited to be starting her new position with better hours and more pay. It would allow her to spend more time with her friends and family after work, and, beyond all of this, she was really excited to start a new journey and generally loved to learn new things.

But it was Wednesday morning at 8:50 am and the instructor was in the early stages of going over what he said would be "71 wonderful years of company history." 71! Sam was easygoing, generally, and respectful, but 71 years was a long time and was not going to tell her how to have her salary direct deposited, or make sure she had correctly filled out the vision care form online.

The instructor's words filtered through her wandering mind and she heard "this company history is a story of corrupt management and whistleblowing accountants, and it is the reason we have such a large financial auditing department at this present time."

Sam sat up a little straighter. Hmm, this was interesting. This is about my specific job? I thought the whole thing was going to be about the company, not my own role as an accountant... Sam was engaged.

CHAPTER PURPOSE AND ORGANIZATION

In both of these scenarios, learners had a high degree of something I will be referring to as *global motivation*, each wanting for different reasons, to learn the content in addition to satisfying the requirements of their job. Also true in each of these cases, the learners had no initial, or *immediate motivation* to engage with the lesson or module in that moment, on that day, in that week, on that particular topic. In both scenarios, the instructor did not rely on global motivation, instead actively and purposefully using immediate motivation to engage the learners in the classroom in that moment for that topic. That intentionality on the part of the instructor, to utilize immediate motivation is a practice I refer to as *motivational immediacy*, and it is the focus of this chapter and the backbone of this entire book.

In the following pages, the case will be made that for a set of powerful reasons, effective instructors must facilitate learner engagement in the workplace by fostering a situation for the learner in which there is immediate, situational interest, and by extension, motivation. This must be continuously facilitated, moment-by-moment throughout the entirety of each teaching-learning situation. If that sounds exhausting, it is. Most things done well tend to require great effort, but there are some practical things that can be done to promote this sort of immediate motivation, and they will be shared in this book.

Going further, this immediate, situational interest, and motivation is developed or diminished within a tension field of complex individual motivational goals, including the motivation to *avoid* certain activities and outcomes. Therefore, an effective instructor must take into account the various reasons (conscious or unconscious) that learners may resist engaging in any given learning situation. The following propositions will be made in this order:

- Learners do not learn without feeling
- Motivation is not unidirectional; Learners are also motivated to *not* learn
- A lack of means-end fusion (MEF) leads to learner disengagement
- Global motivation isn't enough – immediate motivation is key
- Instructors must practice motivational immediacy

MOTIVATIONAL THEORY FROM A DIFFERENT ANGLE

The direction from which one approaches something has a lot to do with how one sees it upon approach and arrival. Rosen (2006), a legal anthropologist, described theories as "a series of lenses through which to view different features of the same thing" (p. 53). Motivational theorists, such as Wlodkowski and Ginsberg, have traditionally approached human learning motivation primarily from the side of how to foster motivation in students (Wlodkowski & Ginsberg, 2017) or in an abstract theoretical sense (i.e., human learning) (Taylor, 2017).

My approach in this book has been to begin the journey from the perspective of the individual learner's motivation to *not* learn; to *not* engage. The distinction is subtle here and seldom discussed or written about, but it remains an important subtlety because it starts with the premise that learners are already motivated in the classroom right from the beginning – they just may not be motivated to do the thing you are hoping they will do.

At the conclusion of Chapter 2, the connection was made between passive resistance and the learners we commonly call "unengaged." It naturally follows that an understanding of learner resistance is key to understanding how to foster learner engagement.

Beginning the journey this way, means that learner motivation is approached from a slightly different direction and therefore, those taking the journey will see a different set of features revealed as the destination draws near. In this sense, the concepts in this book are not an intentional refutation of anyone else's work. Indeed, it should be seen as a companion guide to other motivation literature, not a replacement. And, to quote Wlodkowski and Ginsberg, the instructor "...must consider the learners' perspective fundamental. 'Seek first to understand' is our watchword" (2017, p. 43).

LEARNING RESISTANCE AND MOTIVATION

In Chapter 2, learning resistance was defined as a state in which a learner is not open to learning in a specific learning situation as demonstrated through either active rejection or passive disengagement (Taylor, 2014, p. 60). Defined this way, resistance has, as its more positive opposite, *engagement*. Learning engagement, or rather, engagement with the learning *situation* (though not necessarily acceptance of the learning content) is considered a psychological process, specifically the attention, interest, investment, and effort students expend in the work of learning (Marks, 2000, pp. 154–155). While resistance and engagement fit nicely together, conceptually speaking, motivation is less easily "snapped to grid" within the resistance-engagement continuum. Reeve (2015) defines motivation both in a technical manner as "those processes that give behavior its energy and direction" (p. 9), and also in a more colloquial sense by saying that motivational study is for understanding why people "do what they do" (p. 8). It would seem then, that motivation plays a role in both resistance and engagement. This provides the substance for one of the claims I have promised to make in this chapter – the dual nature of motivation. Simply put – learners are never unmotivated. Instead, learners are always motivated either to learn or to not learn. One must admit that it may be feasible that there may be a technical middle ground where motivational neutrality might exist, but I would also cry foul if too much of a fuss was made about that possibility because it is more theoretical than practical. Students generally have a reason to checkout or to check-in (Illeris, 2017). This idea will be returned to shortly with regards to *avoidance motivation*, but first a word about emotion and affect.

PROPOSITION # 1: LEARNERS DO NOT LEARN WITHOUT FEELING

When looking at motivation, it is important to delineate the related concepts of emotion and motivation. There has been a growing emphasis in the sciences on the role of emotion in cognition over the past ten years (Damasio, 2012; Immordino-Yang, 2011). Reeve (2015) defines emotion as "the synchronized brain-based systems that coordinate feeling, bodily response, purpose, and expression so to ready the individual to adapt successfully to life circumstances" (p. 342). He goes on to point out that emotion acts as: (a) one source of motivation and (b) a sort of formative assessment of how well one's motivation is serving one's goal of adaptability to life events. He further identifies four parts of these "systems" as *Feelings, Bodily Arousal, Sense of Purpose,* and *Expressive Behaviors* (p. 342). These components interact and produce emotions which influence the levels of motivation any individual has in a given situation.

Damasio (2003) in a very creative work, *Looking for Spinoza: Joy, Sorrow, and the Feeling Brain,* addresses emotions from a neurological perspective and weaves it together with some of Spinoza's philosophical ruminations on the same topic. Damasio's work is particularly useful when examining the role of emotion and feeling in resistance to learning because he makes a clear distinction between the physiological emotion and the more cognitively-based feeling. Spinoza made a theoretical distinction between emotion and affect and Damasio essentially uses the word feelings to represent the Spinozian concept of affect.

In his work, emotions are considered:

> "…complicated collections of chemical and neural responses, forming a pattern; all emotions have some kind of regulatory role to play, leading in one way or another to the creation of circumstances advantageous to the organism exhibiting the phenomenon; emotions are about the life of an organism, its body to be precise, and their role is to assist the organism in maintaining life" (Damasio, 2003, p. 51).

Feelings are defined in contradistinction as "the perception of a certain state of the body along with the perception of a certain mode of thinking and of thoughts with certain themes" (p. 86). The key point here is that while the terms are often used interchangeably, there is a distinction that is very useful not only in understanding learning resistance, but also in mitigating it. Simply put, emotions can be used to refer to the unconscious, neurobiological response, while feelings are the cognitive assignments we make to those feelings. This is undoubtedly a much more complicated dynamic and there is a great degree of highly detailed information explaining the interworking of these two. However, the most noteworthy application of the distinction between emotion and feeling is that human beings have some ability to cognitively assign, that is, to think about and make a decision about, just what a given emotion we experience might mean. This can be more easily grasped when thinking about a more concrete exemplar – ancient war drums. Most would agree that hearing a beating war drum does not lead one to pick a side in a given conflict. A beating war drum merely helps one march more energetically on whichever side was chosen to begin with. The neurobiological experience set off by the auditory sensation of the drums causes one to "feel" more energy toward a given end, and step more quickly. Perhaps Shakespeare knew something of this when he wrote Timon's words, "follow thy drum…" (Shakespeare, 1936 [1623], p. 1066). So, while there are physical emotions that might be outside the control of the individual learner, there is some capacity in that learner to channel that emotion in a certain direction and the totality of that channeling is feeling – how that individual feels about it. Damasio's (and Spinoza's) distinction is a valuable one because it allows for some cognitive control within an emotional domain. Acknowledging the cognitive aspects of what we commonly refer to as emotion and affect interchangeably, provides space for the practitioner to more purposefully influence and direct what would otherwise be almost entirely unpredictable. The terms *affect* and *feelings* will be used interchangeably in this chapter.

PROPOSITION # 2: MOTIVATION IS NOT UNIDIRECTIONAL – LEARNERS ARE OFTEN MOTIVATED TO NOT LEARN

The first sign of a problem shows itself pretty early on in almost any "everyday" conversation about motivation, no matter how well-read the speaker is about motivation, academically speaking. "My students are just not very motivated," and/or "I need to figure out how to motivate my students." Before the academician can object, I will add a more nuanced and, in fairness, accurate statement such as, "I need to figure out how to *foster* more motivation in my students." Witty and inspirational quotes aside about "fires that need to be kindled" (popularly attributed to W. B. Yeats but with no valid citation), and Lewis about deserts that need to be irrigated (Lewis, 1996/1944, p. 27), this type of statement exhibits the same error as the first set and constitutes the proverbial exit ramp to a very long way around to learning.

Approach and Avoidance Motivation

This chapter will take motivation from the angle of approach and avoidance goals because that is where a study of learning resistance leads. If one is to start with the learner's experience and perspective, that is, be learner-centered, then one must take a much closer look at just what, exactly, the learner might be motivated to do...or *not* do, in any given learning situation.

Classical Approach-Avoidance Motivation

Elliot and his colleagues (Eder et al., 2013; Elliot, 1999, 2006, 2008; Elliot & Church, 1997; Elliot & Covington, 2001; Elliot & Harackiewicz, 1996; Roskes, Elliot, Nijstad, & DeDreu, 2013) have written so prolifically about approach and avoidance motivation and have done so for long enough, that it is nearly impossible to provide a succinct overview of any given aspect of it without simply quoting them directly. They write briefly about the long history of approach and avoidance dynamics:

> The origin of the approach-avoidance distinction may be traced back to the ancient Greek philosophers Democritus (460–370 B.C.) and Aristippus (435–356 B.C.), who espoused an ethical hedonism that proscribed the pursuit of pleasure and the avoidance of pain as the central guide for human behavior. The first thinker to straightforwardly articulate a psychological hedonism, in which the pursuit of pleasure and the avoidance of pain not only represented an ethical proscription but also a description of how humans actually tend to behave, was the British philosopher Jeremy Bentham (1748–1832). Bentham (1179/1879) offered the following strong dictum in his Introduction to the Principles and Morals of Legislation: "Nature has placed mankind under the governance of two sovereign masters, pain and pleasure. It is for them alone to point out what we ought to do as well as to determine what we should do... they govern us in all we do, in all we say, in all we think" (p. 1). (Elliot & Covington, 2001, p. 74).

They go on to cite Bowlby (1969), Eysenck (1967), Freud (1915), Heider (1958), Hull (1943), James (1890), Jung (1921), Lewin (2013), Maslow (1954), Miller (1944), Murray (1938), Pavlov (1927), Skinner (1938), Thorndike (1911), and Tolman (1925) (all cited in Elliot and Covington, 2001), all of whom identified the importance of the capacity for a learner to feel motivated to avoid learning in a given situation rather than attempt it.

This is a reflection of the early beginnings of the conversation, not the end, but it is worth noting the early and continuous line of thinking across dimensions and fields of study. Indeed, this is why Elliot makes a point of frequently stressing its history (1999). Also noteworthy, is a distinction between more classical conceptions of approach-avoidance and more contemporary conceptions. Classical conceptions examine the dynamics involved in choosing to engage in a given behavior or to avoid a certain behavior (Lewin's work is one of the better examples of what I am referring to as classic), while contemporary conceptions tend to focus on competence-based achievement goals (Elliot's work is an example of more contemporary focus).

In 1935, Kurt Lewin provided one of the earlier coherent psychological treatments of the concepts of approach and avoidance in relation to pedagogy. This is not the first time Levine has made an appearance in a workplace learning book. Odiorne & Rummler (1988) draw at length from Levine's work. In addition to further elucidating the tension within a learner regarding whether to approach an activity or avoid it, he identified a number of implications and practical manifestations that are worth noting, despite how long ago he wrote of this.

First, he pointed out that there is a very real dynamic at play in a learning situation in which the learner is subjected to "...a thrust away from the task...," and that the learner "...shows a tendency, corresponding to the negative valence, to hold himself as aloof as possible from the task" (2013/1935, pp. 205–206). This, of course, even 80 years later will sound very familiar to any active instructor or professor.

Second, he tipped his hat to the nuanced complexity of the learning situation and of approach-avoidance motivation in general, saying that, "... an identical action may in one case be a punishment, in another a reward, according to the total situation in which the [learner] is placed" (pp. 195–196). He further acknowledged that both the situation and certain acts themselves could influence the learner to approach or avoid, and that in order to understand it fully and accurately, "...the process concerned [must be] considered in its relation to the whole present concrete situation" (p. 198).

Finally, he pointed out that a learner operating in the tension field between approach motivations and avoidance motivations, experiences discomfort, which often prompts the learner into "going-out-of-the-field" altogether (p. 213). Going-out-of-the-field can be represented by a physical exodus or a psychological one.

This point is especially powerful because it seems to suggest that even in the face of the struggle between competing drives, the learner may choose to reject the opportunity to engage, never mind the direct effect of the avoidance motivation itself. That is, short of choosing to avoid a learning activity simply because of the technical influence of an avoidance motivation proper, the learner may simply choose to checkout on the basis of having competing motivations to begin with. It would seem then, that in the face of a conflict between approach and avoidance motivation, the game may be fixed slightly in the direction of avoidance and nonengagement. Nearly eight decades later, Leggett et al. (2016) suggest that "the automatic evaluation of stimuli on a positive-negative affect continuum may be closely linked to action" (p. 1164), giving a contemporary nod to the idea that even the evaluative process itself influences behavior.

While contemporary work on approach and avoidance motivation has become increasingly focused, nuanced, differentiated, and empirically supported, it has not refuted the essence of these original ideas, and has instead built upon them. There is "broad and unanimous agreement…that the approach-avoidance distinction is integral to an understanding of emotion" (Elliot et al., 2013, p. 308).

Approach motivation can be defined as "the energization of behavior by, or the direction of behavior toward, positive stimuli" (Elliot, 2006, p. 112). Conversely, avoidance motivation may be defined as "energization of behavior by, or the direction of behavior away from, negative stimuli (p. 112). Energization here is used to mean a "spring to action" (p. 112).

Bass et al. (2019) discussing approach and avoidance systems, use the terms *appetitive motivation* and *withdrawal motivation* (p. 2). Approach motivation has been associated with behavioral activation systems, while avoidance motivation has been associated with behavioral inhibition systems (Gable et al., 2003; Nikitin & Freund, 2015) and encompasses both behavioral reflexes and instrumental actions (Eder et al., 2013).

These approach and avoidance processes are essential for successful adaptation to the environment (Elliot, 2006) are formulated and functionalized through an evaluative process and, "positive/negative valence is conceptualized as the core evaluative dimension" (p. 112). Contemporary research, however, has found that "beneficial/harmful; liked/disliked; desirable/undesirable can be construed as functionally equivalent dimensions" (Elliot, 2006, p. 112). This would suggest that for the human learner, these naturally occurring, functional evaluative judgements include preference and affective judgements, not just survival judgments.

Adding yet more gravity to this dynamic, there is an immediacy connected with these processes and, "an accumulating body of research indicates that persons evaluate most if not all encountered stimuli on a good/bad dimension (Osgood et al., 1957), and that they do so immediately and without intention or even awareness (Bargh, 1997; Zajonc, 1998)" (Elliot & Covington, 2001, p. 78). The short time frame is of vital importance because it weighs heavily on the notion that many educators have that good educational impressions can be made in the long run. While many tout the conventional adage regarding the instantaneous nature of first impressions, when it comes to teaching, we are often content to start slow and boring, and let the totality of the course speak for itself. The very tight window for making such an educational impression is addressed in detail in Frye et al. (2017).

These judgements can be influenced by both situational and dispositional factors (Roskes et al., 2013), which, again, makes a great deal of sense when compared to the literature on learning resistance.

Unfortunately, for the instructor, it gets much more complicated and, well, difficult, than this. Research and theory spanning nearly a century and summarized by Elliot and colleagues, elucidates a learning dynamic in which learners make almost immediate and often unconscious evaluations that lead to motivational decisions to approach (engage) or avoid (disengage or avoid engagement) any (and every) particular learning activity/situation. Given this, one could hope for a strongly rational and unbiased mechanism by which these evaluations are made, but this is not the case.

Deeply influential in the evaluative process are approach-avoidance behavioral dispositions (Corwin, 1921; Lewin, 2013/1935). An approach-avoidance temperament can be considered a "general neurobiological sensitivity" (Elliot & Thrash, 2002), and these dispositions rest, in part, on the learner's experience (Elliot et al., 2013). In the area of social approach and avoidance research, Nikitin and Freund (2015) provided empirical support for an "anticipatory effect" that leads to a "biased interpretation of social information" in which the learner attaches negativity to otherwise ambiguous information (p. 385). Social dynamics are important given that most of life experiences take place in a social context and against the backdrop of social history (Elliot, 2006).

As mentioned above, earlier theorizing of approach-avoidance motivation tended to focus on the directionality of general behavior, while much of the more prominent recent work has situated the approach-avoidance constructs within what are called achievement goals (e.g., Elliot, 2008). This is very often confusing for those not familiar with this particular line of inquiry, mainly because of the terminology, but is less complex than it at first appears.

Most contemporary scholarship on approach-avoidance motivation looks only at behaviors that one is *engaged* in so that they may actually accomplish a given task. In other words, while original approach-avoidance concepts focused on the dynamics involved in a learner actually avoiding an activity altogether, contemporary work tends to look only at those who are engaging in an activity, and then tries to figure out whether or not they are engaged in that activity primarily to accomplish something or to avoid something.

When someone is engaged in an activity to achieve something, the motivational drive responsible it is referred to as *achievement motivation*. Conversely, when someone is engaged in an activity for the purpose of avoiding something, the motivational drive responsible is referred to as *avoidance motivation*.

A simple example of this would be a student in a class who spends hours studying every night of the week and scores high marks on every test. This student is unquestionably engaging in the appropriate and desired behavior for the class, but the question remains as to whether the student is engaged in this pursuit in order to *approach* a goal (i.e., respect from the instructor or classmates, or a personal sense of self-worth), or to *avoid* an outcome (i.e., failing the course, or looking "stupid" to the instructor or classmates).

To provide more contrast, one might consider two different learners in a class who may both choose to *engage* in a learning task such as answering questions in front of the class. Both may engage in the task, but one of the learners may be doing this to impress the instructor and other members of the class (approach goal), while the other may be doing this to avoid looking foolish or unknowledgeable to the instructor or members of the class (avoidance goal). Even once a decision is made to move toward an activity, the motive for that forward movement can be either the result of an approach or avoidance motivational goal. Theories that focus this way are referred to as achievement motivation theories (Elliot, 1999; Schunk & Zimmerman, 2007), the terminological key in the literature being "achievement," which connotes an assumption of engagement in a learning activity.

This more modern line of inquiry is certainly meaningful and has provided quite a large range of practical implications for teaching and learning, but it has a significant limitation. Specifically, it steps over the initial and primary avoidance behavior possibility, namely that of choosing to not engage in the first place. This possibility isn't a stretch and, in fact, is very consistent with the earlier work on approach-avoidance motivation.

The connection between classical and contemporary scholarship lines is evident in that Elliot and his colleagues, while primarily focusing on the achievement motivational aspects, frequently start, historically speaking, with the more fundamental approach-avoidance motivation idea and then move on to the achievement-oriented analysis. Despite the focus on competence motivation and achievement goals, that work still continues to contribute to the broader conception of approach-avoidance motivation, particularly in the clarification of terminology and improved coherence of related constructs.

The concern in this book is primarily with the initial motivational disposition of whether or not to engage authentically in a given learning activity at all, and the previous chapter provided substantial support for the reality that students choose not to engage in learning situations of all types. However, the achievement-oriented approach-avoidance motivational scholarship is important as well because of the potential negative effects experienced by learners even when engaging in the learning space, but doing so via an avoidance goal (Ferris et al., 2012; Nikitin & Freund, 2015).

The implications of all of this are vital in understanding how to facilitate engagement in learners. There are five unavoidable elements to consider. First, learners will often choose purposefully to not engage in a learning activity or activities. This choice to not engage should be considered a motivated behavior in and of itself. Further, to consider why we want them to do what *we* want (how to motivate them to engage) without honestly considering the reasons *they* have for wanting to do what they want (motivated to *not* engage) is to marginalize the student.

Thankfully, there are many practical ways to connect with individual learners, even in very large classes, that will allow the instructor to come to understand these individual dynamics. Some examples of these are individual interviews, online "check-in" posts (even for face-to-face courses), and student journaling. These will be addressed in detail in later sections of this book.

Second, these decisions are based in part on immediate and often unconscious processes and have an automaticity (Elliot & Covington, 2001). This immediacy cannot be overlooked, is a vital consideration in attempting to formulate efforts to facilitate learner engagement, and a key factor in my claim for the necessity of striving for what I am calling motivational immediacy.

Third, these decisions to approach or avoid are also influenced by dispositional factors, such as temperaments, and are developed in part by social contexts and histories. Judgments are not unbiased, and social avoidance tendencies lead to negative interpretations of ambiguous cues.

Fourth, even those learners who choose to engage in the learning activity (achievement) may be doing so with avoidance motivation being the underlying motivation. Avoidance motivation has been linked to many different negative outcomes and effects including to a reduction in subjective well-being (Dijk et al., 2013).

Fifth, all learners – every single one – are subjected to a tension field in which they are faced with competing approach and avoidance motivations. This tension field, itself, can be uncomfortable enough to cause learners to end up "going-out-of-the-field" either physically or psychologically. The five of these implications taken together provide a rather narrow window for optimal learning. That leaves the instructor with the question of how one might: (a) facilitate engagement in the first place, (b) facilitate it via approach goals, where possible, on the part of the learner, and (c) foster a learning environment in which the tension between approach and avoidance motivation, as experienced by the learner, is minimal enough to avoid causing the learner to checkout.

This information on approach and avoidance motivation will connect tightly with the idea of immediate motivation, which will be introduced a few sections further on, but first there is one other motivational dynamic that needs to be drawn into this discussion.

PROPOSITION # 3: A LACK OF MEANS-END FUSION (MEF) LEADS TO LEARNER DISENGAGEMENT. INTRINSIC VALUE DEFINED STRUCTURALLY

One thing all of these cognitively and socio-cognitively oriented motivational theories have in common is that they tend to focus on internal constructs and their relevance to the human learning situation and the social interactions involved (Perry et al., 2007). As such, they have tended to focus a great deal on whether or not motivation is extrinsic or intrinsic. This distinction has classically been treated as a difference between whether an individual's drive is derived from within the person (intrinsic) or from outside the person (extrinsic). The terms *intrinsic* and *extrinsic* motivation have been heavily used and researched over the past decades (a quick database search will reveal approximately 10,000 academic journal articles) and results have helped clarify some basic tenets of motivation. However, while it has been a useful dichotomous construct, there has been some ambiguity regarding the meaning and use of the terms.

Kruglanski et al. (2018) have focused on a very different conception of extrinsic motivation and that nuanced view has very important implications for the instructor, particularly against the backdrop of learning resistance. They point out that historically, intrinsic and extrinsic motivation were differentiated according to the structure – the relationship of the behavior to the purported goal. Over time, however, popular discussions have shifted toward what they refer to as content-oriented definitions. Content-oriented definitions tend to focus more on the content of the motivated behavior itself (what is it and why is it done). This has given rise to confusion at times because any given behavior can be arguably intrinsic or extrinsic, depending on how one argued, philosophically, about it. Kruglanski et al., claim to be returning and defining the word structurally and in a way that they say is *content-free* meaning that focus shifts back to the relationship between the motivated behavior and the end goal.

This can seem rather pedantic and perhaps more technical than necessary, but it is important because it opens up a line of observation and inquiry that is not available to someone who is seeing intrinsic as related only to the reason one sets out on an end goal. While pointing out that their ideas have historical roots, they nonetheless provide a clearly-stated alternative conception of intrinsic (and extrinsic) motivation by attaching it to what they refer to as MEF.

MEF

With every motivated behavior there is an attached goal. The behavior, in this sense, is seen as the means, while the goal is considered the ends. The means and the ends, as we all know, are not always nestled up closely together, and our everyday life would tell us that goals that are realized sooner tend to motivate more than goals that are set much further out. This is why it is much easier to skip meal to finish a high priority task at work, than it is to pay off a house ten years early by skipping one meal a week for 20 years.

Kruglanski et al. (2018) refer to motivation being intrinsic if there is proximity (fusion) between the means and the ends, something they call MEF. Intrinsic motivation then, defined this way refers to, "…the relation (or fusion) between any goal and the activity meant to serve it" (p. 167). The range of time between the activity of the means and the accomplishment of the end, they define as the *intrinsicality continuum* (p. 167).

Tying together Gestalt principles and drawing empirical evidence from multiple disciplines, the authors make a solid case that there are at least three powerful antecedents for MEF – (a) repeated coupling of the means activity and the end goal in the perception of the learner, (b) linkage uniqueness, meaning that the link between the activity and the goal is distinct enough that there is a significant reason to engage in it over and against a different activity, and (c) similarity, meaning that the activity is in some way similar to the goal of the learner.

PROPOSITION # 4: GLOBAL MOTIVATION ISN'T ENOUGH – IMMEDIATE MOTIVATION IS KEY IMMEDIATE AND GLOBAL MOTIVATION

It is almost weekly that one of my graduate students, a student in a workplace training classroom, or someone I am in casual conversation with, mentions that their students are generally very motivated for this reason or that. Military instructors are regularly telling me that their students are "highly motivated" because they want to be pilots, airmen, soldiers, marines, sailors, and so on. College professors are frequently saying that their students are highly motivated to earn a graduate degree, and instructors in the workplace will often say that their learners are highly motivated to get promoted, ensure job security, etc.

When one understands motivation to be only globally related to learning ventures, then an option becomes available for that educator to marginalize their own role as an instructor in fostering motivation in the learner, in the moment. When at its best, this view allows for the instructor to sort the learners in any given learning space between those who are motivated (globally) and those who are not. This at least allows for some clear responsibility on the part of the instructor to attempt to foster motivation in that "unmotivated" group – *if* that instructor doesn't feel as though nothing can be done for that group because they are some sort of outliers for the group as a whole. But when this view is not dressed up in its' Sunday clothes, it has an almost entirely negative effect because it provides the instructor with a reason to cut loose the unwieldy burden of trying to motivate any learners. They already are motivated, of course.

The problem with this line of thought is uncomplicated. It is an unsupported assumption that those who are motivated to earn a college or university degree, get a raise, obtain a certification, or fly a military aircraft, are also motivated to learn any particular thing from a particular professor, or instructor, on any given evening at any given moment in time. Human learning is a moment-by-moment dynamic; learning is sewn tightly to motivation, and therefore motivation to learn (or not) is also a moment-by-moment dynamic.

Since I have taken the time to share the potential harm in viewing learning motivation strictly as a global construct, I will also share the potential benefit is in viewing learning motivation as an immediate construct. When the instructor sees the motivation of the learners in the classroom or online learning space as something immediate to the teaching moment, then the instructor identifies automatically with the role of motivation facilitator as a basic and necessary part of the teaching responsibility. Being motivational as one teaches, in this case, is not going above and beyond, but just, well, teaching. Here again we can return to Wlodkowski and Ginsberg (2017) in remembering that instructors should, "think motivationally, plan for intrinsically motivating lessons as a *continual process* (p. 45, emphasis added)" and that "every instructional plan also needs to be a motivational plan" (p. 45). Teaching ceases at once to be the transmission of some sort of technical content and transforms into everything that we, as educators, always say it is – an individual construction of meaning and transformation.

Again, going back to approach-avoidance motivation, one can see the importance of immediacy in training and learning because "humans, like protozoa, exhibit *immediate*, constitutionally ingrained approach and avoidance responses to certain classes of stimuli" (Elliot & Covington, 2001, p. 78, italics added), and that these responses are "...based in the *immediacy* (if not primacy) and automaticity of many approach-avoidance-based motivational processes" (p. 77, italics added). It is for these reasons that Elliot and Covington "...contend that approach-avoidance is not just an important motivational distinction, but that it is fundamental and basic, and should be construed as the foundation on which other motivational distinctions rest" (p. 74). Strange how often it is not invited to the party.

The Relationship Between Global and Immediate Motivation

My thinking began with the somewhat premature view that Immediate Motivation was the most important type of motivation. I was challenged on this view by one of my students and had to spend some time thinking about a more accurate view of the relationship between the two.

I do maintain that Immediate Motivation is pervasively overlooked, to the serious detriment to learning efficiency, but think one can have a better understanding of the one when it is discussed in conjunction with the other. Global Motivation and Immediate Motivation are related in at least three ways. First, Global Motivation is very often the reason that the learner is exposed to the learning situation (and instructor) in the first place. So, unless one randomly engages in some sort of street preaching-esque mode of unsolicited teaching, Immediate Motivation might not matter much until a learner has a reason to be in the classroom to begin with. In that sense, Global Motivation might set up the opportunity for Immediate Motivation.

Second, Immediate Motivation can, on the other hand, give rise to Global Motivation. An example of this would be a situation in which a person becomes deeply interested in a new topic, field of study, or concept, because of the deeply interesting presentation of it in the immediate sense. If someone is flipping channels and comes across a documentary on something that is not of general interest, but which has such noteworthy visuals, and/or is being presented by someone with a riveting presentation voice or manner, one might tune in long enough to develop a broader interest in the subject matter.

Even more basic than this, would be a child who is visited at school by a firefighter in full turnout gear, and decides that very moment to be a firefighter. Sometimes these sorts of dynamics remain only for a short while but sometimes they become a lifelong quest.

Third, while it may not be factually true that one sort is truly more important than the other, it is an everyday reality that those who are globally motivated have a complete lack of interest at a given point along the way and completely tune out, learning nothing, while those who have no significant global motivation at all, can be drawn in by a particularly good speaker, an exceptional picture or video, or a lively group conversation. This latter condition gives rise to learning, even in the absence of global motivation. If this is true, then pedantic arguments aside, there is a powerful reason for instructors to spend more time focusing on (and fostering)

Immediate Motivation and to stop relying on Global Motivation to shove their learners across the finish line.

PROPOSITION # 5: INSTRUCTORS MUST PRACTICE MOTIVATIONAL IMMEDIACY

To be clear, what is being suggested here is a motivational construct, not a communication construct, per se, but my choice of the term "motivational immediacy" was drawn in part from the construct of *teacher immediacy*, which is drawn from the communications discipline. This being the case, a brief overview might be useful.

Teacher immediacy is a term that refers to "perceptions of psychological closeness between the instructor and students" (Kwitonda, 2017, p. 384) and is based on the "immediacy principle" discussed at length by Mehrabian (1971). The immediacy principle was stated, quite simply and directly by Mehrabian as the dynamic that "people are drawn toward persons and things they like, evaluate highly, and prefer; and they avoid or move away from things they dislike, evaluate negatively, or do not prefer" (p. 1). Notice here the similarity with regards to approach-avoidance motivation.

Cabranes-Grant (2018) attributes the original usage of the term "immediacy" to Kierkegaard. According to Cabranes-Grant, by immediacy, Kierkegaard was referring to "the experience of presentness" (p. 6).

There has been a lot of scholarship on this over the years, much of it in the communication field (Anderson, 1979; Burroughs et al., 1989; Estepp et al., 2013; Kelly et al., 2015; Kwitonda, 2017; LeFebvre & Allen, 2014; Mehrabian, 1969, 1971, 1981; Plax et al., 1986). The concept of Immediacy is often addressed in terms of verbal and nonverbal immediacy (Baumann & Sidebottom, 2018), and the practice of engaging in instructional practices in an effort to bring about immediacy is referred to as teacher immediacy (Bialowas & Steimel, 2019).

Teacher immediacy has been identified as a tool to mitigate learner resistance, and in Chapter 2, I provide some strategies for fostering immediacy, but my point in bringing it up here is only to introduce the genesis of my own adoption of the term "motivational immediacy."

It is time to draw all of the pieces of this puzzle together. Taking into account that Immediate Motivation is vital for addressing learner resistance, maintaining MEF, and fostering, where possible, approach motivation, it is my contention that the instructor who wishes to facilitate consistent and authentic learner engagement must strive for motivational immediacy. *Motivational immediacy* can be seen as a *state* of being in a moment-by-moment motivational relationship with the student. Defined as an *action process*, motivational immediacy is the practice of purposefully adopting as a part of one's instructional method, the consistent, pervasive, and habitual attempt to connect with each individual learner and ensure that the learner is motivated in the immediate sense, regardless of whether global motivation is present or not.

CONCLUSION

The answers we get are seldom greater than the questions that they belong to. When we ask the question "what must we do to motivate our learners to engage?" our answers may be useful, but they will never be complete. This is because the question those answers are predicated upon is based on a misunderstanding of the situation – namely, the assumption that unengaged learners are in a state of motivational stasis and we need only to nudge them in the right direction. A better question might be, "what are our learners motivated to do, and why?"

FROM RESISTANCE AND ENGAGEMENT TO EFFECTUAL LEARNING

Chapter 4 takes the information about learning resistance from the previous chapter, and the information about motivation in this chapter, and puts them together in the conceptualization of *effectual learning*. Effectual learning is considered learning that includes both acquisition of content and acceptance of content.

From Learning Resistance to Efficient and Effectual Learning

Safety instructors everywhere are onto something. It is not that all of those who teach workplace safety classes do everything right, but there is an essential truth that they seem to be aware of that the rest of us would be well-served to learn. Those who have been tasked with the thankless job of teaching the rest of us that we should not stand on the top step of the ladder, are fully aware of something that most instructors miss. They are fully aware that first, we already know not to stand on the top step of the ladder, and second, that we are damn well going to do it anyway.

What then, is their game? Is the training a joke? A trivial bit of bureaucracy? A litigiously-oriented liability check? Sadly, at times, workplace training can be all of these things, but it doesn't have to be. When standing before a group of employees and providing instruction on something the group already largely knows and already mostly ignores, the only recourse for the serious instructor is to "go big or go home," and attempt to foster a post-training condition in which the learners actually change the way they believe. Beyond learning something new, they come to believe that something is *good* and ought to be acted upon.

The instructor who teaches this way holds a different view of teaching and training on the whole, and rather than seeing it as the process of telling people stuff they didn't know, they see it as a process of convincing people that those things ought to be believed and acted upon. What helps those who teach workplace safety classes to adopt this broadened perspective, is that they are working with content that is quite often naturally dismissed by both those who have been on the job for a long time (and survived thus far) and those who are new (who have not seen anyone hurt on the job yet). A common method for pulling off the impossible is to appeal to the emotions, and by extension, interests, of the learners – most often by sharing near

DOI: 10.4324/9781003144137-5

over-the-top videos of workplace training disasters. There is not a great deal about this in the professional texts, but a simple walkthrough of safety training classrooms all over the world, will reveal instructional material that, on the one hand, is moving, but on the other cringeworthy. The point here is not to endorse gruesome videos in the classroom, although there may certainly be contexts where that is appropriate, but to point out that these instructors intuitively know that they must make the learners feel something in addition to thinking something.

ENGAGED LEARNERS

A learner is engaged when they are open to learning and willing to put their back into it. It is not, as has been noted, a gullible and blind acceptance of anything the instructor may present. Engagement is not synonymous with buy-in, but it is almost always required for buy-in to occur. Kraiger and Mattingly (2018) refer to Mayer's (2008) claim that a learner's first step is to "select" what information to focus on and suggest that, "from a pedagogical perspective, manipulating the instructional environment so that the learner engages in the relevant content is thus critical to facilitating learning" (pp. 14–17). In cases in which someone who was resistant to a learning situation later learned something intentional, there was doubtless a point in time in which the learner ceased being resistant and became engaged, if only reluctantly.

Despite this distinction between engagement and buy-in, every teaching act has an intentional purpose to bring about not only the acquisition of content, but also the acceptance of content. That is, we want those in training classes to not only understand the technical aspects of what we teach them to do, but we also want them to believe that the things we are teaching them *ought to* be done. So, while understanding learning resistance is important, it *is* so particularly because it leads to a clear need for motivational immediacy. And, in turn, motivational immediacy is useful especially because it allows the instructor to foster both acquisition and acceptance in the learner of the learning content. It is a means to an end, not the end.

The most principled instructors are wary of tricking learners into something without the learner's individual agency intact, but also know that the best way to foster the acceptance of meaningful learning content is to foster openness and engagement in the learner to begin with. The best instructor will believe in the value of what is being taught and therefore, believe that if the learner will approach it with an open mind, engagement with it, and apply reason, the content will be accepted. It is true, of course, that in the training world the instructor is quite often stuck teaching something that does not, on the face of it, seem worth it even to the person teaching it. Frye et al. (2017) addressed this particular problem specifically:

> Regarding passion, of course, it is much easier to suggest what, than to suggest how. Our experience in the training world has been that very often professional trainers will tell us that their students (employee-learners) are highly skeptical of the importance of the content. Our immediate follow-up question is, "Do you agree with them?" Sadly, there is quite often an awkward pause and the truth is immediately clear on the face of the trainer. There is no practicable way to fake passion. The best that can be said here is, again, what we say to these professional educators – "figure out a way to believe in what you teach or stop teaching it. You must believe it is useful or they will not believe it is useful." Passion is not passive; passion leans forward with its face in the wind. Passion is passed through to practice in the form of energy and motion. Passion is not monotone; passion is not motionless. Passion does not stand behind a lectern or sit in a chair. In fact, passion doesn't stand still much at all. Simply put (although not at all simply done), "own" what you teach, know why you teach it, feel deeply about its importance, and then share that honestly and directly with your students. True passion will always make its presence known without us helping it across the street (p. 340).

ACQUISITION AND ACCEPTANCE

A great deal of energy and focus are extended toward whether or not our training means are, in fact, producing our transfer ends. Much of the assessment activities that are employed at both the individual and program levels, are designed to confirm or disconfirm the achievement of the desired outcome. While it makes sense that one should ensure that ends are achieved through a given set of means, doing so does not ensure that the means are at all *efficient* at producing the desired ends. The question being addressed here then is not merely whether or not our training results in learning, but whether or not our training results in as much learning as possible in any given situation. The distinction between wanting learners to learn the bare essentials and wanting learners to learn as much as they possibly can as effectively and efficiently as they can, is a defining factor in both instructor and program excellence.

How efficient, then, is our effort to facilitate learning? Are we slopping effort, energy, and financial resources out of the training bucket with each awkward step we take? Unfortunately, one thing I run into routinely when trying to make the case to someone that they need to facilitate more engagement with learners, that they need to mitigate learner resistance, and that they need to practice motivational immediacy, is a counterdemonstration about how fixing what is *not* broken is not always (or even seldom) worth the effort. "Look" they will say, "we have been doing this for 20 years – it is working – we don't need to reframe the entire way we conceptualize training and learning."

Many years ago, a colleague challenged my efforts by pointing out that the learning objectives in the program we were discussing were being met, at least moderately well. One of the biggest impediments to improvement is a feeling of contentment with the status quo. Jim Collins opened his book with the often quoted "good is the enemy of great," (2001, p. 1) and a similar statement has been attributed to John D. Rockefeller, nearly a century before Collins – "don't be afraid to give up the good to go for the great" (Bannerman, 2006, p. 24).

Engagement and learning resistance scholarship can sometimes legitimately focus on the near impossibility of certain teaching situations and attempting to foster learning through them, but the focus here is increasing the efficiency of what might be already successful effort. Good instructors do not become great instructors while being content with being "good."

So, do we need to do anything at all with all of this talk of learning resistance, learning engagement, and motivational immediacy? Acquisition and Acceptance – so what? One of the criticisms of academic ruminations is that they so rarely converge on some practical path and even more rarely produce a practical action of some sort.

No matter the debate over whether learning is inseparable from motivation and therefore two different facets of the same thing, or whether they are two distinct phenomena that cannot be disentangled (Rogers & Illeris, 2003), the implications are the same. Learning without some sort of motivation simply does not occur (Illeris, 2017; Taylor, 2017). Given this linkage between resistance, engagement, and ultimately acceptance, the most authentic learning, the most practical learning, and perhaps therefore the only meaningful type of learning, involves both the *acquisition* of knowledge and the *acceptance* of knowledge. Acquisition is easy to measure usually, but acceptance nearly impossible, which is probably the most salient reason that it is so often bounced off the cart somewhere along the journey. The point here is that "that thing" we want them to learn is not simply a thing that they need to know, but rather a thing that we deeply want them to believe they *should* know.

Taking all of this together, if motivation is seen as both globally and immediately focused, and if it is the responsibility of the teacher to work to facilitate motivation in the learner at every moment during every teaching situation, then training is a tremendously difficult process that requires significant modifications in approach. And, of paramount importance to the trainer, the entire concept of employee learning must be reconceptualized.

EFFECTUAL LEARNING

Wenger's (2000) assertion that words help us focus on features of something that we may have taken for granted and missed, is in play here. In order to convey the key concepts of the principles in this book I am introducing terms and using them throughout. I have tried to build a case here for the need for learning that includes both acquisition and acceptance, and after speaking and writing about this for a while I began to think of a way to encapsulate both of those factors together in a way that differentiated that type of learning with all of the other references to it that so often include only one. I use the term *effectual learning* to refer to any form of learning that includes both of these components. The word effectual is very close in meaning to the similar, and more common word effective.

In digging a little on this, I found that while the words are very similar and many sources show them to be the same – with effectual being the more antiquated or obsolete term – there is a difference. Merriam-Webster provides a distinction in claiming that the word effective means "producing or capable of producing a result," while effectual "suggests the accomplishment of a desired result especially as viewed after the fact" (https://www.merriam-webster.com/dictionary/effectual). Effectual then, seemed to fit very well with what I was trying to convey because the very reason I am speaking about learning that must include both acquisition and acceptance, is because it is the only way that learning will produce any sort of desired effect after the fact. This "after the fact" sort of effect is referred to by many different names such as learning transfer, training transfer, and, to use more constructivist terms, transformational learning that results in meaningful behavior change (Mezirow, 2000) and shared meaning making (Lave & Wenger, 1991). The point is, the thing most all of us want but have so much trouble facilitating, is long-term, after the fact, behavior change. Again, no matter what one's theoretical position on training and learning, there is generally a consensus that the instructor wants some sort of lasting change in behavior – after the fact. It is this ultimate goal that has spurred the extensive body of literature related to the various aspects of training transfer.

My claim here, is that in order for this to happen, we must foster both Acquisition and Acceptance of the learning content, whatever that may be, and I am therefore referring to learning where both of these dynamics are present as *effectual learning*.

LEARNING EFFICIENCY

When we speak of efficiency, even in common language, we are not discussing whether or not something is being accomplished but whether it is being accomplished in a more or less optimal way. *Learning efficiency then is the degree to which any given learning experience results in effectual learning.* By extension, teaching efficiency, or instructional efficiency, can be considered teaching that brings about effectual learning.

FIVE PRINCIPLES FOR FOSTERING EFFECTUAL LEARNING

All of the content in the first five chapters of this book can be boiled down to the following five principles of Effectual Learning, Learning Efficiency, and Motivational Immediacy, summarized in the pages that follow.

1. You never teach groups – you always and only teach *individuals*...who might be together in groups sometimes.
2. *Connection* is the "underneath" of all effectual teaching.
3. You must engage in *Motivational Immediacy* as you teach.
4. You must foster both the *acquisition* of content and the *acceptance* of content.
5. Focusing on the negative *is* positive – focusing on the learner's strengths while ignoring their needs is not human-centered teaching.

You Teach Individuals, Not Groups

Before I even start this one, I need to make certain that my point is not misconstrued. The point being made here is not connected academically to the argument regarding where the individual leaves off and society begins. That is, this is not a statement about the individual over and against society. The role of the social has been clearly acknowledged in other places, but to be practical, and from an instructional perspective, it is useful to speak of it in the following way.

There are many cringeworthy educational clichés out there, but none of them are more troubling than "teach to the middle." I was speaking at an event a number of years ago when someone used this line to address a question someone was asking about how you can reach a diverse group of learners in the classroom. To be fair to both the cliché itself and to those who use it, the sentiment can seem very much to be a practical truism and as such, it both rolls of the tongue and tumbles into the ear with the same ease. The fact of the matter is, we do have very diverse groups of learners in our classrooms and trying to reach them all on an individual basis is, on the face of it, impossible.

So, maybe to some extent, that phrase speaks to a certain truth that must be admitted. But it also tends to convey a meaning that mustn't. To realize that an instructor in a learning space with a large number of learners and a limited amount of time to teach a set amount of content, simply cannot fellowship in real-time with each individual learner is probably healthy. But there are ways that an instructor can teach to the individual rather than the group and to embrace any sort of cliché that stifles our awareness of that is a dangerous move for any instructor who wishes to be exceptional.

Mitchell (1988), when writing about focusing on individual learners in the workplace, wrote, "It is the most time-consuming and, therefore, the most inefficient. It is, however, the most effective way to learn, which is why so much training in American takes place on the job" (p. 17). It is interesting here that Mitchell, while speaking for individualized attention, referred to it as inefficient. If, indeed, it is as he claimed, the most effective way to learn, then it might be the most efficient way to engage the learner so long as it is true learning that is sought in the first place.

Teacher immediacy (Kearney et al. [1985] is a related notion that has impact in that it is related to the student's perception that the teacher is "immediate" (in that present moment and time). A significant amount has been published on this construct and the suggested modes of practice reveal that there may be ways to convey immediacy as a perception beyond the limitations of physical immediacy (Plax et al. [1986]). It is difficult to find any mention of "instructor immediacy" in the workplace training literature but that is a shortcoming of the workplace training literature, not the concept.

It would take more than a few chapters to lay out an exhaustive and airtight case for why each individual learner learns their own situatedness, but the concepts provided in the first section of this book should provide a moderately compelling case to shift our teaching perspective toward one that focuses on teaching individuals rather than groups. Husserl (1970/1954) adopted the concept of the lifeworld, and used the term to describe the highly unique individual experiential world, and it is a good word to use here when discussing the need to teach individual learners. This was similar to Kidd's (1959) use of the term *life space.*

Each distinct lifeworld brings with it a distinct set of interpretive structures, learning needs, teaching preferences, and practical applications, and the only way you can teach effectively is to address those individual needs, preferences and applications. There is simply no way this can be done if you are "teaching to the middle."

This claim needs to be accompanied with a set of concrete teaching methods – some way to provide evidence that it can actually be done – in order to pack the punch that I want it to. I will take a big step in that direction with the second section of this book (Chapters 7–12), but even so, I would point out that the inability to do something well does not undermine the fact that we ought to be doing it at all. For the time being, the *how* needn't get in the way of the *what*, and the *when* doesn't need to diminish the reality of the *why*.

You Must Connect

Given that one must teach individuals if one is to foster effectual learning, the key to teaching an individual is connection. Pascal wrote, "Let no one say that I have said nothing new; the arrangement of the subject is new" (1958/1670, p. 7), and admittedly, the case for connection has been made many times over the years (e.g., Brady, 1975; Horton et al., 1998; Kotinsky, 1933; Lave & Wenger, 1991). But it must be included in this list of five principles because it is an indispensable part of the method and process for fostering effectual learning. Connection in the sense that I am using it here has to do with relationship, fellowship, and community with the other. It is Brady's (1975) convalidating relationship and Peter's and Armstrong's (1998) collaborative relationship. It is the underlying mechanism by which an instructor is able to take the intended content of the teaching situation, and match it up to the distinct needs, preferences, and applications of each learner in your course; to meet them where they are and walk the journey with them.

ENGAGING IN MOTIVATIONAL IMMEDIACY

Depending on the learner's motivation for the end goal of the learning situation to ensure consistent engagement, is not a wise or effective course of action. learners may be highly motivated to earn a training certificate, gain a promotion, have credibility in the workplace, or find another job, but that doesn't mean that they are going to be highly motivated to engage with the learning experience at any given moment during the training course.

To take this even further, the learner's motivation to learn a given subject in a given course still does not ensure a moment-by-moment engagement throughout the course. Any training professional who wishes to foster continuous, consistent, pervasive engagement by the student, will need to ensure immediate motivation. That is, the highly effective instructor practices motivational immediacy – that instructor ensures that they are making each learning moment a motivational moment. Each moment spent in a learning experience has some sort of content, even if that content is experiential or processual, and the motivationally immediate instructor never loses sight of the need to package *incentive* right along with that *content.* Returning again to Gagne' (1965), gaining the attention of the learner is the first training event. Keeping that attention is at the heart of every training event.

Once again, I need to take a minute and admit that this is a great deal more difficult to do than it is to say. But whether or not it can be done flawlessly, it can be done actively, and I will spend time addressing this in Section II.

FOSTERING BOTH ACQUISITION AND ACCEPTANCE

Little more needs to be said here since the focus of this chapter centered on effectual learning, a term I use to connote learning that includes both acquisition of the content and acceptance of the content as valid and meaningful. Teaching simply to promote acquisition results in mostly temporary but always inert knowledge that is rarely applied actively toward any particular end.

RESISTANCE MITIGATION APPROACH (RMA) AS A POSITIVE APPROACH

However, valuable the contributions of positive psychology have been, it is a disservice to the learner to avoid helping with the learner's most basic struggles and problems, instead only working to squeeze whatever can be had from the learner's strengths. When stranded on the side of the road with a flat tire, no one has the patience to be grateful when a passing motorist stops and provides them with a fuel additive that is purported to enhance the car's internal combustion. Give me help with my tire or leave me alone, enhanced engine performance won't help me with my problem.

When a learner has incredible strengths and potential but is continuing to struggle with a particular sort of "flat tire" in our classroom, the only meaningful way to serve this student is to step up beside the student, and work the problem, shoulder to shoulder, and this would require a jack, not a fuel additive.

In this sense, having an approach to teaching that actively seeks out the potential learning resistance and engages in ways that will mitigate that resistance for the good of the student, is a supremely learner-centered and positive approach.

ENGAGEMENT AND EFFORT

The importance of learner engagement in the workplace is not new. Both theory and research have supported this (Bell & Kozlowski, 2008; Kraiger & Mattingly, 2018). Blume et al. (2000, cited in Saks & Gruman, 2018) stressed the connection between increased engagement and training transfer, and Kraiger and Mattingly (2018) cite work as far back as Craik & Lockart (1972) in support of engagement as it relates to later recall. What has been described so far in the first several chapters of this book, is a specific way to think about learner motivation, and about how different ways of thinking about motivation bring with them different ways of acting in practice.

Effectual learning is about both knowing how to do something and also in believing that it is a thing that should be done. There are many forces that converge in the human learning, but in the end, training transfer is about effort on the part of the employee-learner. And, "effort becomes the key determinate of the extent to which trainees' will exhibit the expected behaviors" (Marand & Noe, 2018, p. 81).

Chapter 5

Zones of Engagement

Understanding motivational immediacy in the workplace requires an understanding of the workplace learning space. More specifically, it requires an understanding of the motivational space for learning that exists in the workplace. In order to be able to identify and understand all of the motivational spaces in the workplace, one must be able to first identify and understand all of the learning spaces within the workplace, which I have referred to previously as the zones of intervention (Taylor & Mckissack, 2014).

Most often, when the term learning space is used, it is used in the macro sense to refer to a genre of teaching and learning, such as higher education, community education, or in the present case, workplace education. However, this habit can serve to obscure the important nuances of the more broadly conceived learning space. This chapter will identify and explain the four zones of intervention in the workplace and then follow with how each of these zones can be used to foster engagement through motivational immediacy.

TRAINING TRANSFER

In previous chapters, I focused on learning transfer more directly, particularly in relation to learning resistance and engagement. A few points can be drawn from the training transfer literature that pertains directly to consideration given to the four zones of motivational immediacy addressed in the following pages. First, learning something is not the same thing as doing something. Pham, Segers & Gijselaers (2012) suggest that "learning in training does not automatically result in transfer" (p. 2). The literature, in fact, points to the fact that performance is a more important factor in

DOI: 10.4324/9781003144137-6

the workplace than learning (Burke & Hutchins, 2008; Swanson, 1997). The training transfer literature itself includes the affective (e.g., Ford, Smith, Weissbein, Gully & Salas, 1998); Taylor (2014) addressing the issue from an affective position hints at this when he points out that learning something is more about accepting content than acquiring content. This is an important issue because it makes salient the disconnect between all of the material that training facilitators hope to actually *teach* and what learners in the workplace actually end up *doing*.

Second, the discussion on training transfer provides solid evidence of the continued concern to improve the level of training in the workplace and by doing so to improve the overall efficiency of the training effort. Going further than this idea of efficiency, I have introduced the term effectual learning to refer to learning that includes both acquisition and acceptance of the content. To have learning that is both efficient and effectual, that is, in successful alignment with its intended purpose, it is a perfect fit for the cost-benefit approach to training in the workplace that is so prevalent at the present time.

The particular set of ideas addressed in in the following pages fit well with this emphasis because they are aimed at using more of the resources already in the workplace for facilitating training transfer and for facilitating it more naturally, efficiently, and effectually.

Third, the continued work on training transfer has led to the admission that learning is a situated event and that classroom training and on-the-job learning are not easily disentangled (Burke & Hutchins, 2008; Baldwin-Evans, 2006; Clarke, 2004). Indeed the traditional boundaries have been expanded, and "we must consider training as a system within work organizations" (p. 142). As early as 1995, this realization had led to an examination of factors that had not traditionally been considered in terms of workplace learning and training (Cannon-Bowers, Salas, Tannenbaum & Matheiu, 1995).

These three points provide the impetus for considering a very broad array of novel ideas, paradigms and approaches for workplace training, and for looking closely for new ways of framing things that have perhaps been at least generally understood for some time. The following pages are an effort toward that end.

COMMUNITIES OF PRACTICE

Lave and Wenger (1991) perhaps more than anyone else, disrupted the idea that learning occurs entirely in an abstract, sterile, and unsituated way. They and others (Driscoll, 2005; Illeris, 2007; Wenger, 1998, 2000, 2002) have instead posited that learning is entirely embedded in the social milieu and is inseparable from its context. Wenger's (2000, 2002) conception of learning as a dynamic that is bounded by a community of practice in which the learner experiences learning as *belonging*, learning as *becoming*, learning as *experiencing*, and learning as *doing* leads one to fully consider that learning may take place at all times and in all quarters of the workplace learning space.

If this is the case – that is, that employees are learning at all times in every facet of the workplace, then it must further be considered that learning is also being *facilitated* at all times and in every facet of the workplace. The natural next link in this chain is to reason that if learning is being facilitate at all times and all places within the workplace, than learning motivation is also in play and, therefore, motivational immediacy is necessary.

THREE DIMENSIONS OF LEARNING

Illeris (2007) speaks of two axes of learning: the *acquisition* and the *interaction*. The acquisition axis is in a reciprocal relationship between what he refers to as the content dimension (knowledge, understanding, skills), and the incentive dimension (motivation, emotion, and volition). These internal dynamics, together making up the acquisition process, also interact in a reciprocal fashion, with the external environment. This intersection of the individual and the environment, Illeris refers to as the interaction process. The interaction process connects the individual learner with the social nature of learning, which results in the third dimension of learning (social). The external environment (social) which is made up of both the social (localized social situation) as well as the societal, encompasses all of the extant theory on social aspects of learning while, in a more holistic sense sees these social dynamics as inseparable from the internal processes.

Illeris calls all educators and scholars to draw back from their daily focus and see the learning phenomenon as it actually is a complex dynamic, the many valid parts of which cannot be disentangled from one another in practice, no matter how much that may be done in academic pursuit.

Illeris (2017) points out that Wenger, while providing some wiggle room for internal learning and acquisition (cognitive) processes, does so from firmly within a social learning perspective. As such, Wenger's point of departure mirrors to some extant earlier attempts by those operating solidly within a given position while trying to explore and make note of the others, and as such it is subject to the same limitations. Illeris stakes his claim as having approached the human learning process from some position neutral of these two (internal cognition vs. social learning), acknowledging the existence and essential nature of both the individual

Individual Context

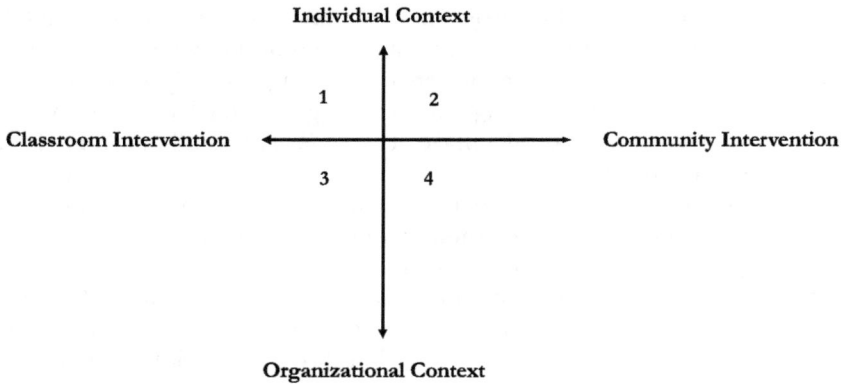

Classroom Intervention   1   2   **Community Intervention**

                              3   4

Organizational Context

Figure 5.1 *Zones of intervention and motivation.*

and the social as an "interplay" which cannot be "disentangled." Whether or not one can operate in some sort of orientation vacuum when approaching the learning dynamic, it might appear reasonable to purport that perhaps, emphasizing one aspect of human learning over another is something of an academic exercise rather than a practical one.

In a workplace learning adaption of his original perspective on the dimensions of learning, Illeris substituted the environmental side of the figure with social dimensions in line with the workplace learning spaces (see Figure 5.1). Instead of *social* and *sociality*, he includes *production* on the one side and *community* on the other, referring, respectively, to the dynamics involved with the purpose of the workplace itself – production, and the general social situation as it is altered by being bounded, at least to a certain extent, by the workplace. These ideas do not venture far from his ideas in conceptual terms but provide added levels of specificity for the workplace learning space.

The importance of Illeris in the presentation of the zones of intervention and motivational immediacy is that in order for all the zones to be clearly recognized and utilized in efforts to improve the workplace for both the employer and employee alike, all dimensions of human learning must be acknowledged and understood. The zones suggested here are, in fact, simply the logical conclusion of zooming out on the learning process and seeing all of its many different dynamics, not the least of which are cognitive, affective, and social.

Looking at Wenger and Illeris together leads up to a very basic understanding about learning – that learning is *everywhere at all times*. Taking this as an assumption, one could reasonably consider that if learning is taking place in all places and at all times within the workplace community, then teaching and training, at least in some form, might also be taking place in all places and at all times. If this is the case, and we wish to foster engagement in employee learners in the workplace, than we must be motivationally immediate at all times and in all places as well.

The ideas presented in the following pages, what I am calling the *zones of motivational immediacy*, represent an explicit way of viewing workplace learning that can provide practical opportunities to facilitate greater levels of learner engagement, less resistance to learning, and therefore greater levels of training transfer and organizational growth. Before examining the zones of motivation, it is necessary to first understand the *zones of intervention*.

THE FOUR ZONES OF INTERVENTION

The idea of workplace learning zones takes the ideas of Wenger and Illeris as a theoretical backdrop and provides a more practical level of specificity for the workplace training practitioner.

Axis of Learning

Taking both Illeris' (2011) and Wenger's (2000, 2002) depictions of workplace learning as complicated integrations of personal, organizational, and environmental factors and assuming that as such, such learning is generally not bounded by the walls of a classroom, the zones of learning presented here represent four "distinct" spaces in which learning takes place continually in the workplace.

The model suggested here consists of two different axes: the *context* axis and the *intervention* axis. Each of these axes will be discussed below and then in the subsequent section, the individual zones (quadrants) will be identified and discussed.

Context Axis

Looking first at the context axis, (see Figure 5.1), one can see that it extends in a range from the *individual context* on the top end to the *organizational context* on the bottom end. To be sure, this figure is an oversimplification and viewing these two as polar ends on a range is useful in analytical terms, but one should keep in mind the two overlap in any given learning experience.

Simply put, the individual context refers here to individual learning as distinct from organizational factors. While it is true that individual learning cannot take place in a vacuum, it is a helpful distinction because it places focus on the internal cognition of individual leaners. Or, to more accurately account for the social context in individual learning, the individual context focuses on the individual leaner in the workplace and how that learner interprets and processes information and social interaction.

The organizational context, on the other hand, focuses specifically on the organization as a whole and the collective learning process of the employees. To return to the theories described in earlier sections of this chapter, Illeris (2011) speaks more cleanly to this individual context, even while including the social and environmental dynamics as important dialogic features, while Wenger (2000, 2002) speaks with more clarity toward the social or organizational contexts of learning.

Individual Context

The individual context, as noted above, places emphasis on the individual learning processes and, in keeping with this, on teaching methods and processes as they address the learner on an individual learner, distinct from the more socially-oriented organizational aspects of learning. Illeris (2017, 2011) addresses the individual learner from a multidisciplinary perspective and in doing so provides a somewhat comprehensive analysis of learning on an individual level.

Organizational Context

While the individual context focuses on the internal processes as they interact with the environment, the organizational context focuses specifically on the organization as a whole and the collective learning process of the employees. This is similar in many ways to informal learning ideas (e.g., Dale & Bell, 1999).

Classroom Intervention: An attempt to solve a problem through classroom training.

Community Intervention: An attempt to solve a problem through changes in the workplace community.

Individual Context: Used here to indicate a focus on solving a problem through addressing the behaviors and effects of individual employees.

Organizational Context: Used here to indicate a focus on solving the problem through addressing the dynamics, phenomena, and effects of the organization (i.e., systems and culture).

Intervention Axis

Classroom Intervention

A classroom intervention is an attempt to solve a problem through classroom training. This is the standard approach to solving workplace problems through education and training. It is important to note here that the word classroom does not necessarily refer to an actual room, in the traditional sense, but includes that format along with online and blended formalized training courses in the workplace. This form of intervention typically arises because the management identifies a problem of some type and then determines that the need can be addressed through employee training. While this can take many forms and much could be said about it, little more will be said here because it is the subject of the greater part of all workplace training literature extant today. When on focuses on the proportionally large amount of resources placed behind this type of learning and compares it with the proportionally small amount of practical workplace learning (transferred) that actually occurs through this avenue, the efficacy of more global workplace learning approaches becomes attractive.

Community Intervention

A community intervention is an attempt to solve a problem through changes in the workplace community/organization. This type of intervention is also commonly used and is therefore not a "new" intervention per se. Efforts along these lines are usually represented by workplace signage, programs, awareness campaigns, and employee reward systems. It may be that this form of intervention is not used as often as it could be but the ideas being presented in this chapter have more to do with the power of the complex when put together rather than any individual pole on an axis. Taking these two axes into account, the presence of four resultant quadrants comes into focus. It is these four quadrants that the rest of this chapter is concerned with.

Workplace Zones of Intervention

The two axes identified above form four zones in which the interaction of the two axis poles create a set of dynamics that have significant implications for those who wish to make full use of all educational and training opportunities in the workplace. The four zones are (1) applying a classroom intervention to address the individual context, (2) applying a community intervention to address the individual context, (3) applying a classroom intervention to address the organizational context, and (4) applying a community intervention to address the organizational context. *All four of these zones are spaces in which learner engagement can be fostered and in which motivational immediacy must be present.*

Zone 1: Classroom Intervention-Individual Context

To ground these ideas, an example can be used in which a company determines that unsafe practices exist within the organization, as evidenced by large numbers of employee accidents and injuries. In an effort to change these practices, a workplace-wide training program is "rolled out" providing information on safety practices, appropriate and inappropriate behaviors at work, and processes by which an individual can work more safely. This is a typical method for addressing a very typical problem in production industries. One can easily envision the horrific videos and pictures that employees may be exposed to in such a training course for the purpose of driving home a need to avoid certain practices (e.g., leaving protective guard plates off of machinery) and to adopt others (e.g., wearing eye protection). By attempting to apply an intervention in a formal classroom structure while operating from an individual context, those making the decision are operating on a basic set of assumptions. For instance, one must assume that formalized class or course structures are an effective method for changing the behavior of employees over time; that there is some sort of long-term training transfer. Also, there must be an assumption that changing individuals is the way to change the community. These assumptions are not necessarily faulty, although it is not difficult to find statements to the contrary. A lack of training transfer is widely discussed in the literature (see Grossman & Salas, 2011, for a review), as is the debate over whether societal change is best sought through the self-development of the individual or society as a whole (Brockett, 1997).

Zone 2: Community Intervention-Individual Context

Continuing with the safety problem above, an example of this type of intervention would be a situation in which the company decided to promote an awareness campaign in which signage was posted throughout the workplace, and emails were sent out to everyone promoting safety practices and discouraging unsafe problems. Again, just about everyone has seen this type of "buckle-up" campaign in the workplace in some form or another. Both this zone and the previous zone have in common the focus on the addressing the problem through the context of the individual. Assumptions implicit with this approach are that this type of marketing style education will be effective with the organization's employees (i.e., they will read them and internalize them), and, like the previous zone, that change is best sought through the individual employee.

Zone 3: Classroom Intervention-Organizational Context

Like Zone 1, Zone 3 uses the classroom or structured course setting to address problems. The difference here is that the organizational context is taken into account when developing the content and focus for the educational course. Carrying forward the safety training from above, the approach would be to "teach" or "train" employees about the safety problems and the necessity to eliminate such practices in the workplace. But in this case, rather than just addressing the harmful practices that need to stop and the safe practices that need to replace them, the course will focus on the system and structural causes of unsafe practices, and also the ways a workplace can engender such behaviors *structurally* and *organizationally* (similar in some ways to Argyris & Schon's [1977] double-loop learning). For example, if employees of a package delivery service are told to sign a policy indicating that they are not to walk on the conveyor belts while they are moving, but then are placed in workplace situations where no other option is available (i.e., stopping the belts jams up the entire process for a large number of workers and the production process itself), they will very likely go the practical route rather than the policy route. Again, this is consistent with Lave and Wenger's (1991) ideas of learning within a community. Since this is also a classroom intervention, employees would be asked to participate and discuss the factors that might lead them to engage in the unsafe practices in question. They might further be asked to collaborate to identify solutions to some of these problems. Additionally, the employees might be asked to also consider how their own role as a part of the environment might facilitate unsafe practices in their fellow employees. This type of focus is perhaps addressed most effectively by those writing about systems thinking (Senge, 1991; Senge & Lannon-Kim, 1991). Of vital importance when using this zone, is that employees be given a true sense that they can speak their mind, that their input will be given fair consideration, and that they will not be penalized in any way for providing candid feedback in the first place.

Zone 4: Community Intervention-Organizational Context

Addressing the community through an organizational context lens is the fourth zone from which workplace interventions can take place. It is similar to Zone 3 in that it focuses on the organizational and systemic, but in this case, not only are the organizational factors taken into account, the actual interventions themselves are directed at the organizational structures themselves. The focus in this zone is not the individual, though the individual certainly is a factor in any group, but rather the organizational dynamics that shape a workplace. In the parlance of Illeris'(2007) global learning model, this would concentrate more on the interplay of the *social* and the *sociality,* and in his workplace model, the *production* and the *community* aspects of the social dimension (2011).

It is the overarching dynamics and nuances that develop when many individuals are placed into one domain and required to work together on a regular basis. An example of how an organization would deal with the safety problems we have been discussing using this zone would be to identify all of the core structures and social dynamics of the organization that permit, foster, and in some cases maybe even require unsafe practices, and then "design them out" or at least put in place a series of changes that will, over time, remove or limit their negative effect.

For instance, if the engineering of the package production line requires that stopping the conveyor system jams up the production process, reengineering the system in a way that permits employees to be able to remove packages without stepping upon to the moving belts would greatly diminish the practice. Perhaps there are bottle necks or the machinery is old and frequent jams occur, which require employee intervention. Looking more at person is that poor supervision, micromanagement, or excessive pressing for higher speed and production is causing the unsafe practices. Perhaps an overemphasis of Taylorist production methods is causing a problem. Understaffing could also be a cause.

It doesn't take a great deal of thought to realize that this fourth zone could be a touchy one. It would be easier in most cases, and perhaps less painful for management, to simply train the bad behavior out and the good behavior in. Like all the zones, this zone has inherent assumptions at the base of it. Among them are the assumption that changing the organizational structures will serve to modify the individual's behavior in the final analysis, and also the assumption that a great many of the safety problems are the fault of the organizational structures to begin with.

PRACTICAL IMPLICATIONS FOR THE ZONES

When looking at learning this way there are several noteworthy implications for learning in general and workplace learning in specific. First, if learning occurs in these four zones and actions can be taken in each of the four zones that will ultimately facilitate learning, then it must follow that all actions taken by managers, supervisors, and trainers in the workplace that touch these fours zones are in themselves teaching acts, whether intended to be or not. This is a daunting idea because it removes intentionality from a great portion of teaching that actually occurs. As mentioned earlier and depicted in Figure 5.1, the largest zone of intervention is community learning in the community context. This raises the uncomfortable question of what exactly might be being taught on a day-to-day basis since almost every act, if not every act, taken by administrators in the workplace is a teaching act. This would mean, for instance, than when a policy is drafted, whether its purpose is to address some new dynamic or to react to an old dynamic, the writing and implementation of that policy will bring about some sort of change in the social workplace community.

So, the key point here is that while some of the very best opportunities to address problems in the workplace, educationally speaking, come through the ability to address them in the workplace community through the systemic context, a different way of thinking about workplace management is that in real-world experience, *all action is teaching action.* Wenger (2000, p. 2002) pointed out that this organizational type of learning is the most potent type of learning so it must concern the workplace leader that at all times the learner is being taught through the most powerful of all mediums while the organization's main line of agency through teaching is through meager classroom interventions.

Second, the zones provide a rubric through which workplace management and educators can plan for holistic and effective training programs that have a real-world effect. Addressing learning transfer from all four zones rather than only one or two is certain to increase efficiency. Furthermore, if each of these areas is a space that some form of teaching takes place, then each of these zones is a place in which learning engagement and motivational immediacy is important.

The third implication is a combination of the first two in that the most effective workplace interventions must include multiple dimensions in which training is facilitated. Newer, more effective, fairer, and more mutually beneficial policies can be implemented by using the four zones, but at the same time, a very close examination of what has been taught unintentionally through the lesser-known zones must be undertaken to locate practices that have "taught" employees to be, as a community, as they presently are. It may be the case that for every action taken, several more actions need to be modified or rescinded. Once leadership understandings that it is engaged perpetually in teaching acts is will be compelled to attend to ongoing unintended instruction while at the same time planning purposeful counter instruction going forward.

The fourth implication, and the one most closely connected to the concepts addressed in this chapter, is that if there are four zones of teaching and learning, there are four zones of motivational immediacy.

FOUR ZONES OF MOTIVATION

My original use of the term *zones of interventions* was the result of my belief that ultimately, teaching aims at intervening in the environment, engaging in some sort of mediation, and facilitating learning in an individual. But, if each of these zones is a place of learning, then each of these zones is a place of teaching. And, of course, if each of these zones is a place of teaching, then each of these zones is a place where motivational immediacy can be brought to bear.

Zone 1: Classroom Intervention-Individual Context

Classroom teaching, whether physical or virtual, is the focus of a number of chapters of the second section of this book. Zone 1 is the one in which we traditionally focus the most attention, despite it likely being the area of the least amount of learning in the workplace as well as the weakest of all types of learning that occur in the workplace. It does, of course, have the distinct advantage of being controllable, and that alone can be said to balance out its power in terms of purposefully fostering change in individual employees and the organizational culture as well.

Specific, practice-oriented concepts and methods for both promoting motivational immediacy in the classroom, and being motivationally immediate as an instruction, are included in Chapters 7–9, and so it is unnecessary to include more here.

Zone 2: Community Intervention-Individual Context

Zone 2 also represents an area of training that is commonly associated with employee learning and change, but one which seems to fall under the realm of marketing as often as training. The reason for this is simple – marketing principles are designed to catch someone's eye, be emotionally evocative, and prompt toward some sort of action that would otherwise likely not have been chosen. Interestingly, that is a very close match for what I have proposed as the true purpose of training. The tendency is to think about training as the straight-up knowledge and ability to either know something or do something. Although this is certainly a part of training, to stop there is to miss a vital factor and therefore to have training that languishes over time, never quite being as efficient as it could be, and rarely, if ever except by accident, being effectual.

Marketing skills and strategies are outside the scope of this discussion and also outside the scope of my own expertise, but fostering learning and change in adults in the workplace is not. The following thoughts are not meant to contradict sound marketing advice, but to expose the connection Zone 2 learning has to the other three zones and therefore to workplace learning as a whole.

A key here is to ensure that your signage and other sorts of devices, such as slogans, mottos, and symbols, are motivationally immediate. They are not a disconnected series of marketing tools to prompt behavior change; they are a significant part of a global instructional complex that the organization as a whole is promoting. As such, no single part should contradict or work against any other part. The power of the zones is that intersection, not their individuality.

Remembering that motivational immediacy is about fusing the means and the ends for the learner (i.e., making the learning item of immediate interest rather than later interest), Zone 2 campaign items should be a fit with the employee learner's immediate world, and as such, must connect to the *other* three zones of intervention and motivational immediacy. A witty slogan on a sign will only be absorbed and be of interest the reader to the extent that it is understood clearly and bought into soundly. Simply seeing the sign often enough should not be the end game of the intervention itself.

A no-smoking sign, for instance, to use an "oldie but goodie" first of all, tells every employee what they already know. If this is the case, one must ask what the real intended purpose of providing it is. If it is a legal artifact (like a no trespassing sign), it is outside the educational realm entirely and can be left alone so long as it is fulfilling its legal purpose. However, if it is intended to actually change behavior, then it must be in alignment with all of the other pieces of workplace training. The sign will do little but anger an employee if there are no designated areas to smoke (and maintain a 35-year habit that is terribly difficult to break), and no breaks from the shop floor to do so.

Likewise, a "no cell phones in the work area" will not be a meaningful instructional tool if the breakroom has no secure storage for them, employees don't have time to get their phones on breaks and check on family and vital life details, or other structural impediments to having access to phones and a way to secure them before returning to the job are available.

An employee of a large shipping organization once shared that he and his colleagues were faced with signage all over the place (and honorable mention in training sessions) indicating that under no circumstances was any employee to ever mount the parcel conveyor belt and walk on it. This, he said, was a joke among all of them because when the belt jammed up, which it frequently did, there was simply no other way to clear it and keep things moving without hopping up and clearing it manually – which of course everyone did with the supervisors jumping in with them, or at least pretending they didn't see it. The signs, in this case, were teaching the employees something – ignore, make fun of, and a big key here – do not be motivated to learn from them in a meaningful way. Learning transfer was not on the playing field. The need to clear the parcels on the jammed belt was more immediate than the instructional bit about not getting on the belt. And, likely, it always will be. The parcel shipping service situation is worth bringing back up in the discussion of Zone 4 below.

As a final note in this section, the power of the zones of motivation lies in the manner in which the point out and reveal the connections they have with the integrated, holistic, workplace instructional effort. Just as the classroom in Zone 1 can render any given signage a waste of space, so too, can any given sign (and its regular effect with employees in the workplace) pre-emptively undermine training efforts in the classroom. Each zone absolutely must be taken into account both individually and in relationship with all other zones. This mindset and the resulting modifications will shift the workplace learning situation toward motivational immediacy in a significant way.

Zone 3: Classroom Intervention-Organizational Context

Zone 3 has us back in the classroom, but with the boring stuff. Many employee learners (and, for that matter, those in other educational domains as well) often groan at any mention of being exposed in a training class to the historical, cultural, theoretical, and philosophical aspects of whatever the learning content may be. This is almost overwhelmingly due to the fact that we have been doing it so badly for so many years. The more abstract the learning content, in fact, the more naturally distant we allow it to become from the day-to-day lives of those we teach. This is the fault of our instructional strategies, not of the content itself.

Teaching in the classroom, with the purpose of changing employee behavior, but doing so by facilitating a deep, conceptual, cultural, and historical understand of the reason things are as they are in the workplace, is not alienating if it is done well and for the right reason. Motivational immediacy requires that each thing being taught – at each moment along the way – be connected constantly back to the immediate lifeworld of the learner. This may seem like a challenge if you are talking about the original founder of the company, 80 years ago, to a group of assembly line factory workers at an auto plant, and it is, but all good instruction is challenging.

The key is, as it nearly always is, to ask why. Why are you teaching it? Why are you sharing that particular piece of company history? Is it because you happen to enjoy history for the sake of it? If so, there is your problem – go home and read a book. Is it because you have been told you *have to* even though you don't care at all? If so, there is your problem – go sit down and figure out how it could be relevant to the employee learner now, and then come back and do it right. Buy into it yourself or you will never be able to get your learners to buy into it (Frye et al., 2017).

Telling employees not to allow friends and family into the work areas will likely have more buy-in if it is connected to some of the stories that resulted in the rule being adopted. How does that rule relate to the "we care about you and your family" mantra the organization tries to convey more than a slippery marketing device, if it doesn't square with a rule like that (think cute signs posted around from Zone 2). If grocery store employees are working at the only store in the state that requires them to offer every time to carry bags out to the car for customers, there is power in the historical, cultural, and philosophical narratives that shaped that policy. The problem is that it so very often is not connected firmly to the individual employees' present life and work (and concern, anger, frustration, anxiety, happiness, pride, identity). Knowing policy is about knowing policy, teaching policy is about knowing *people*.

Consider how many movies released at major theatres in the United States are historical documentaries, and then compare that to how many box office hits are related in some way to historical fiction. The same can be said about books. One can look up the sales volume of history books and compare it with the sales volume of historical fiction. Having done so, one might infer that there is a great deal of interest in personable, human-interest stories. What there is a great deal less interest in seems to be technical history books largely containing fine-grained factual details. These are of interest only to the specific subgroups that value those things. I have offered this as a clearly anecdotal item, because the essence of it is that the more relatable history is, the more everyone seems to be interested in it – that is motivational immediacy on display.

When providing instruction in a classroom, but attempting to address more systemic, global, cultural, and structural problems in the workplace involve the learners in the process. Allow the employee learners work together to connect dots between what they like about the everyday environment of their jobs, and the shaping factors that might have caused them. Allow them to connect the dots, to offer up ideas, about how the things they really dislike about their job environment could possibly have been shaped by the history and sociocultural aspects of the organizational development over time. Did it have to be that way? What can be done to change these things? Again, in this zone, as in all the others, the employee must be at the heart of the discussion. The employee is living culture, living history, and the embodiment of a living philosophy. Seize on these things, start where the learner is, know where you want to end up, and walk the journey with them.

Zone 4: Community Intervention-Organizational Context

This final zone is the trickiest for the average instructor, training director, or curriculum designer. This is because, at least at first glance, is soundly "above the pay grade" and therefore, just simply not our business. Zone 4 is largely about company policy, decisions made in the middle and the top, but rarely if ever at the bottom. This zone rests most heavily on the idea that every act in the workplace is a teaching act.

Understanding the realities of the hierarchical nature of most workplaces, the point of this section is not to make unrealistic suggestions that a classroom instructor or training director begin to push-back on management decisions in earnest and with vigor. Much of the decision-making at high levels in an organization are not up for grabs, with respect to those with "boots on the ground" in the employee training arena.

What is important, however, is that the trainer be deeply aware of the influence and connection all of the various company policies have on the learning goals that are being sought in the classroom. This is true of both the written rules as well as the unwritten "secret" rules of engagement that crop up anywhere enough humans are together in an organized effort. Perhaps the unwritten rules are even more important because they might be more flexible in terms of shaping long-term change. Either way, every instructor must be fully aware that they are only one part of an instructional team in the workplace, with the other members being, collectively, the other zones, and specifically, those in places of authority throughout the organization.

Returning to the examples of the jammed conveyor belt, the no cell phones on the shop floor, and the no-smoking signs, the same questions should be asked. Are there ways to make minor adjustments to the environment (physical or social and emotional) that can make the content of the class (i.e., follow these rules), more motivationally immediate? Are you able to talk to those in places of authority in the workplace and make reasonable suggestions for minor modifications that would make following the rules easier and more likely? These should be considered instructional activities because they are instructional activities.

In the event that the instructor has absolutely no sway whatsoever, in changing company policy, having secure storage added to the break room, having an additional outdoor smoking area added, or having more personal protection supplies in more locations for ease of accessibility, then at least the instructor can find ways to relate to the employees and work with them to find solutions. The moment one determines that the training situation is not one of getting people to know stuff (they probably already do), but to accept that they should do stuff (buy-in), it becomes clear that one more PowerPoint slide is simply not going to cut it. People want solutions.

Perhaps a group problem-solving facilitation that sought to help the employees find some solutions to the difficulties they have adhering to a given training policy might in the end be an authentic training class that results is actual long-term training transfer (e.g., employees start wearing their protective gear, or connect a bolt the correct way). It likely would be more so than a traditional lecture during which employees are provided clinical knowledge to acquire (and likely ignore).

These four zones of motivational immediacy are meant to be examined together, with their many intersections being analyzed in an effort to make training efforts more authentic, holistic, and meaningful. Motivational immediacy brings employees face to face with their own lifeworlds and how those lifeworlds are connected to company policy, procedure, and technical knowledge.

Chapter 6

Training Through Conceptual Change Frameworks

In his book on training, Mitchell (1988) starts out by saying that "The how-to's of this book are all directed toward shaping and controlling the learning environment to facilitate change" (p. 4). Mitchell goes on later to say that this is true because one "cannot create learning. [One] can only create an environment that is conducive to it" (p. 19). The first section of this present book on motivational immediacy has built a case that training is about both acquisition and acceptance. If training is about fostering a change in the paradigm of the learner, rather than just adding content to the existing paradigm, and if it is about facilitating effectual learning that includes both acquisition and acceptance, then the training methods adopted by an organization must serve these purposes. Methods used both in the physical classroom and online must serve the latter as well as the former. One pathway for fostering effectual learning can be found in Conceptual Change Theory (CCT). The theories themselves are complex enough to be off-putting, but the practical purpose for which they can be employed is worth the effort required in coming to terms with the theory.

INTRODUCTION TO CONCEPTUAL CHANGE LITERATURE

CCT is perhaps more accurately thought of as a cluster of theories that in one way or another attempt to explain the learning of complex knowledge as a process whereby former learning must be significantly modified at best and completely unlearned at worst. Learning, in this case, is a, "changing [of] prior misconceived knowledge to correct knowledge" (Chi, 2013, p. 61). There are a number of ways this is explained or

DOI: 10.4324/9781003144137-7

approached, each with very different but related concepts about how information and conceptual knowledge are acquired and retained. *P-prims or phenomenological primitives and coordination classes* were promoted by diSessa (1983, 1993). Chi (1992, 2013) and Chi et al. (1994) described a process whereby new concepts are assigned to different ontological trees and branches on the same tree, and Posner et al. (1982) wrote at great length about a mechanism for conceptual change that they refer to as the *Conceptual Change Model.*

Conceptual change theories are similar in many ways to the idea of Transformative Learning (Mezirow, 2000) but distinct in a functionally important way. While Transformative Learning is generally focused on learners coming to a place where their own implicit frames of reference are made explicit to themselves, so that they can examine them and assess them for appropriateness, CCT is focused, perhaps more instrumentally, on simply working to foster a specific conceptual change in the learner in order that the learner may better and more accurately interpret and learn a specific piece of new information. All of the various theories of conceptual change tend toward a pragmatic goal of paving the way for the learner to be able to more accurately understand new and technical information.

All of these different views of conceptual change share familial roots in terms of theory but have different foci. In this chapter, I will focus on only one approach to CCT, referred to as *Framework Theories* (Vosniadou, 2013).

Framework Theories are nomological networks of understanding, within which a learner interprets and makes meaning of all new experience. This "framing" from which they derive their name is viewed as a fundamental aspect of human learning because it is through this framework that all new information receives its meaning. It is at this juncture that framework theory approaches to conceptual change link up with other views, such as ontological category (tree) approaches. Ontological trees are categories of things that carry whole collections of characteristics simply because of the tree upon which they hang. "Categorization is an important learning mechanism because a concept, once categorized, can 'inherit' features and attributes from its category membership" (Chi, 2013, p. 62).

This is spectacularly important when looking at how a given learner's view of what their in-service training is all about, because a particular educational or training program can also potentially "inherit features and attributes from" (p. 62) that learner's negative perception (whether accurate or not, as the case may be).

The use of an improper framework results in a consistent skewing of conceptual understanding of the new material. In order to either ensure the proper conceptual understanding to begin with, or to correct for improper understandings post hoc, a process must be facilitated in which the learner identifies the framework error, drops the erroneous framework, and adopts or preloads the new framework. In her research on this particular dynamic, Vosniadou (2013) looked specifically at grade school students in science courses and noted how a solid conceptual understanding of electricity came only after students abandoned the view (framework) that electricity was matter and instead came to see it as a process. When all of the specific nuanced interpretive elements and characteristics specifically associated with physical matter were dropped and all of the interpretive elements and characteristics specifically associated with processes were adopted instead, students began to demonstrate empirically that they had a more accurate conceptual understanding of electricity. This same dynamic was demonstrated in learning situations in which children were trying to understand that the earth is round (and that therefore some people stand "upside down" on it), with the same effect. In the latter case, it was a matter of abandoning the framework that viewed the earth as physical matter and seeing it instead as an astronomical body.

In each of these examples, all of the various conceptual information individuals bring to bear on a given learning experience were used to either assist in fostering an accurate view of a given concept or to further entrench a misunderstanding of the concepts. Furthermore, these inappropriate framework theories can actually facilitate sustained novel errors in future thinking. That is to say, not only will present understanding remain erroneous, but future information will be coded and understood improperly as well. It is, to use common parlance, quite literally the "gift that keeps on giving."

In all of these cases, the practical take-away is that efficient teaching of any sort of conceptual material requires that individual framework theories be taken into account, addressed, and in many circumstances actively molded in an effort to foster a framework change. These ideas will be connected more firmly to learning resistance in the next section.

The frameworks, pictured in Figure 6.1, through which learners interpret new concepts are portrayed by a series of nested boxes (frames) each being subject to the conceptual constraints of the frame it falls within (Vosniadou, 2013). The outer-most box is referred to as the *Framework Theory* and consists of the learner's ontological and epistemological views of the world that they are employing at the given moment, to interpret the new information. Inside this, there is the *Specific Theory*, which the learner is applying in a more focused way to interpret the new concepts. Specific theory factors include Observational and Cultural Information and individual beliefs. The third and most constrained box is the *Mental Models*, which are the conceptual understandings, visualizations that the learners arrive at, for the new information.

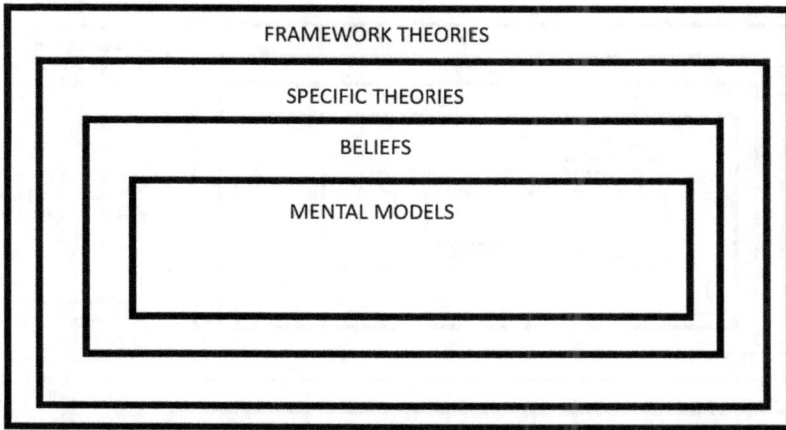

Figure 6.1 Embedded frameworks.

Source: Adapted from Vosniadou (1994, 2013)

FRAMEWORK THEORIES, RESISTANCE, AND THE WORKPLACE LEARNING CONTEXT

The interplay between conceptual change theories in general, framework theories in specific, and learning resistance comes into sharp focus when considering the possibility that learners in a given training environment preload frameworks upon entering the classroom. Looking back to Chi's (2013) statement and applying it to a different context, it is possible that adult professionals enter a given training event with certain predispositions that cause the ensuing training content and methods to "inherit features and attributes" (p. 62) from the associated, a priori conceptual framework. These frameworks along with all of the associated characteristics and elements are then brought to bear as the learner interprets and comes to understand the content of the course as it is presented in some way.

Although Vosnaidou's work has been consistent with much of the conceptual change research in that it focuses on the frameworks through which learners come to understand specific concepts taught within specific learning contexts, it is useful to expand that view, to zoom out, and consider framework theories that bound the learning context itself. Figure 6.2 shows Vosniadou's framework model (Frame B) in the center of a larger framework of the same structure. This outer conceptual framework (Frame A) represents the series of conceptual frameworks that learners use to interpret all individual content within a given training context. For instance, if an employee feels like the company's mandatory annual training is "busy work," that concept will determine all interpretations that are constructed

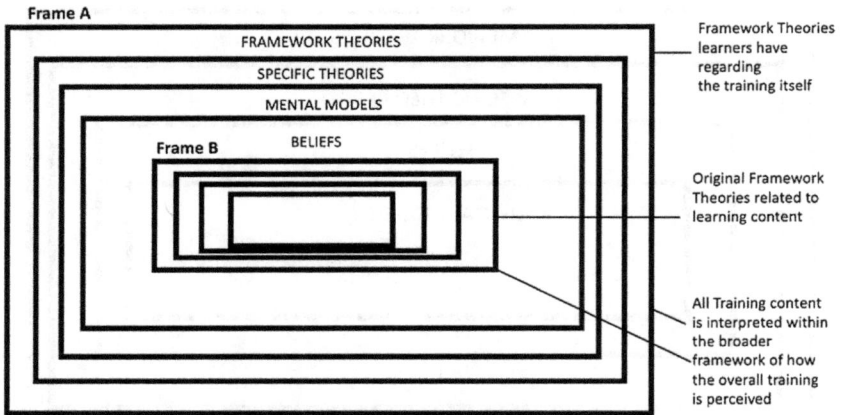

Figure 6.2 *Context and content frameworks.*

Source: Adapted from Vosniadou (2013)

by that learner regarding any given content taught during the class. No matter how important the learning content, if the learner perceives the entire enterprise as a waste of time, it is very likely that the magnitude and importance of the specific content will go unnoticed. Many pieces of treasure have likely been lost simply because they were buried in what was perceived to be a rubbish heap.

AN EXAMPLE IN THE WORKPLACE

Years ago, while sharing the potential applicability of using conceptual change framework theories to understand the attitudes and perceptions in workplace mandatory training contexts, I populated the frames formulated by Vosniadou with common sentiments that I had heard expressed for many years by both colleagues and acquaintances in various workplace contexts. Following is a brief overview of those categories and perceptions. Immediately following the anecdotal viewpoints below, the same framework will be populated from a qualitative study and it may be interesting to see the similarities.

In the outer box (see Figure 6.3) referred to as Framework Theories, there were the ontological and the epistemological views of those regarding annually-scheduled in-service training. Ontological views had to do with what the learners perceived to be what "was" about in-service training (i.e., what is real), while epistemological views had to do specifically with what criteria learners used to determine whether or not they would accept training content as valid and worth accepting and putting into practice.

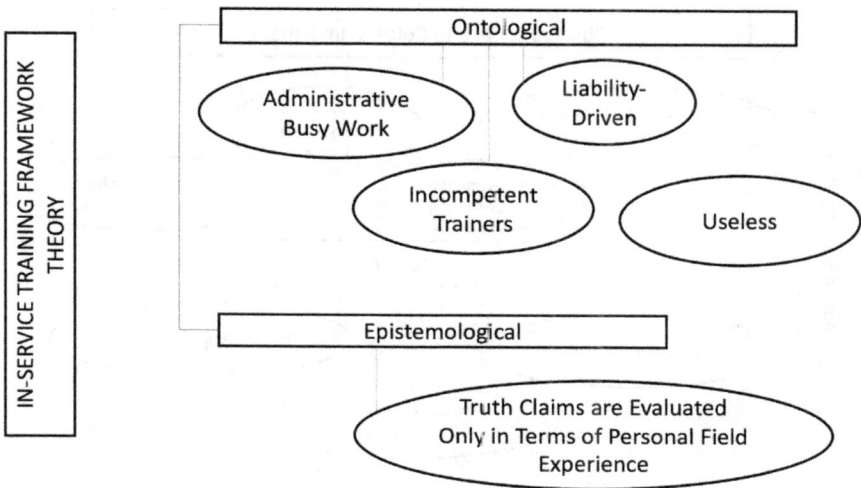

Figure 6.3 *In-service training framework theories.*

Source: Adapted from Vosnaidou (2013)

In my experience at the time, and this has not changed in the years since, when asking employees what they thought about their in-service training, the most common responses were "it is administrative busy-work," "it is just something we do to avoid liability," "the trainers are incompetent," and, tragically, "it is completely useless."

When asked what criteria was used to determine if the training was useful, worth it, or high-quality, responses were most often "if the content doesn't line up with my own experience 'on the street' or 'on the shop floor' then it is not worth listening to."

The next "nested" box in the Framework Theories taxonomy, is the *Specific Theory* (see Figure 6.4). When asked about general workplace cultural beliefs related to in-service training, the most common responses tend to be things like, "this required training was some sort of 'knee-jerk' reaction to office or social politics," "Assessment for training is a complete joke," "trainers are often the 'goody-goody' or 'kiss-up' type who don't have enough experience to be worth listening to," and "training classes are quite often a sort of punishment for having done the job the way it had to be done."

These cultural perceptions then lead to learner beliefs that "training is a waste of time," "the training is sometimes even dangerous," and ultimately, "the training is offensive."

All of these ontological, epistemological, and cultural viewpoints lead to the most narrowly-focused nested frame, those originally labeled as *Mental Representations* by Vosnaidou, but changed to *behaviors and cognitions* in this

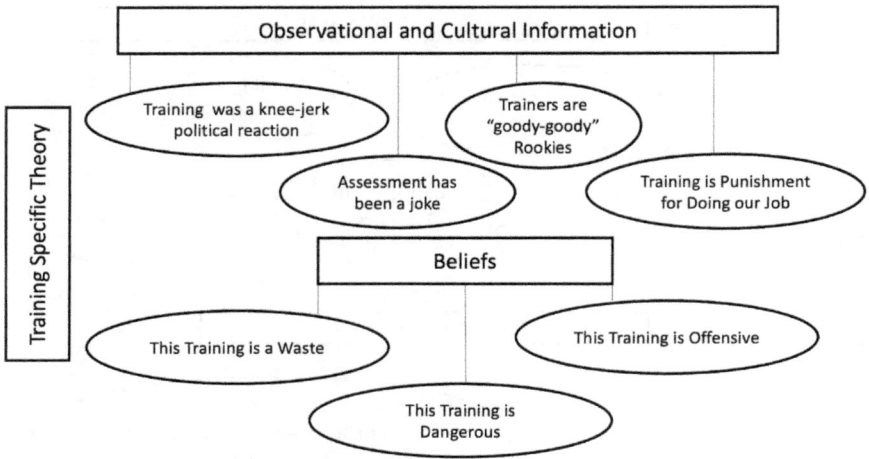

Figure 6.4 In-service training specific theory.

Source: Adapted from Vosnaidou (xxxx)

scenario to align with my own work on learning resistance and engagement (see Figure 6.5). When it comes to how all of these views play out in the workplace, in training classes, learners most often say that they "check out," "work on something else," or "try to mess with the instructor."

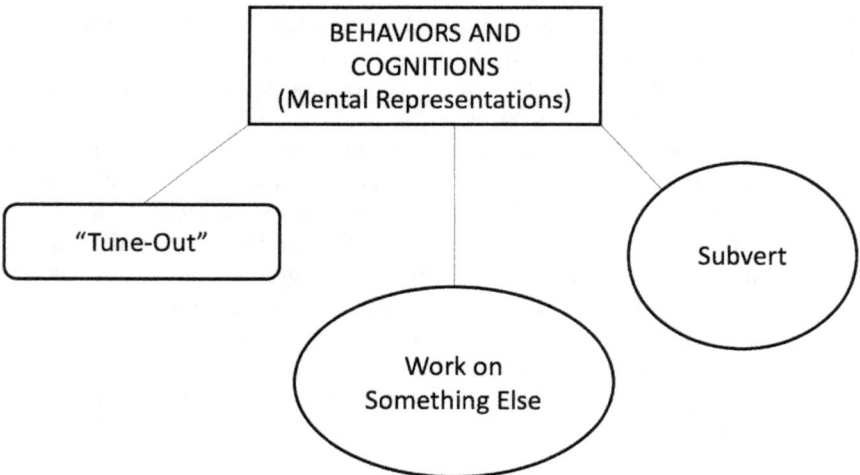

Figure 6.5 In-service training specific theory (Continued).

Source: Adapted from Vosnaidou (2013).

While these words may ring true for many readers, anecdotal information is always limited in that it has a folk-tale nature about it, and, like all fish-stories, anecdotal stories tend to grow with time. It is for this reason that, years later, a colleague and I (Taylor & Frye, 2020) set out to conduct a study in an attempt to actually populate these frames with real data, from employee learners.

RESEARCH FROM THE WORKPLACE

The context of the study was mandatory training in the workplace, and school teacher in-service training was the focus of the study. Each year, professional school teachers have some form of mandatory continuing education to remain up-to-date in their profession, and this training is often referred to as in-service training. A total of 13 teachers participated in the interviews, conducted over a two-day period. The participants reflected the ethnic diversity of the school system, and ages ranged from early 20s to late 40s, with experience levels varying from new teachers with one to two years of experience to veteran teachers with over 20 years in the classroom. The educational level of the teachers was consistent with the experiential level, with eight of the teachers holding a Master's degree. The teachers represented a wide variety of schools: from inner-city to suburban, from predominately low-income to above average income, and from low-performing to one of the highest performing schools in the state. Participants were interviewed one at a time, and audio recordings were made of the interviews. These recordings were later transcribed verbatim. The teachers were asked very broad, open-ended questions about their general perceptions of in-service training (e.g., "tell me about in-service training" and "talk to me about how you determine whether or not a training class is 'good'?"). Two different qualitative researchers independently coded the information before comparing notes and working to find commonalities. Here are the predominate themes that were clearly shared across the data:

Figure 6.6 shows that the employee participants in the study, when asked about their required, workplace in-service or continuing education courses, responded that they believed that training should be useful and hands-on, that learner choice is essential, that the employee's time is valuable, that training should be contextualized to their specific working conditions, and that those who teach such courses should have experience doing the job they are teaching about (i.e., in this study, it was that they should be school teachers, not administrators or experts from outside the practice of teaching).

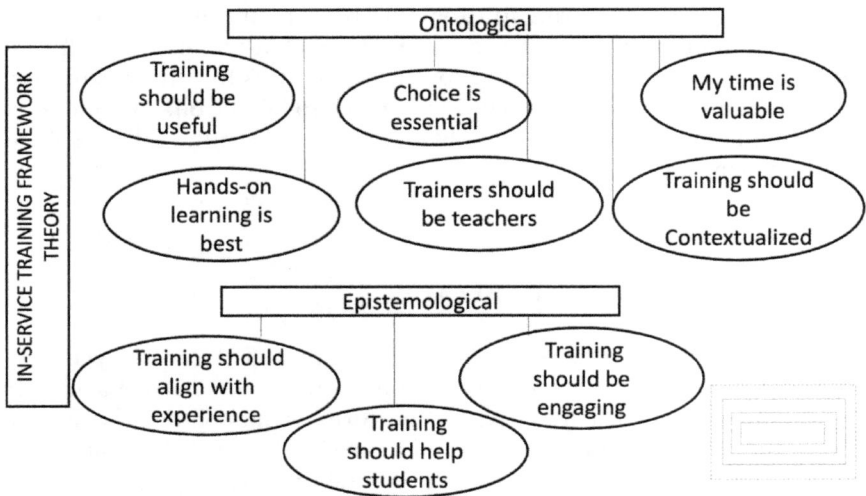

Figure 6.6 *Teacher in-service study framework theory.*

Epistemological views were sought by asking study participants what sort of criteria they used to determine whether or not they "accepted" the course and the content as legitimate and valid. Some of the responses to this were expected, such as claims that training should align with personal workplace experience, and that the training should ultimately be helpful to the participant's students. Surprisingly, employee participants continued to include the notion that in order to be viewed as legitimate and worth paying attention to the training should be *engaging*. This attachment of engagement to the judgment of whether or not a course and the content within the course was acceptable, valid, or worth paying attention to should be eye opening for the trainer, especially because the participants in this particular study were, themselves, professional educators. This represents yet another practical connection between learning engagement and learning resistance, and the ways the trainer chooses to teach a course.

When asked about personal observations and the culture of their workplace with regards to in-service training (see Figure 6.7), participants shared that those teaching the in-service courses did not care about the employee learners themselves.

Additional themes included the ideas that repetition is the norm, trainers are quite often not connected to the training content, that the participants (and their colleagues) make very quick judgments about whether or not a particular training session or course would be valuable

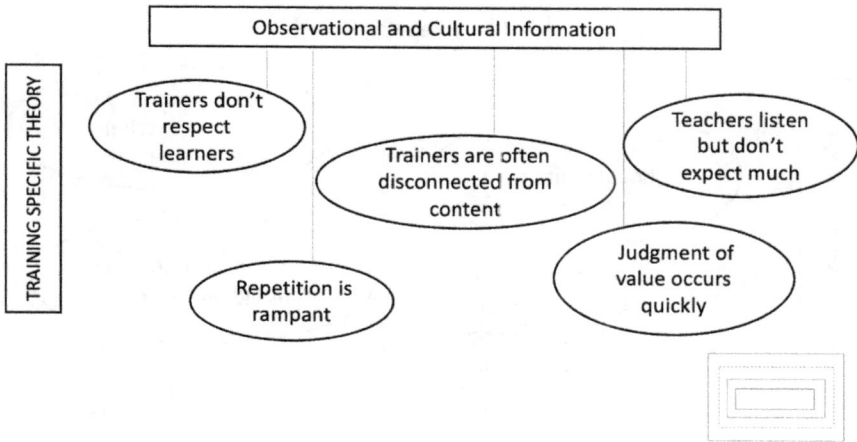

Figure 6.7 *Teacher in-service study training specific theory.*

and worth engaging with, and that those in these courses generally attempt to listen but don't expect much, right from the outset.

Figure 6.8 represents the general beliefs that the study participants had formed over time, given those previously shared outer conceptual frames. They seemed to share what they believed training should be over and against what it was in their own routine experience. Themes included that training content should relate to what the teacher does, administrators are not good trainers (repeated from earlier questions as well), that administrators do not respect the employee learners time, and that, although these employees (teachers) remained hopeful, they expected to be disappointed.

The culmination of all of these viewpoints was that the employee learners in this study actually attended these mandatory in-service courses, they responded in these ways, according to their own words: they were hopeful for something good, but expected the worst, they always, no matter what, took something else with them to work on, and while in the training class, they most typically just "checked out." Figure 6.9 represents these themes.

The practice of taking something else to work on was so prevalent, that it was brought up multiple times by nearly all participants and was even provided as one of the primary things that they tell new teachers by way of advice, about upcoming in-service training courses.

Beliefs

TRAINING SPECIFIC THEORY

Training content should relate to what I do

Administrators don't respect teachers' time

Administrators are not good trainers

Teachers are hopeful but expect to be disappointed

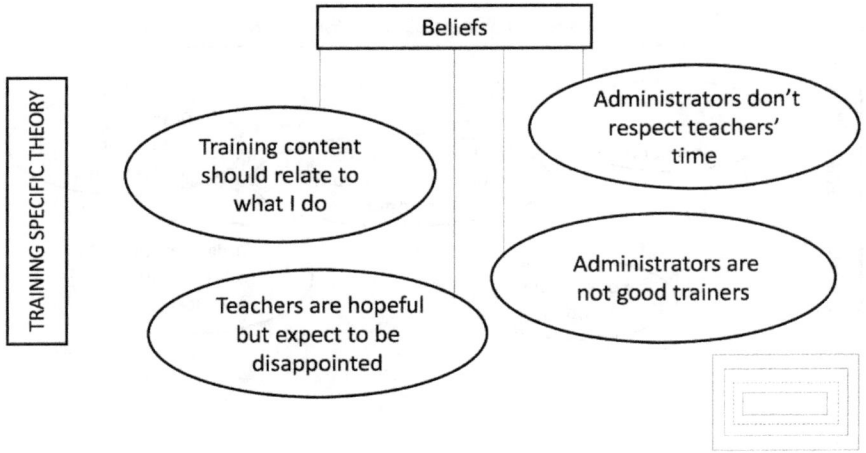

Figure 6.8 *Teacher in-service study beliefs.*

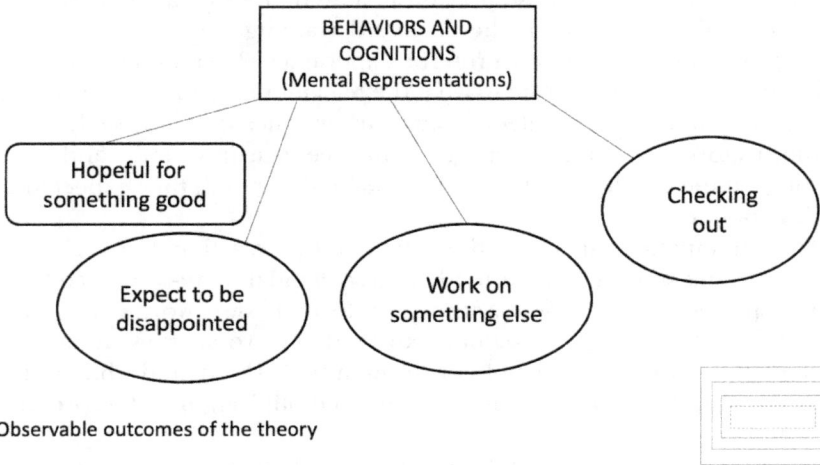

BEHAVIORS AND COGNITIONS
(Mental Representations)

Hopeful for something good

Checking out

Expect to be disappointed

Work on something else

Observable outcomes of the theory

Figure 6.9 *Teacher in-service study behaviors and cognitions.*

UTILIZING CONCEPTUAL CHANGE FRAMEWORKS
TO MITIGATE RESISTANCE

Taking into account the power of conceptual frameworks for interpreting and encoding (or not) new learning experiences, it is clear that one of the most significant and necessary steps to increase learner engagement and to reduce learning resistance in workplace mandatory training is to purposefully facilitate a complete reframing of the training experience for the teacher *before the learning content is even presented.* There is a very real linkage here, between the statement I have just made, and the very similar ones in the chapter on lesson plans and curriculum design. This idea of building conceptual change into the learning content as a part of the learning content is absolutely essential for reducing resistance, improving engagement, and increasing the effectual learning that occurs in workplace training courses.

If the evidence indicates that learners, in any given learning context, have the tendency to preload interpretive conceptual frameworks through which they learn (or not) the content of the course, then evidence might likewise indicate that the content in any given course simply cannot be, effectively speaking, any more important than the introduction of a context for the intended learners. If this is true, then *shared* content should always be accompanied by *developed* context, and significant time would need to be devoted to each. Certainly, one might question how much time can be dedicated to "setting" the context and preparing the learner for the content, particularly when time almost always seems to be of the essence in the teaching/training world. Conversely, however, one might also question whether ten minutes of content that is actually learned might well be worth more than three hours of content than no one accepted, thought about, or internalized.

Despite the tendency for this type of discussion to sound hyper-theoretical, it is concrete and practical. If there is content to share; if a facilitation of understanding is sought; if the material being taught is worthwhile; then, teachers and trainers alike simply must attend to specific concrete methods for setting the context for the pending content, and for ensuring that the conceptual frameworks held by the learners are in sync with the intentions of the teacher.

Returning to Mitchell (1998), it is important to understand that "unless each trainee comes to realize the worth of the material you are teaching – that is worth changing for – [they] will redefine the situation to exclude you from the group and will dismiss the norms of management in favor of the norms of whatever subgroups [they] can create or join (pp. 23–24). It is, therefore, absolutely essential that the individual learner in any training situation has an interpretive framework that aligns with that of the trainer, at least in regards to the content being taught. In order to do this, practically speaking, the trainer must be able to have an understanding of the learner's conceptual framework going into the training, how that may differ from that of the trainer's own framework, and a method for bridging the gap between the two. Rainbird (2000) rather strongly claims that it is an "illusion" to think that employees and employers are on the "same page" (p. 1), and a failure to act purposefully to get everyone onto the same page at the very outset of every single training endeavor will result in a very likely failure to have learner outcomes that match those intended by the instructor.

INACCURATE VERSUS INCOMMENSURATE PREEXISTING KNOWLEDGE

Chi (2013) has pointed out a distinction between *inaccurate* knowledge and *in conflict with* or *incommensurate* knowledge. It is relatively easy to understand what is meant by inaccurate information, but incommensurate knowledge is more difficult to grasp. Simply put, incommensurate knowledge refers to information that is incorrect, but is so because it is viewed through a paradigm that is internally consistent, but not aligned with the reality of the situation.

An interesting example of this can be taken from the post 9–11 law enforcement workplace. Public law enforcement has long held public safety and order as its primary goal. When this is the case, decisions about how to deploy resources can be made largely along the lines of whether or not the public will *be* safer. In the aftermath of the 9–11 attacks, and the shifting of the collective American mind toward acts of terrorism, both domestically and from abroad, what became at least equally important for a while was that the public *felt* safe.

The paradigm of making people be safer is entirely different from the paradigm of making people feel safer. Sometimes both can be achieved with the same policies and implementations, but often one receives the immediate focus at the short-term expense of the other. Given that terrorism is about evoking terror, it was natural for those in places of leadership all over the United States and many other countries, to begin making moves with the public's *perceived* safety in mind. Individual law enforcement personnel, however, were slower to make the mental shift, having been steeped in the mindset and practice of attempting to provide actual safety for so many years and individually, in many cases, for so many generations.

A specific occurrence of this dynamic was the internationally adopted practice, particularly in the UK and the United States, of having law enforcement wear brightly colored, reflective, mesh vests, so that the general public could more readily see and notice the presence of police. This was entirely aligned with the paradigm of making the public feel safe, but in many situations completely out of alignment with the mindset of actually making the public *be* safe. My point here, of course, is not to validate or criticize a particular policing method, but to point out that police officers being told that they needed to be more "obvious" everywhere, was a difficult pill to swallow, and arguments often were centered around the idea that this would not actually make anyone safer (i.e., because anyone "up to no good" would actually want to know where all law enforcement officers might be at a given moment in time). In order to bring this group of employee-learners around on this idea, it was vital to ensure that the overarching job paradigm was shifted from one of only keeping people physically safe, to one of also making them feel safe, emotionally.

Chi (2013) went further and broke the two types of misconceived knowledge into four subtypes, where are *false beliefs, flawed mental models,* ontological *category mistakes,* and *missing schemas.* A reading of Chi will quickly reveal the complexity of CCT and its varied applications, but for the purposes it is being employed here, what is vitally important is that simply having bad information (false beliefs) is a much simpler problem to fix, than one involving flawed mental models, category mistakes, and missing schemas.

False beliefs refer to simple pieces of information that are incorrect and which, by simple clarification on the part of the instructor, can be changed by the learner. The distinction between flawed mental models and category mistakes is real enough, but not important to address here. It is an appropriate oversimplification to group both together and say that they refer broadly to incorrect paradigms, through which new learning content is being interpreted. These incommensurate forms of knowledge are considered robust in that the learner is very often resistant to conceptual change when they are present (Chi, 2013). The missing schemas sub-type is essential for this discussion, however, because it represents an important linkage to the practical applications of understanding CCT.

There are two conditions that must be present in order to bring about conceptual change in an employee learner in these sorts of situations (Chi, 2013). First, when a learner is trying to learn something but is doing so while having a conceptual paradigm that is incommensurate to the point that the trainer is attempting to make, the paradigm of the learner must be changed *before* the new information is shared. That is, it must be brought to the attention of the learner, that their paradigm is not adequate for interpreting the new information correctly. Second, the learner must be familiar with the necessary (correct) paradigm, in order to embrace it and use it to interpret the new information.

FACILITATING CONCEPTUAL CHANGE IN THE CLASSROOM

It is at this point again, that the entire essence of this book can be reduced to four words – listen to the learner. Stephen Covey's fourth rule to seek first to understand and then to be understood has a direct connection to teaching and is woven throughout every single practical application in this book – you cannot reach the learner if you don't know where the learner is. We "find" a learner, by learning how the learner is seeing the world, both globally and immediately, at the time we are attempting to convey information.

The following and final section in this chapter provides some practical tips for facilitating conceptual change in employee-learners, but it is important to point out that these learning and teaching principles are extended throughout the other chapters in the second section of the book. This is true because teaching well is a cradle-to-grave task, meaning that it requires attention from the moment a sharable idea comes to mind, all the way through until the learner is using that knowledge in an applied setting in the workplace. This includes thinking, planning, curriculum, instructional methods, and assessment practices.

Three Rules for Facilitating Conceptual Change in the Workplace

1. Understand the box – Know what the learner's paradigms are.
2. Build the box – help the learner construct the necessary paradigms.
3. Test the Box – assess the paradigm in addition to the content itself.

Understand the Box

The very essence of understanding the relationship between a learner's motivation to learn, and teaching, is to understand where the learner is, mentally speaking, to meet them there and to walk the journey with them. My use of the word "box" here refers to the paradigm (conceptual frame) within which all new information will be interpreted by the learner. In order to make sure that the learner is going to grasp the point you are trying to make, you must be able to understand the mental models (filters) through which the learner is going to hear what you are saying. In this sense, it is true that it matters more what the learner hears than what you say. Training is not about getting a dart somewhere on the board, but about hitting the bullseye every time.

Some Methods for Understanding the Box

One simple method for achieving this is to have employee learners discuss a new topic in groups and then report out on what they understand the *content* and the *context* to be, both for the training course itself and for the particular content at hand. The content is what we typically focus as both training directors and training instructors in the classroom, but it is important to remember that the conceptual frameworks through which learners interpret content are themselves embedded within the conceptual frameworks through which the learners interpret the purpose and value of the training context itself.

Having these groups discuss and share what they believe the importance level to be (of the training program and the content itself), and how they believe the content could be applied to their job, will provide vital information about the mindset and of the learner. While this method is not novel, the purpose of it goes far beyond being an icebreaker, or a way to simply start conversation about a topic in a training class. Its express purpose in this context is to give the learner space to share what their conceptual frameworks are for the training as a whole, and for specific targeted content, and then to *listen.*

Another way to accomplish this is to have employee learners engage in regular reflective journals during which they are asked to describe both what they think about the content, but also what they *feel* about the content. Asking the learners to be open and clear about how they feel about both the context and the content will surprise even them, because learning and particularly training, is so often associated only with think and do. Knowing what your employee learners feel about it, however, will provide highly predictive information about whether or not they are likely to do it.

A third option is to have employee learners break down their understanding of the topic in a way that will reveal the conceptual assumptions they are making. It is possible to infer the conceptual framework or paradigm of a learner by the ways that they explain the content itself. This takes advance thought, but is possible to do. Having learners do this can be very helpful in making sure that they are going to do the right thing for the right reason, and doing things with purpose for the right reason at the right time and with the right conceptual understanding, will provide a natural line toward training transfer.

Build the box
Some methods for building the box

Start with the big picture, and then scale down. Get everyone to agree to a general set of assumptions before moving forward into the learning content. It is important to use the information that you have gleaned from the steps above (having the learners think and share their understandings and perceptions of the content and context). Chapter 8 specifically addresses how to do this, but what is important to know at this point is that you simply cannot rely entirely upon a script that was designed before the learning situation, because each set of learners has a different set of conceptual frameworks.

You must be willing to, and able to, think on the fly, as it were, and connect the new data that you have just received for your learners, and to deliver your content in a way that takes that data into account. To be an effective instructor, one must be able to bring learners into a state of broad consensus with regards to the conceptual frameworks (i.e., paradigm) that the content itself requires. In order to get them from point A (their framework) to point B (your framework), you must understand the box (both theirs and yours) and use that information to situation them, conceptually speaking, in a mutual space.

A second step in this process is to make sure that for each new piece of information and especially for each new set of concepts, you explain each piece of information in connection with its relationship to the whole. The fact of the matter, mixed bag that it is, is that the learner will always connect it to a whole of some sort and if you don't do it as the instructor, then the whole the learner attaches it to might be quite different from the one you, as the instructor, had in mind.

Test the box
Some methods for testing the box

Again, I am jumping the gun a bit to discuss practical applications in the theory section of the book, and these topics will be addressed in much more detail in later chapters, but a few simple things can be shared here that provide a more concrete outline for understanding the ideas shared in this chapter.

Set up ill-defined problems. Ill-defined problems are problems that have no clear answers. The power of ill-defined problems is two-fold. First, they are a pretty close fit with the real world, where nearly nothing is simple and textbook-like, and second, they absolutely require learners to put their understanding cards on the learning table. That is, rote memory, guessing, and lucky choices don't accomplish much and are almost immediately revealed. The only hope of providing a cogent way forward is to have a conceptual understanding of the thing in the first place.

Building on this, make employee learners explain *why* they make the choices they make and what types of circumstances could make their answer incorrect. By having them explain under what circumstances their own answer would be clearly a bad answer, they are forced to provide their own conceptual frameworks even more starkly. And, again, knowing what they understand is key to facilitating an understanding in them of what you are trying to teach.

MOTIVATIONAL IMMEDIACY: CHANGING THE WAY WE PRACTICE

Chapter 7

Instructional Methods and Lesson Plans

> It is very important that you understand the difference between your perceptions of people's problems and their perceptions of them. You shouldn't be trying to discover your perception of their perception. You must find a way to determine what their perception is. You can't do it by psychoanalyzing or being smart. You have to ask yourself what you know about their experience and cultural background that would help in understanding what they're saying.. . " (Horton et al., 1997, pp. 70–71).

With highly emotive training content, it is always much easier to see the merit in all of this talk of motivational immediacy, connecting with the learner, lifeworlds, etc. It is a much heavier lift, so to speak, when talking to someone who is engaged in the sort of technical training that is oriented around mechanically-based, one-way-to-do it content. For these instructors, there is often a bit of reasonable push-back in the form, typically, of wanting to know if this all isn't just a bit of a complicated overstatement of a much simpler sort of thing.

All of the basic cognitive tools of the instructional trade, such as primacy-recency, cognitive load, see-one, do-one, teach-one, and others, have been time tested in many ways, and little can be added to the straight-up skills-based instructional strategies that teach a skill and test a skill. There may be some truth in this, at least in a comparative sense and matter of degree. Surely it is less complicated to teach an employee how to use a simple tool properly, than it is to teach someone to be more conscientious, or team-centered. This hard-soft skill divide is not a novel idea.

For this purpose, and because of its' tight connection with the purpose of this chapter, that I will share a paraphrased conversation that I have had in a workplace training situation many years ago. What is important about the conversation is that it was concerned with training purely mechanical

DOI: 10.4324/9781003144137-9

skills, and that it took place with an experienced mechanic who was teaching the skills that he had used himself for many years.

TRAIN WHEELS, TECHNICAL SKILLS TRAINING, AND FEELINGS

Many years ago, while in a train-the-trainer session with subway train mechanics, the question came up about whether or not all the "complicated talk" about emotions, buy-in, and other sorts of what were thought to be nontechnical factors, were necessary or practical for technical training. I didn't agree with the statement that these factors were nontechnical, but there was a reasonable sentiment being expressed and it was the first time it had been brought up in a class I was teaching, so I remember it clearly. I asked the following questions and the conversation went this way:

Me: What is it you teach, specifically?
Rail instructor: We work on the rail wheels of the trains.
Me: Okay, let me ask you a few questions then. Is there a way to put the nuts (or whatever you call them) on in a way that will hold, but which is bad for the threads of the posts?
Rail instructor: Yes, you could.
Me: Is it possible to put the nuts on in a way that is damaging to the tools, in the long-run?
Rail instructor: Yes, it is possible.
Me: Is it possible to do this work in a way that is less safe than it should be, for the mechanic and for those in the immediate area?
Rail instructor: Yes, it is.
Me: Is it possible to do this work in a way that can result in unsafe working conditions, in general? Like, not putting the tools away, not wrapping and stowing power cords, not cleaning spills, or other things like this?
Rail instructor: Yes, I guess it is possible.
Me: So, for all of these things that a mechanic can do properly, or not do properly, would it be because they don't know how to do it, or because they don't feel like being bothered with it for some reason.
Rail instructor: Smiling, well, I guess maybe a little bit of both, but mainly they don't feel like doing it right.
Me: So, even with a highly mechanistic, technical task, there is an entire dimension that is connected with what someone feels like doing and what they can be motivated to actually do, even when no one is looking.

It is certainly true that more technical skills might be less emotively-driven than soft skills, but attitude affects all levels of our work, and nearly every task we train for in our training classrooms has two components – a *know-how* and a *want-to*. This chapter, and this book as a whole, is focused on the want-to rather than the know-how. No matter how technical the training may be, no matter how straight forward the task, there is a want-to side that requires attention on the part of the professional training instructor. The following ideas are meant to be focused on an individual lesson plan, for a given training class. For discussion on more formal curriculum design, Chapter X examines those areas.

POSITION THEORY

Imagine a scenario where an instructor is standing in a classroom, or leading a virtual training program, and believing that their role is one of support, help, and servant-leadership, while everyone else in the classroom is thinking of the class as punishment, and of the instructor as a weapon of the bureaucracy. It is not difficult to understand just how wide the gulf would be in this situation between the instructor and learner. This scenario would be inefficient, at best, and unpleasant and personally harmful at worst. Position Theory with its idea of storyline is a very useful tool for developing a lesson plan that will be motivationally immediate and foster engagement and effectual learning on the part of employee learners.

The work of Harre' and Langenhove (1999a) can be applied in many different directions, but it is being bent in only one direction here, and that is in the direction of reaching individual learners in a classroom and helping them learn. For a more in-depth examination of position theory, I recommend a full reading of Harre' and Langenhove's work.

Harre and others writing about position theory have written with the assumption that "psychology is the study of discursive practices" (Harre' & Langenhove, 1999b, p. 15), and positioning can be considered "the discursive construction of personal stories that make a person's actions intelligible and relatively determinate as social acts and within which the members of the conversation have specific locations" (p. 16). This definition carries many similarities with teaching, particularly when considering learner engagement and resistance from the perspective of the learner.

A position can be compared to the sociological construct of role. However, while roles tend to be more stable, static, and long-term constructs, position is a quickly shifting status that can change multiple times within a conversation and, in many ways, is a discursive phenomenon in the sense that it is constructed largely through speech acts. This distinction is easy to see when comparing a typical role, such as parent, spouse, and employee, to a position such as victim, accuser, or temporary confidant. The power of this construct for the teacher is that it breaks the teacher out of one overarching role (teacher) and allows for a discussion of all of the moment-by-moment relational shifts that occur discursively (positions).

In a conversation, then, a position "is a metaphorical concept through reference to which a person's 'moral' and personal attributes as a speaker are compendiously collected" (p. 17), which is a somewhat complicated way to refer to qualities such as "powerful or powerless, confident or apologetic, dominant or submissive, definitive or tentative, authorized or unauthorized.. . " (p. 17). Key to the discussion here, since position is embedded in discursive acts, is that "one can position oneself or be positioned" (p. 17) and both are typically happening at the same time. The dynamic space this phenomenon creates accounts for much of the teaching-learning continuum and that continuum is largely a discursive one. One's position is what makes one "hearable" (p. 17) in one way or another, and as such is of vital importance when addressing any teaching act, and fostering engagement, particularly.

Figure 7.1 shows the position theory triad (Harre' and Langenhove [1999a]) in which there exists (a) the speech act itself, (b) the position of the speaker, and (c) the storyline of the communication. Each of these acts upon and is acted back upon by the other two in ways that shape all communication acts, including educative ones. This is a relationship similar to Bandura's (1986) triadic reciprocality, but with different factors. Bandura refers to several domains (behavior, personality, and environment) that act on and are acted back upon in a discursive way. This is noteworthy because Bandura's work is so fundamental to human learning theory and his notion of environment included, among other things, human interaction with others.

The speech act (locutionary in the figure above) is subject to variation even without position and storyline, and one can see this by taking a simple

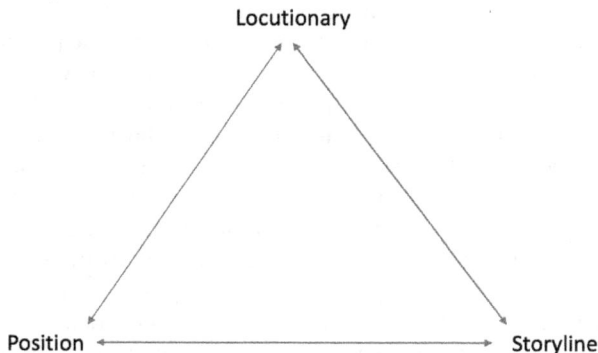

Figure 7.1 Position theory triangle.

sentence and speaking it multiple times while placing the emphasis on a different word each time.

I want you to go to the store.
I *want* you to go to the store.
I want *you* to go to the store.
I want you to *go* to the store.
I want you to go *to* the store.
I want you to go to *the* store.
I want you to go to the *store*.

The emphasis and inflection placed in each of these words is an example of locutionary dynamics, but the body language that would accompany such statements would also have effect. Saying each of these statements while laughing, frowning, or pointing angrily might change how each of the above sentences is taken.

Position, whether one is trying to position oneself, position others, or is being positioned by others, drastically affects the meaning of the speech act. Take for instance, the following statement: "please stop talking." How would the meaning change if spoken from someone in different positions? How would it be hearable in different ways? Suppose an instructor says it. What about an employee learner? While one can consider instructor and learner to be a more long-term situation that might be better referred to as a role, position is a more powerful conception because even the official instructor in a classroom is always being positioned as the teacher, proud parent, griping employee, or "sold-out" middle management, depending on whether they were sharing technical content, rambling on about their kid's piano recital, complaining about how the IT department is woefully inept, or telling employees what they must do differently in the workplace. The learners will pay different levels of attention depending on the nature of the communication, and the *position* from which it is heard.

Storyline can be understood on a basic level, based on its namesake, known to all of us from very early childhood. Each person interprets events from within a narrative, which means that every event may have many narratives attached to it. Applying this to teaching and learning, the storyline in position theory refers to the contextual narrative held by the learner, into which the instructor is communicating.

Taking all of this together, "positioning can be understood as the discursive construction of personal stories that make a person's actions intelligible and relatively determinate as social acts within which the members of the conversation have specific locations" (p. 16). In one particular way of looking at things, this could be considered the teaching-learning space within which the instructor works. The question arises here, for sure – what does this mean then, for those who wish to make a practical difference in the classroom? It means that the instructor is often teaching specific content without any awareness that the learner is perceiving the entire situation from within a very different storyline than the instructor.

For instance, a communication expert called in to provide customer service training skills to front line workers in a technology firm may think that she is offering a great opportunity for the employees to hone their verbal skills, and improve their productivity and job satisfaction. The employees, on the other hand, may think that they are being punished for the company's poor fiscal quarter, and that management is bowing to pressure from the Board of Directors and forcing them to sit through the training. The instructor views her own position as a helper, a developmental resource, and a key to enhanced job satisfaction, while the employees are viewing her as "the punisher."

In this case, the disconnect itself is problematic, but the most important viewpoint for how the content is taken in, interpreted, and whether it is internalized and used in the future (transfer) is the employees viewpoint. Those receiving punishment are not particularly open to guidance and advice, especially from the person issuing the punishment.

Position theory is useful when considering ways to foster engagement with learners and the "inherently dynamic character of positioning" (p. 28) fits what has already been discussed about the learner's tension field between drives to engage in learning and drives to avoid it entirely (Lewin, 2013/1935), and the rapid decisions concerning approach and avoidance motivational dispositions (Elliot, 2008). The practical value of this will be fleshed out in the CONNECT method below, and I will provide examples in the following pages, but to make all of this clearer, a more concrete example will be used in tandem, throughout.

Here are examples of two different ways the class could be interpreted and the position I was potentially assigned by the students for each:

Scenario #1

Learner's Storyline

I have worked really hard for years and have not received a pay raise in a very long time. On top of that, I am now being supervised by someone who started after me and doesn't even really know how to do this job. The economy is tanking, the company has made stupid decisions, and now I am being called out as the scapegoat, the problem that needs fixing.

Instructor's Position

Outsider, getting paid lots of money to tell me how to do my job even though they have not done my particular job at this particular company.

Instructor's Communication/Locutionary

Everything said will be interpreted by this position through this storyline.

Scenario #2

Learner Storyline

I am a professional customer service specialist with many years of experience. She is going to use her outside expertise to help me develop strategies for being more successful here. I work hard and do a good job, but I am being provided an opportunity to develop my knowledge and skills and improve my skills. This will help me be more productive, open new opportunities for promotion in the future, and make this job more satisfying.

Teacher Position

Collaborator and subject-matter expert in customer service, Consultant, Professional Equal, and Supportive Coach.

Communication/Locutionary

Everything said will be interpreted by this position through this storyline.

In each of these two scenarios, the same content is being taught, by the same person, with the same skills, and to the same people with the same skills. But the storyline is quite different between the two and it is easy to see how speech acts might be interpreted very differently in the former than the latter.

The question then, is what to do with this. The theory itself is terribly complicated, but the application is, thankfully, not. The takeaway is very similar to those of conceptual change theory discussed in Chapter 6. One of the first things to consider when planning for a training session is what the storyline of the employee learners is likely to be. It is true that everyone in the class will not have the same storyline, although workplace culture often tends toward a number of shared storylines that have been developed over time and steeped in hallway and watercooler conversations.

Considering the significant storyline or even several prominent storylines is an early step in the process of figuring out how to ensure that your position is what it needs to be for the training and that the locutionary acts you engage in (speaking and body language) will convey the meaning that you intend. As a practical application, the instructor needs to include changing the storyline – setting the appropriate storyline, as a legitimate part of the lesson plan design process. Simply put, building the story line needs to become part of the content.

The remainder of this chapter provides an overview of a specific approach that I have found to be effective over the years, in getting around resistance, connecting with learners, and fostering openness and engagement, even under less than perfect circumstances, like teaching professionals how to do their jobs when you have never done their job. With only a few short detours, I will continue to use this customer service training to give structure to the steps being introduced.

Because the power of acronyms has survived throughout the decades (and perhaps centuries), I have arranged the steps into an acronym as a simple memory tool. In other work, I have used the term OPERATE (Taylor, 2022), but I have used connect for many years as well and favor it because the word "connect" fits well with the concepts of motivational immediacy.

C-O-N-N-E-C-T THROUGH LESSON PLANS

Consider your primary objective. The primary objective is vital in all training situations. It is vital because there are likely many different objectives, but they are not of equal value and, importantly, some may contradict others. In a training class for public transportation rail operator instructors, a debate between instructors developed because certain instructors were requiring bus operators to read publicly in class from a policy and procedure book as part of one of their classes.

Several instructors did not like this practice because they said that quite a number of rail operators were not able to read out loud well, particularly in public while nervous, and that to force them to do so was unnecessary and caused them disruptive stress which might ultimately get in the way of their learning. The opposing team, so to speak, felt that reading in public was something that the bus operators would be required to do at some point, and therefore good practice to have them "buck up and learn how to do it" while still in training.

In a situation like this, knowing what the primary objective is for a particular training class session is very important because it will provide the answer for this sort of dilemma. When asked what the primary objective of that training situation was, the instructors answered that the primary objective of that particular training session was for the rail operators to become familiar with all of the basic policies and procedures for their job.

In this scenario, if the primary objective is to learn the policy, to become familiar with it, and to understand what it means, then all instructional decisions must be made in accordance with whatever will advance that objective in the most efficient way. If other secondary goals can be met at the same time without conflicting with or diminishing the primary objective, it is okay to work toward them as well. But in the case of the reading aloud task, reading aloud (for the purpose of teaching them to read aloud) was working in direct conflict with and opposition to the goal of becoming familiar with the policy.

Anyone who has had to read aloud in a group before knows that a couple of things are going on while a few others are decidedly not. First, while everyone else is reading their part, you are counting how many people there are between them and you, and then trying to count out and find which paragraph or section you are going to have to read. Second, you are trying to scan for trouble words and tricky phrases, to sort out any problems before you have to read it. Third, while you are actually reading it, after having not heard what anyone else was reading before you, you are actually so focused on reading the words properly in front of you that you finish without any real idea of what you read. This may be a bit of an exaggeration for some, but near enough for most of us.

In this case, the learning to read aloud objective was not the primary objective and therefore needed to be cut loose. Perhaps it could be the primary objective at another time. Or perhaps it could even be a secondary objective during a class where it would not trip up the primary objective.

Returning to the customer service training scenario above, the primary objective may be to work with the front-line employees to develop techniques for dealing with difficult customers. In that case, all subsequent decisions must be considered over and against that primary objective to ensure that they forward that objective rather than contradict it.

Obtain thorough information on learners. A fundamental practice for being motivationally immediate is to *listen* to the learners. This may be difficult when planning a lesson because in some cases the instructor may not have had a great deal of interaction with the learners, and in some cases there will have been none. When there is personal, first-hand knowledge, of course, this should be used. For training situations where there are multiple modules or session, it is vital to speak with the learners about their thoughts and ideas and, yes, their feelings. We often might not like to ask those questions because we tend to get what we ask for, but they will help the instructor make better decisions, to be more relatable, and to be more motivationally immediate.

It will be discussed in more detail in the next chapter, but taking every opportunity before class, during breaks, and between sessions to fellowship (yes, I am using that word on purpose) with the employee learners in your class so that you can learn from them will provide you with lots of important information about storyline, preexisting conceptual frameworks, and what they think they know, do actually know, and really need to know.

Beyond this, there are many ways to make reasonable inferences and predictions based on prior interactions with employees in similar situations and reasonable attempts at empathy.

Navigate with empathy. Empathy is a key word here, not sympathy. Sympathy may help as well, but it is not entirely necessary. The difference matters. While empathy understands what others are going through, sympathy feels bad for them. Sympathy likely will make you a better instructor, but empathy is required to be good at all.

Empathy is what will help an instructor arrive at a reasonably inferred idea of what the learner's storyline is for the training, along with other motivational factors that play a major role. Empathy is what will help one with the next step below, but before moving on, it is probably worth addressing an objection that is sometimes raised on this point. One might wonder if it is a good, or even ethically right, idea to try to "assume" what the learner may be thinking and feeling before you even teach a course. Admittedly this sounds, on the face of it, like something that should be avoided. However, it is the responsibility of the instructor, of all teachers of any kind, to do just that.

Educators make loads of inferences and make an equal number of assumptions about learners, learning situations, content, and just about every other aspect of teaching. If you are teaching a class, you are making an assumption (in most cases, at least) that there is a need to know. Instructors make assumptions that employees need to know things, assumptions about what those things are, assumptions about how best to communicate them, and assumptions about how to best manage the next group of students.

To be fair, we are often wrong about them and have to adjust all along the way. That is also a part of being a good instructor. So yes, making some reasonable predictions about what your learners might be thinking and feeling will make you a better teacher – if you make plans accordingly. And, as things move forward, you will be listening very closely to all sorts of different cues your learners will give you and in the event you are wrong, and you often will be, you will be able to adjust on the fly because you will have motivational immediacy at the very front of your mind the whole time you are teaching.

Note all potential resistance. This step is the culmination of the empathy step and obtain thorough information from the learner step. Given all of the information you have either gleaned or inferred to the best of your ability, you consider all of the possible reasons that any one of your learners might actually be motivated to ignore you, tune you out, disagree with you, and determine in their mind that they will never be doing that thing you have suggested in class.

Why would a good instructor engage in such a negative task? The answer to this question is easy, really. The good instructor will engage in this because it is a deeply learner-centered approach and is not negative at all. They seek to listen and understand the learner's point of view. They seek to connect with the learner where they are and to make the journey from there. They acknowledge that human motivation is not binary and goes with equal energy in either direction with regards to learning. As a professional, you are aware that your learner may in fact be motivated to *not* learn. In order to unmotivated such learners to not learn and, in turn, motivate them to learn (often two different steps, but sometimes the same), you simply must be aware of what their motivations might likely, or even possibly be.

In the example of the customer service training class discussed above, there are a number of potential reasons an employee learner might resist.

- The learner may think they already know all there is to know about their job.
- The learner might think they know more than the instructor about how to do their job.
- The learner might believe that they are being unfairly punished for something outside of their control, such as a bad fiscal quarter or atypically difficult customers.
- The learner might believe that the instructor's "theory" is not applicable to practice.
- The learner might believe that instructors (and management) are out of touch with the day-to-day operations.

These factors and others may be in play during the class and making an attempt to catalogue them in advance will prepare the instructor to connect more easily, quickly, and effectively to the learner, address those concerns, and get past them.

Engineer all content to preemptively address resistance. Taking all of the reasons above that a given group of learners may be motivated to resist rather than engage, the very basic, important, but often overlooked step, is to add responses to each and every one of these directly into the lesson plan, *as part of the content,* and use them to slowly but surely bring each learner to a place where their resistance has dropped and they are engaged with the content, with their classmates, and with you as the instructor. In practice, the five concerns listed above will now become an authentic and irreplaceable part of the training content itself.

The Learner May Think They Already Know All There is to Know About Their Job

The training content now must have the employee learner's blind spots or knowledge and skill limitations built into the list of learning objectives. This awareness may be facilitated by group discussions in which members work together to find difficult workplace problems that they have experienced and a related set of questions or by sharing a case study that involves an ill-defined problem and then having a class discussion to expose weak areas.

Whatever the actual method that is used, motivationally immediate training requires that these steps and the related purposes be considered a part of the content, not merely some preparatory exercise leading up to it. The practical purpose of seeing it as part of the content is that a failure to do so – to see it only as a pre-content exercise – leads far too often to it getting cut when time is short.

The Learner Might Think They Know More Than the Instructor About How to Do Their Job

This may be a common problem, but it is one that also must be addressed as part of the training content. Simply rattling off all of one's accolades is not going to cut it – only a few care and most don't pay any attention. That is, sadly, how learners often respond to what they consider routine parts of any training course. This is tough for those who are stuck teaching a course that they are not passionate about (see previous point in Chapter 4 about figuring out how to be), but for those who are deeply interested in what they are teaching, and, perhaps more importantly, deeply interested in having someone else *learn* about that something, sharing the personal story behind that passion and interest will go quite a bit beyond a simple listing of credentials. This, again, does not sound very technical or "shiny" but, also again, human learning is not about technical content or acumen. It is about human connection.

**The Learner Might Believe That They Are Being Unfairly
Punished for Something Outside of Their Control, Such as
a Bad Fiscal Quarter or Atypically Difficult Customers**

This would seem even more like something that should be considered, if at all, as a preemptive step to prepare the learner, rather than a part of the training content itself. Thinking back to what the research on conceptual frameworks (Chapter 6) has revealed about how humans learn, every bit of training content is heard, interpreted, made sense of, encoded, and loaded for future use (or not) within a conceptual framework that already exists in the learner's mind. If you don't "build the box" before you fill it, the learned content is very likely to not look anything like it does in the box you are teaching it from information on position theory and the storyline learner's hear training content through.

**The Learner Might Believe That the Instructor's "Theory" is
Not Applicable to Practice**

This is a simple one, although it seems supremely difficult to pull off in practice. No theory should ever be taught without a relevant application and to do so is to do both the learner and the theory an injustice. The trick here, like in most other areas, is less about coming up with great ways to teach this and more about finding ways to foster conditions in which learners discover it. Use discussion and group exercises to develop the connections. Something as simple (and perhaps silly) as having a competition between groups of employee learners to develop a scenario for which the theory would apply and a true workplace anecdote to make the point. Most of the time, the employees are going to have more knowledge and skill in this area than the instructor does. And, even if they don't, they will find their own experiences more meaningful and valid then they will the instructors.

**The Learner Might Believe That Instructors (and Management)
Are Out of Touch With the Day-to-Day Operations**

The great news about this one is that if the instructor uses group facilitation heavily in the training, carefully creating circumstances through which learners come to the conclusions they need to and weaving in expertise and the requisite technical knowledge where natural gaps occur, the learners won't be much concerned about the instructor's credibility in the first place. They will be busy thinking they had all of the answers, even though it was the instructor who expertly led them there. Training is not about the teacher knowing the content; it is about the learner coming to know the content.

What makes this particular part of the "connect" process work, and what makes it different than other approaches that also suggest preparing the learner, is that the motivational immediate mindset considers these real-time adjustments to learner perceptions as part of the training content itself. This step is metaphorically much like the old Western movie idea of "heading them off at the pass."

Connect to your learners in situ. This step is easy for some and tremendously difficult for others. Motivational immediacy is well immediate. That means that the effective instructor most be immediate to the individual learners at all points during the class. Faces must be read, body language must be interpreted, and responses must be assessed and clarified. This may sound daunting to some, and it can be challenging, but this is why motivational immediacy is more about changing the way we think, than about any particularly practice. The moment one really accepts that teaching is about working with people, knowing people, understanding people, and communicating with people, it becomes a natural step to stay in touch with each and every learner the entire time one is teaching.

Talk to your learners. This step should be easy but isn't for many of us. Small talk is required, icebreakers may be expected, but authentic inquiry into the lives, minds, and especially "hearts" of our learners is a difficult proposition. I have spent nearly 20 years now asking different groups of people to (a) share who their favorite teach was from their entire life, from birth to the present time at any level and form of education, and (b) explain why. In all of the years I have been asking the question a few things have been true 100% of the time. First, in every single case, the person remembers the name of the teacher, no matter how far back the experience was. 65 year-olds remember the name of their third grade teacher (Ms. Jones) from that town they only lived in for one school year. Second, in absolutely no cases was the reason that the teacher new a lot about their subject area. Discussion reveals that this is not because that isn't important, just expected and assumed. In every single case, it was a teacher who connected with them individually, as a human being, met them where they were, and walked some sort of a journey with them. And, it is accurate to say, they are still walking the journey with them all of these years later, even if unaware.

COGNITIVE, AFFECTIVE SOCIAL (CAS) WORKSHEET

The worksheet depicted in Figure 7.2 is designed to be used by both instructors and employee learners alike. The instructor should use the worksheet before each training session, ad with each significant content

Learning Dimension	Classroom	Field	Effect of F on C	Effect of C on F
Cognitive				
Social				
Affective				

Figure 7.2 The CAS worksheet.

point within a lesson. The learners should be given the opportunity to use the worksheet during class, when possible, for two reasons. First, it will help them experience effectual learning (acquisition and acceptance), and second, because they will typically be much better at this than the instructor, especially if they have been on the job for any significant amount of time.

The worksheet takes into account a number of different things. First, it takes into account the three dimensions of learning described by Illeris (2002). The terms used – cognitive, social, and affective – have been changed by Illeris (2007, 2017) in his later work, but I have retained them because I think they are clearer, in terms of their application to practice.

Second, the worksheet takes into account the effect that the classroom discussions will have in the workplace, which I have labeled "the field." When practical issues are discussed in the classroom, and the instructor is providing a comprehensive package of content to the employee learner, that "learning" is not static and isolated in a vacuum. It will have to intersect with all of the fluid and constantly changing dynamics of the workplace. For instance, when an electrician apprentice is told quite firmly not to ever use his lineman's tool as a hammer, it will have a very clear and present effect on the job the next day when the foreman and the other six electricians on the jobsite tell him to "shut up and use the tool" to knock that plate off.

Third, the worksheet takes into account the effect that actual experience in the workplace has on the classroom. In the workplace training room, it is very common for the learners to have logged hundreds if not thousands of hours in actual workplace activity. That puts technical and often "canned" training knowledge to a true test and one for which it is very often ill-prepared. An employee who has been reamed out by her more senior co-workers for kicking the brick out of the external door that was propped open for a smoke break at 2 am will smile at your very serious (but in her mind, trivial) line 5, slide 26 mandate to "never prop an external door open for security reasons." The employee absolutely will prop the door open again (read, zero transfer), and ironically, she will do so especially because it will ensure her personal security.

In Practice

For the sake of providing a concrete example, consider the case of the lineman's tool. More accurately, it should be called lineman's pliers. More accurate still, it should be referred to as electrician's pliers, but no matter – each trade has its oddities. Lineman's pliers are well pliers. But they are used on the jobsite so frequently and for so many things that if one hangs out with electricians for only a short while, honorable mention of one sort of another will come up. Simply put (and for electrician's, I am trying to make a point and apologize for any minor inaccuracies), electricians have learned over the years, in the school of "hard knocks" probably, that these pilers are robust enough that they can be used, in a pinch, as a stand in for a hammer. Hammering, however, even with a hammer, takes its toll over time. When the hammering is conducted by something that was not designed to be a hammer, the vitality of the something is greatly diminished. It takes little imagination to understand that the thing being hammered might also suffer an indignity or two when being struck by something that was not designed for that purpose. Because of this potential damage, by both the tool and the recipient of the hammer strike, it is a routine part of apprentice training to be told to not, under any circumstances, use the lineman's tool as a hammer.

Cognitive

It is a gross oversimplification to split these three dimensions apart because they all interact with one another, and there is a cognitive context to both the social and emotional. However, for the sake of practical use, the cognitive dimension refers to the more clearly recognizable aspects of cognition and learning concepts and skills. This category would include all of the train-the-trainer information related to human skill acquisition (e.g., primacy-recency, cognitive load, etc.).

The cognitive part of the learning task is the easy part, relatively speaking. It is the most controllable, most stable, and least robust to change. It is strange then, that this is the dimension of learning that the training profession nearly obsesses about. It may actually be natural to focus on this area especially because it is controllable, relatively stable, and robust to change, but if we do so we are, in essence, ignoring the dimensions that require the most effort and focus if we wish for success.

Using the example of the lineman's pliers, it is easy to see that the more straight-forward part of the training process would include sharing the proper information with the learners – that they are not to use the tool as a hammer (or any number of various other purposes) – and to perhaps share why that is the case. There may be more here, but for the sake of clarity, and because this is the one area of workplace training that is reasonably effective, I will leave it at this.

Social

The social is where the learning process starts to become complicated and where the training process begins to become halting at best and completely unsuccessful at worst. The social dimension has everything to do with the peer work dynamics while on the job. For every workplace there is a general culture of both community and of the work task itself (Illeris refers to this as production in his model, 2017). Each of these exerts tremendous pressure on employee learners to come into compliance with those cultural practices in the workplace.

Although this is empirically well-grounded (Illeris, 2017; Wenger, 2000), it is anecdotally obvious as well. A large share of the training content is often related to changing a number of different, entrenched practices in the workplace. There is the way employees are taught to do things and "the way we do it out here." Going back to Salaman and Butler (1990), it is not that employees don't want to learn from training, just that they have already learned too well in the workplace.

In the lineman's plier situation, apprentices will readily share how they are expected to use the tool anyway they are asked to use it, and to do it quickly without offering up their "two cents." While there are some job sites that have more by-the-book supervisors, most often, the apprentice is working with a seasoned professional in the trade, and in these instances, most will admit that there is no way they are going to buck the system out there "where it matters." And, if a professional trainer is fair, they have a good point.

In this case, the power of the social will outrun the cognitive nearly every time. When working through this worksheet then, before a class, it becomes immediately obvious that simply transmitting factual knowledge and expectations to the employees will be woefully ineffective. If the instructor is working for effectual learning (acquisition and acceptance), then two things are clear. First, something has to be done out in the workplace to shift this practice (see zones of intervention in Chapter 5). Second, if one has any hope of actually swaying the opinion of a learner strongly enough to make that learner resistant to the powerful peer pressure on the job site, then the instructor must be motivationally immediate.

It may not be 100% effective, but if there is any hope of changing this behavior, it will require a very frank conversation among the employee learners in the classroom, and the instructor absolutely must provide a safe space for honesty. Discussions need to be facilitated around these dynamics in the workplace without the learners being penalized for admitting their jobsite transgressions related to the tool use, without it getting back to their foreman that they have been open about these things, and without it being held against them in the future. Having authentic conversations about these practices may not fully change them, at least immediately, but there is no hope of doing so without them. As per usual, PowerPoint slide number six, with the little verbal diatribe attached, is not going to cut it. It is a waste of time.

Affective

It is in this affective domain that the other two meet and produce something difficult to control and predict. Not only do emotions regarding the content and job itself affect the learning choices of the employee, but all manner of incidental emotions that have little to do with the workplace, co-workers, or the training content at hand. Gino and Schweitzer (2008) found that incidental anger (anger that was not related to the situation at hand) resulted in study participants being less willing to take advice from others. Again, providing space for the learner to share their own conceptual frameworks, their own storylines, and their own experiences, opinions, and yes, feelings, is the only way forward to getting very complicated human beings to change the way they see any aspect of the world enough to transfer it to long-term practice in the workplace.

Effect of Field on Class

The question here, for the instructor first and then for the instructor to draw from the learner, is "what is the effect of that job site dynamic on the employee as they are sitting in your classroom hearing you talk about how to use the lineman's tool?" And, an easy further step, "what would you do in their place?" (empathy). Simply thinking through this should provide some insight in how to make the point more powerfully with the learner. Likewise, facilitating a discussion with the employee learners themselves about this dynamic, how it affects them, etc., will greatly improve the chances that they will change their behavior on the jobsite, although it will certainly stop short of guaranteeing it.

Effect of Class on Field

Finally, there is the consideration of what the effect of the classroom discussions will be in the field, on the jobsite. This one may seem silly, given that the whole point of the training is to have the person end up doing what you are teaching them to do in the class. However, as all training professionals know, this is sadly, just not always the case. There are many ways that training in the classroom can end up playing out on the job and in order to predict it at all well, and adjust for it in advance is to plan for all of the contextual elements of the jobsite.

For instance, the employee learners, if they have been on the jobsite before, can share with you that, in the case of the lineman's tool, the apprentice is going to be told to shut up and do what they are told. And, if they share that it was how they were taught in the classroom, they are going to be told another few things that I will leave out here. If this is a reality of the work, and if it can't be controlled, then it is disingenuous to not discuss it with the learners and plan accordingly. To fail to do so (slide 6, line 4) is to risk having your learners lose respect for the training (and other training courses down the road – remember conceptual framework development). Further, it makes for inert training that is more of a checked-box, than a learning experience for the employee.

Putting the Pieces Together

In this case, the situation seems somewhat hopeless, but at least by talking it through *with* the employee learners, rather than talking *at* them, there is the possibility of first, working out a strategy together for using the tool properly (perhaps there is a way to make sure a proper). Using the worksheet to think through these sorts of dynamics with each topic in the lesson is hard. Doing so, however, will provide a great deal of information about the true context you are speaking into, help you learn more about the learners in your classroom, and provide ways to potentially navigate situations is ways that the learner may, at least in the long-run, end up doing the right thing, and encouraging those around them to as well.

Chapter 8

Motivational Immediacy in the Classroom

All of the chapters in this second half of the book are meant to provide practical applications for the concepts and principles in the first half. It is important to realize, however, that the point of the book is not to introduce new methods for doing things, but to foster a new way of *thinking* about all of the things we already do.

That is not to say that there are no new ideas out there, and perhaps some will be found in the following pages, but the power of motivational immediacy is that it provides a set of principles that can make a significant difference even when applied to the things we are already doing in our training rooms. The essence of this entire chapter is that the instructional expert must in every case, consider the exact purpose of the particular method being used, and to ensure that it is used in a way that connects the learner to the content in motivationally immediate ways.

The key to understanding how to best facilitate engagement for both in-person and distance learning situations is to grasp the essential commonalities that underlie both. The common thread between the two learning spaces and all of the span between is the learner. The human learner is present in both contexts, and motivational immediacy is about the learner. Therefore, motivational immediacy is not radically different between the two environments. Likewise, it is not bounded by, nor is it automatically assisted or hampered by the use of technology. How we connect to the learner might differ, but the fact that we must connect remains the same.

Before these different learning spaces can be discussed with any hope of a truly practical outcome, a very frank analysis of the reasons each are chosen in the workplace (and anywhere else, for that matter), must be sorted through.

DOI: 10.4324/9781003144137-10

MOTIVATIONAL IMMEDIACY AND THE CHOICE BETWEEN F2F AND ONLINE

There are many different reasons that a course might be taught online rather than in a physical classroom. Like all decisions, the one made in this context can be a reasonable and good one made with the authentic interest in the learner and hopefully the intended learning, or it can be fraught with short-sightedness, ill-fated thriftiness, or misconceived notions. Online learning utilized for the right reasons can be an extremely powerful tool, but used for the wrong reasons can render the entire effort a complete waste of time, educationally speaking.

It can be less expensive. While initial setup is often significantly expensive for companies, the long-term savings that are naturally experienced in relation to the reduced need for physical space, on-site, nonmobile training staff, and other logistics having to do with face-to-face learning, can make distance learning an attractive choice.

It can allow for more accessibility. Distance learning opens up the ability for a large number of individuals operating from a large number of different geographic regions, to participate without having to travel, find lodgings, and other tiresome, expensive, and often prohibitive requirements. Asynchronous distance learning further allows individual learners across multiple time zones to participate at their own optimal times.

It can reduce liability. Distance learning run through online platforms allows for digital tracking and enforcement, providing companies the ability to both ensure all of their employees complete the training, and to automatically collect digital records of measured outcomes indicating (perhaps) that the learning content has been successful.

It can be less work. Whether it should be less work is another question entirely, but is a question for later. Using a training method that reduces the overall long-term labor makes as much sense as making cost-effective choices. However, just as the term cost-effective connotes something that is fiscally wise but also effective, labor choices must be made with the same consideration for effective practice. Interestingly, this is a relevant consideration in almost all areas of the working world. The decision regarding how much effort to invest in any given project is governed by its connection to the respective output for those various levels of effort. Some shortcuts are inconsequential and therefore wise, while others are catastrophic and must be avoided.

It can allow for more control. Online platforms provide a training department with the ability to strictly control what goes on in the virtual classroom. Asynchronous learning is typically structured in a way that organizes content, delivers it in a very specific way, and offers the ability to set tight limits to the flexibility of individual instructors to add their own preferred content. Synchronous distance learning allows more flexibility but also is more easily and systematically monitored.

It can ensure more consistency. The ability to control brings with it the ability to force a strict consistency across the curriculum, across sites, and across geographic regions.

While each of these can be very positive effects of distance learning and could merit making a decision to do so, there are considerations that should be addressed either before making the decision or to review decisions that have already been made.

Honest Decisions

First, it is essential that those making these decisions be brutally honest about the real reason that the choice is being made. Second, those making decisions about distance learning must understand that when it comes to educational matters, the various reasons one has to make a decision are most often not evenly weighted. That is, each reason should only be viewed over and against its value in serving the primary purpose of the endeavor to begin with.

If one is using distance learning strictly to save money, but casts it as an effort to provide more accessibility, the entire educational mission is at risk of failing because consistently fostering learner engagement in ways that bring about deep, long-lasting, applied learning (transfer) in the workplace, requires that trainer or training director act with purpose and intentionality and in a clearly informed way. Working under false pretenses might be considered unethical but also has far-reaching consequences for the learning endeavor itself. Perhaps the clearest example of this would have to do with federally required personnel training of some sort, for which there is a real liability risk for the company. The digital learning experience might provide the easiest way forward with regard to ensuring that everyone gets it and everyone passes it (and is effectively recorded as having done so), but this can run entirely counter to the intended purpose of the training itself.

Passing it, is not at all the same thing as learning it, as was extensively addressed in the first section of this book. Because of this, the very moment when you have most easily and thoroughly documented the training material may also be a moment marked by abysmally low effectual learning. This may be a minor problem if those in charge of the training do not think that the required training is actually important beyond being able to say that everyone has had it. It if is seen as something truly beneficial, however, then distance may not at all be the best choice even though it has some nice features with regard to liability.

Conceptual Change

Most Resistant

Low Emotional Disruption — — High Emotional Disruption

Least Resistant

Rote Memory/ Procedural Skill

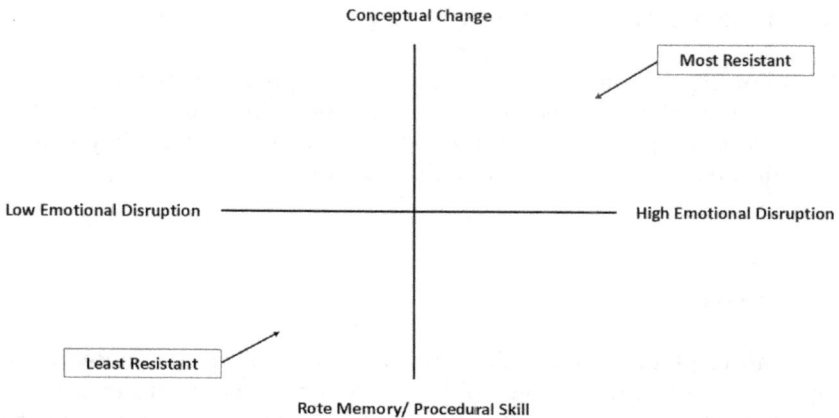

Figure 8.1 *Range and strength of learning resistance.*

Source: Adapted from Gold (1995)

Having employees actually experience a truly transformative learning experience with regards to harassment behaviors, for instance, might be much better for reduced liability, than being able to say that everyone was trained, after they are off engaged in inappropriate, unethical, and high-liability behaviors. The point here is not that distance learning cannot be used for important training, but that being robust to liability is a concern that must be weighted in comparison to all other reasons. Otherwise, it can be a very short-sighted decision.

When considering these reasons and any others that are not listed here, they need to be considered in relation to their respective capacity to foster motivational immediacy. Is the training going to be more motivationally immediate, and therefore more powerful, if it is offered online? That is the question that needs to drive the decision.

Returning to Gold's notion of emotional disruption (Figure 8.1), when making a decision about whether to offer a course online or in a face-to-face setting, those making decisions about organizational training must consider how significant the level of emotional disruption might be. Likewise, taking into consideration the concepts from Chapter 6 on Conceptual Change and learner paradigm shift, one must also consider the degree to which the required learning will involve significant paradigm shift within the learners. Consequently, if training really is ultimately about people and, by extension, about connection between people, then the more intense the emotional involvement required, and the more radical the perspective shift that is needed, the more connection and involvement between people that must be present.

FACE-TO-FACE APPLICATIONS

The following section is divided loosely into applications before the class begins, while the class is ongoing, and after the class is over. Many applications might transcend these three categories, but they can be generally grouped into these three timeframes.

Before Class

The almost legendary awkwardness that is present in the 20 minutes before a training class begins, can be avoided. Anyone who has been a learner in a workplace training course will immediately relate to the awkwardness that I mention here, and probably most instructors as well. There is the dead silence, the pregnant hush that resides in the room like an artificial climate. There is a person or two sitting somewhere in the room, typically not together, the instructor fidgeting about up front, and each new arrival pausing awkwardly at the door, taking in the environment, conducting a preliminary threat assessment in an instant, before moving to find a seat and look down at something – anything – and hunker down is some proximal amount of emotional safety.

From the moment one takes a seat, there is the twin specter of wanting things to be better, but not wanting to be singled out by the instructor up front or the stranger sitting across the room either. And, since most instructors are trained to do their best to greet employee-learners as they arrive, there often follows the greeting tossed across the room from the front and, possibly, a personable question or comment. This scenario rarely brings with it an easing of tension, because it singles out the learner (who was trying to look down) and forces them to engage across the chasm, in front of the others scattered throughout the room, and ends up being the Karaoke version of interpersonal conversation – without the fun drinks to potentially help things along.

While writing this, a particularly extroverted friend has come to mind who on more than one occasion has shared publicly that he likes people so much that when he enters a public space and doesn't know anyone, he looks around and tries to make eye content with someone – anyone – so that he can initiate a conversation. It may be true that there are those out there who share this mindset, but it is important to note that this does not change the general set of circumstances that are being addressed here. If someone is probing the room with beady eyes, in search of some relief from the silence, it is an attempt to improve the conditions of the situation. And, for the many who do not share this extreme form of extroversion, those beady eyes coming for us in no way serve to improve the situation.

Music

It may be that there are no effective ways to completely eliminate them, but there are a few that can mitigate them. First, the use of music in the classroom. This suggestion can be shocking to those working in more formal workplace classrooms, while, to others, seem like not much of a novel suggestion at all. It is worth including though, because in over 30 years of being a student or instructor in workplace training courses, I have only ever seen music used before, after, during breaks, and during group work and breakout sessions, on a few occasions, and all of the few occasions were by the same instructor and were in workplace training contexts.

The risks, of course, are that selected music might cause offense, that other instructors from nearby rooms (or upper-level managers), might complain, or that a few in your class, who expect a certain gravity to be observed at all times, might be put off. But the potential benefits make it worthy of consideration.

The benefits include the elimination of awkward silence. The power of this function has made it long be a common practice in other public settings including restaurants, shopping malls, and even grocery stores. So long as the appropriate volume level is chosen for the given room, crowd size, and location, having some baseline continuity of pleasant sound goes a very long way to ease tension, eliminate awkwardness and, a key to motivational immediacy, foster a sense of human connection. Given these purposes, it is vital that the right kind of music be chosen. "Oldies" that would be considered "clean" by the average person, are the safest bet, but this decision, like all others, should be chosen with the particular set of learners in mind, rather than a static set of guidelines. Again, here the principle is relatively stable over time – help the learner feel connected, but the specific application can change significantly from setting to setting.

Of special importance and utility is the playing of music during breakout sessions and group work. It is important during these times, however, to ensure that the music is quiet enough that it does not distract the learners from thinking and talking and learning together. Like the first few minutes before class starts, the first few minutes of a breakout group are riddled with awkward moments and transitions. The first thing one often hears in a training room, particularly during the early instances of breakout work, is dead silence born of the average person not wanting to be the lone and very public voice that breaks the silence in such stark nakedness. Music changes this, much as it does in a restaurant when people sit down at a table together.

Purposeful Connection

The time before a class starts is the best, and for many, the only time that the instructor can meet the individual learners in the room, connect with them personally, and begin to get an idea of where they are in terms of their job, their life, the content, and more general things, like what sort of day they are having. Every bit of this information is absolutely vital for the instructor that intends to be motivationally immediate throughout the training course.

Even while writing it, this seems like an underwhelming statement of the obvious, but it is not, and for a couple of reasons. First, for those who are most obviously "people persons," the point of the conversation can very easily become the *self*. For those instructors who are extremely shy (and, strangely, there are many), the tendency is to avoid such personal conversations that require being "out there." However, for those who are extremely outgoing (and, naturally, there are many), the tendency is to have such personal conversations for the wrong reasons. For the instructor, the idea should be connecting personally with the learner at that moment and, while being authentic and true to your own personal manner, the purpose should be to learn as much as possible about the individual sitting there in your classroom. That knowledge will be a key part of your ability to foster engagement in those particular adult learners in the workplace.

During Class

The following discussion about during class applications could likely run on forever, and as such it should be considered a sampling of applications intended to provoke thought and generate ideas.

IceBreakers – A Wasted Opportunity

Icebreakers are divisive in the classroom setting. That may come as a surprise since they are primarily used to help loosen everyone up and grease the gears of discussion and interaction. But, if instead of using one, the instructor asks the members of the class to indicate by a show of hands who likes them and who does not like them, a startling controversy will itself, for better or worse, become the icebreaker. In my personal experience of asking this question for many years, what has happened most often is that the room is split between two groups of individuals, those who "like" icebreakers on the one hand, and those who "loathe" them on the other.

There are few who fall into a category of "loving" icebreakers, but there are a great many who deeply hate them and fear them. Given that the first 15 minutes of a learning situation is the time during which the bulk of learners make decisions about whether: (a) you are worth listening to and (b) whether they are going to listen to you (Frye et al., 2017), using icebreakers wisely is an essential skill.

The number one anecdotal explanation given for not liking them is what one might expect – personal shyness. And, in fairness, this may be a good reason to use icebreakers, rather than to avoid them. They are, after all, intended to loosen people up, and even those who don't like them will often grudgingly admit that they have that effect in the long run.

The second runner-up is often that they have nothing to do with class, are busy work, and are consequently an annoying distraction. This one is a complaint that we would be wise to listen consider. Icebreakers can be and very often are significant opportunities for connecting with the learner to obtain highly meaningful information that are completely wasted. Icebreakers, when used well, can provide opportunities for learners to identify their personal conceptual frameworks, to admit to and specify areas of bias, and many other vital bits of information that are vital for the instructor who seeks to be motivationally immediate to the learner.

The suggestion here would be to design icebreaking activities that have the learners dig into either the course content itself, their personal views about the content, or their personal views about the class, all of which are important for the sort of interpersonal connection that is required in order to meet the learner where they are and make the journey with them. One particular example of using an icebreaker this way is provided below.

Teach from Their Questions

Instructors are acculturated into a set of practices that focus on what the instructor needs to teach, and consequently tend to avoid, at least overtly, what learners want to learn. This seems like another bit of common sense, and of course, the driving factor in a training class likely shouldn't be the employee-learner's general ideas of what they would like to learn. Part of the problem with discussions about learner-centered teaching in the workplace is that it requires an inflation of an artificial reality – that employees and employers want the same thing (Rainbird, 2000). The binary treatment of instructor-centered versus learner-centered classrooms is problematic because it leaves out the center ground. When this happens, it is the overlapped portion of the Venn diagram that is being cut out of the deal, and that overlapped portion is the point of the whole thing to begin with.

If the question is asked properly, there will nearly always be an overlap between the many questions a classroom full of learners can come up with, and the content you were planning to teach anyway. There is a win-win potential in this case, because the basic psychology of learning indicates that learners engage more when their own questions are being addressed. This is the essential means-ends fusion (MEF) in the classroom. It is the basic building block of motivational immediacy.

At the beginning of the class (icebreaker), the instructor can break everyone into impromptu groups of 2–4, depending on the size of the group. Then, have the learners chat within their groups for a short period of time (i.e., five minutes), to come up with 1–2, or 2–3 questions they have as a group about the general topic of the course. If the instructor is concerned about whether or not anyone cares at all about anything in the class (this unfortunately a reality of the training world from time to time), then the question must be more tightly focused and more context must be set more clearly. For instance, in a class that everyone is likely interested in, like how to avoid serious burns while working closely with a new chemical, a simple question such as "what questions would you like answered during this class?" will work.

In cases where there may be less interest, for instance, in a class about the general employee policies and procedures handbook updates, one might need to ask a question like, "if you were writing an employee handbook, what types of things do you think should be included, and why?" This is a different sort of question, but one which will reveal points of interest, or at least relative interest, on the part of the learners.

After taking five or so minutes for the groups to talk, go around the room and have one person from the group shout out one of their questions, and then either write it on the board or have someone from the class or group do so. Typically, you will find that by the time each group has provided one question, other groups have had most if not all of their questions answered. That is, there is often a significant overlap between the types of questions that learners have in a given situation.

After this exercise, the instructor can move forward with the planned lesson, but will be able to connect bits and pieces of it to all of the individual questions that were asked, and, for the few questions for which you did not plan on providing an answer, you now have the opportunity to address those as well. One of the advantages of this method is that *it does not require that you teach the content in the order that the questions are asked.* The preplanned lesson and supporting materials (e.g., PowerPoint presentation) can be used according to plan, but the instructor can consult the list of questions while moving through the lesson and ensure that each point being made is, whenever possible, grounded to one of the questions the class has come up with. This will have the effect of providing a "feel" that the content was planned in accordance with those particular questions, even if it was not. Additionally, it allows preconstructed courses to be taught to many different groups of learners over time, while molding each presentation to the specific questions of the group being taught. It can personalize an otherwise somewhat distant lesson plan.

Don't Use the Parking Lot

Questions coming from the learner in the middle of class can be disorienting. Beyond this, they can actually derail important points that needed to be made, confuse other learners, and contribute to an otherwise halting stride in the middle of a presentation. There have probably been many ways developed over the years to deal with this eventuality, one of which is the infamous "parking lot."

When an unexpected and unwelcomed questions is raised at an inopportune time, it can be placed somewhere and "parked" there until a more appropriate time for it to be addressed. Of course, there are times when a question is so truly out of square to the space it is asked in, that it is necessary to put off answering it for a while, and there are also questions that are inappropriate enough that they should not be answered at all. This latter situation is much like having a fire drill in the middle of class – it is not good but not much can be done about it when it happens once in a while.

It is worth challenging, however, our designation of "inopportune" time, when general questions are raised from the floor during a class. What is most often meant is that the question does not fit with the flow (read present PowerPoint slide) of the presenter at the time and is therefore inconvenient. It may be that it is inconvenient to be asked an unexpected question, or one that is only connected to the topic in a tertiary way, but it is likewise inconvenient to have our learners disconnect from us, tune out, and fail to learn what we are trying so hard to get them to learn. Also, if the instructor only does what is convenient it is unlikely that effectual learning is on the table to begin with.

A recurrent theme in educational psychology, educational research in general, and workplace training literature, is that learners do not learn well if they are not engaged (Illeris, 2017; Kraiger & Mattingly, 2018; Taylor & Frye 2020), and that learners are more engaged when they have a reason to want to know what is being taught (Knowles, 1980; Kraiger & Mattingly, 2018). Because these are real dynamics involved in human learning, and because we are seeking effectual learning (both acquired and accepted), learner questions need to be taken very seriously. And, further, what motivational immediacy and MEF dictate, is that learners questions must be handled in time and space as closely to their asking as possible.

The takeaway here is that when a learner's question is put in the parking lot to be handled later, say after lunch, what the instructor is, in essence saying to the employee-learner, is, "I am going to take the thing that you are the most personally interested in and engaged with at this very moment, and I am going to answer it later when you no longer care about it." And, sadly, we are really going further than that and conveying, in essence, that "and I am going to put off the thing you are terribly interested in right now, because I am going to press on in sharing something that you don't at all care about in its place."

Surely, we must teach the required content to employee-learners, but it is worth questioning the notion that we should stay on track, even at the expense of stifling the very learning that is being sought. The last thing an instructor should want is for a learner to be badly distracted by a point of confusion or interest, when that particular itch could be scratched quickly, freeing the learner's attention up for moving forward with the planned content.

The name of the game is getting the learner to acquire and accept learning in a way that will transfer later on down the road, and the most effective way to do that is to roll with the contours of the learner's interest, rather than trying to get the learner to roll with the flow our PowerPoint or Prezi slides.

Roller Coasters, Questions, and Means-End Fusion

Training and, for that matter, all forms of teaching are quite often reduced to the act of answering questions that nobody has asked. Motivational immediacy concepts require, in contrast to this, a special emphasis on questions in general, because they represent, or at least should represent, some level of interest on the part of someone in a teacher-learner relationship. The previous paragraphs focused on questions that the learner may ask, but the following focus on the questions that instructor uses in the classroom.

Thinking back to those old and often rickety wooden roller coasters that were so prolific years ago and so replicated today, there was that moment after clicking slowly up the towering peak of the largest "hill" and then cresting the top, there was a moment of stasis, where everything stopped for a moment, the cars seemed to still for a split second, and one might hear a happy shout echo from somewhere below in the park. But that moment was full of energy, despite its stillness, because it was poised for a violent path down the long, harrowing hill, wrenching the breath from everyone and leaving stomachs up at the top. Upon reaching maximum speed, at the bottom of the descent, perhaps after a few twists and turns, there was a somewhat drastic slowing of the cars, until either there was a complete stop or a near stop and the jerk forward could be felt, as the conveyance system grabbed the line and begin clicking forward up another hill.

The difference between the top, the trip down, and the bottom is one of energy. At the top, there is potential energy, as the hill is before with nowhere to go but down. On the way down, there is kinetic energy, in action. At the bottom, there is no energy, and external power of some sort is needed to push or pull.

Human motivation *to learn*, is based, similarly, on these three states of energy – potential, kinetic, and *none*. Roller coasters, old and new, work by using both potential and kinetic energy in the right amounts at the right times. Too much potential and everyone would eventually be "on to it" and stop being interested and excited. Too much kinetic and everyone would be sore enough and stressed enough, not to enjoy it in an optimal way.

Questions are one of the key tools that can be used by trainers and instructors to manage learning energy (i.e., motivation) in the classroom. When learners have authentic, personally meaningful questions, they are in the potential energy stage of learning. They are at the top of the hill and, while waiting for the answer, are in that tiny space in time where the cars have stopped just over the crest and are about to move quickly and fluidly of their own accord. Presenting information via direct instruction, although sometimes necessary and sometimes useful, is the equivalent of the roller coaster conveyance slowly clicking everyone slowly up to the top. How useful it is, depends almost directly upon: (a) how much of it there is in total on the whole ride and (b) how well it is mixed up with the big downhill runs.

This is not a new piece of information, for sure, but the point here is not that questions should be used in training, but that they should be used in a specific way, with specific learners, and at specific times. Using questions in the right way, will help the instructor manage learning energy in an optimal way. Here are three rules for being motivationally immediate in your use of questions in the classroom.

1. First, know what questions are for and why you are asking them.
2. Second, ask the right type at the right time, for the right reason.
3. Third, use questions as a way to share the content you need to share.

Know what questions are for It is impossible for someone to use questions properly with any consistency, if one doesn't know what questions are for. Should rhetorical questions be used in our presentations? Should questions be used to help employee-learners feel involved? Should questions be used to make sure that learners stay involved? Should questions be used to point out gaps in the learner's knowledge? Should questions be used to create conundrums or "ill-defined" problems? Questions can be used for all of these and likely more reasons.

The most common problem, at least in this era, is not a lack of questions for the learner in a training classroom, but the lack of properly used questions. If the trainer must learn how to use questions better, than the trainer must always know what different sorts of things one can be up to with a question. Here are some examples:

Ask the right type of questions. When it comes down to it, asking the right question is often more about when you ask the question and to whom you ask it, rather than what the question is. For instance, the same question can be asked for many different purposes.

Example # 1

The instructor is just using a rhetorical question in a presentation as part of the presentation or (often) as a speaking habit. The following question is being asked: "Why do we need to know this?"

Example # 2

The instructor wants everyone in the class to feel involved in the learning process. The following question is used: "Why do we need to know this?"

Example # 3

The instructor wants someone to wake up, sit up, and pay attention. The following question is used: "Todd, why do we need to know this?"

Example # 4

The instructor wants to point out knowledge gaps in the classroom. The following question is used: "Why do we need to know this?"

Example # 5

The instructor wants to make everyone think critically about why time is being wasted on a particular topic. The following question is asked: "Why do we need to know this?"

Each of these questions was packaged in a set of particular intentions and also expectations on the part of the instructor, with some, for instance,

MOTIVATIONAL IMMEDIACY IN THE CLASSROOM **133**

requiring answers, while others did not. The problem arises, in terms of a reduction in engagement (resistance), when we use questions in the wrong ways or at the wrong times. Additionally, asking the same sort of question too often can cause problems.

Asking rhetorical questions regularly teaches learners not to answer them, and, ultimately, not to listen to them (or anything else being said). Going back to the Zones of Motivation in Chapter 5, we can see how every act during teaching is a teaching act... Asking questions to foster engagement is only every useful if, well, it fosters engagement. This means that every question needs to be a very good one that the learner will think is a meaningful one. Bringing this discussion back around to MEF, if the learner does not see the immediate purpose of the question itself, that is, of it being asked, then it will not be of interest. Asking questions is a teaching *means* that must be immediately connected in the eyes of the learner, to the learning *ends*. A failure to do so, especially repeatedly, will result in your question-asking being one of the things that actually demotivates learners to learn and motivates them to ignore you.

Handouts

The age-old question of whether or not to provide some sort of handout or diagram has its place in the motivational immediacy discussion as well. It has become customary to provide different sorts of collateral for learners to utilize during a class and the confusing morass of information on learning styles has contributed to the pressure that instructors feel to ensure that every possible avenue is provided to the learner. Unfortunately, it is possible to set up a situation in which the instructor is perceived as a needless tack-on to the course material. This hearkens back to that old warning that one not become an usher in their own theatre.

One way to avoid this is to design your instructional supplements in a way that requires that they all be used together, in tandem, in order to deliver the punch that is intended for the learning situation. A handout that has parts of a diagram, but is missing an explanation, or labels, requires that the learner use the handout along with the instructor rather than instead of the instructor.

PowerPoint

Like so many other aspects of the training world, problems arise when automation occurs, practices develop into unquestioned traditions, and then cultural rules encroach upon the scene, forcing everyone to follow a tightly prescribed set of rules. When this happens, at least two things happen along with it. First, the original purpose for doing a thing and in doing it a very certain way, are long-forgotten. The moment the precise reason for doing an instructional thing is forgotten, is the moment the instructor loses the ability to monitor its use and to ensure that it is, in every real-world situation, serving its intended purpose.

The inclusion of PowerPoint slides, or something similar, along with an instructional presentation, has become largely assumed in the workplace (and nearly everywhere else as well). Enough has been written about the appropriate ways to use PowerPoint that it need not be laid out here in all of its detailed glory. What is important, however, and in keeping with the motivational immediacy concepts being presented in this book, is the admonition that – here we go again – PowerPoint is about the *learner*, not the content. The moment the presentation wedges itself even slightly between the learner and the instructor, like an unwelcome third wheel, it needs to go fast.

If using PowerPoint, or similar technology, has developed into an assumption, then we are no longer carefully considering its purpose in each individual learning situation. Further, we are no longer engaged in the moment-by-moment process of checking it against its purpose to ensure that it is working well.

Like the handouts mentioned above, one of the ways to use PowerPoint to increase motivational immediacy, is to create them in a way that requires the learner to connect to both the slide presentation and the instructor's presentation itself. If you need notes, just use notes. PowerPoint should be to increase the power of your presentation, not give the learner an option to opt out to either the slides or the instructor. And, if one wants to really do something crazy, one could choose to skip the PowerPoint entirely for a class here and there. Automaticity and mechanization do not serve individual groups of learners very well.

The question to ask, is whether the presentation aids are helping the learner along with the content, not whether they are helping the content along to the learner. There is a subtle but vital difference between the two, and motivational immediacy requires that the instructor remember at all times, that the very same training aid can foster engagement in learners, or serve in a Pavlovian way to tune them out

After Class

From the perspective of training transfer, it is only when the class is over, that the learner is entering the period where transfer, strictly defined, is even possible. From an instructional standpoint, if the instructional goal is to foster or ensure training transfer of the training content, then it is not until the instructional event is over that it might actually begin.

Recognizing that ending as the true beginning of the application period, it is wise to take the time to talk to learners, individually, as they are packing up and leaving the room, and to establish a way to communicate with them in the future as they have questions or concerns. The employees are a key resource to the instructor, who in many cases, no longer spends as many hours "on the job" due to instructional responsibilities. Asking employee-learners to reach out later on with problems they have run into, examples they can provide for you to use in future classes, questions about something you said, or even arguments they think of later, is one significant way to insert yourself into the learner's long-term transfer process. It will extend your training class far beyond the room you are teaching it in.

THE "UNDERNEATH" OF F2F AND DISTANCE LEARNING

Distance learning in the workplace largely occurs in two forms, prefabricated training videos and synchronous videoconferencing of some sort (i.e., zoom). To a lesser extent there are asynchronous learning platforms like Blackboard and Canvas. While these latter platforms are used heavily in higher education, they are less often used in the workplace. One of the more convenient things about motivational immediacy is that it is what I often call "the underneath" of human learning, meaning that it is a fundamental, foundational construct that undergirds all forms of training delivery modalities.

Because motivational immediacy is the underneath of all forms of workplace training, the key factors that foster motivational immediacy are required across all forms of workplace training – human connection and interaction. Earlier on, I wrote that online learning could be easier than F2F instruction. I have no doubt that those who teach some form of asynchronous learning struggled with that statement because it unquestionably requires more effort to connect with a large group of learners in an asynchronous learning environment than it does in a F2F environment. This is true in the same way that it would be easier to make a big announcement to everyone in your neighborhood, and address their questions and concerns while they are all gathered in one room, than it would be to try to correspond individually with each and every one.

An important factor is at play here, though, in that if one actually had the enormous amount of time and patience it would take to have a meaningful, full-length dialogue with each neighbor in the neighborhood, one-on-one, one could make the argument that it would be a very solid way of going about it. The question, of course, is whether any corners would end up being cut in order to make the task manageable.

MEF in Our Teaching Principles and Teaching Methods

There are learning principles and learning methods. There are teaching principles and teaching methods. When we know why something is the way it is, we know the principle of the thing. When we know the principle of a thing, we can find a suitable method that will allow us to render change upon it. All teaching methods likely started being used at some point for precisely this reason – someone understood something about how someone learned something and set out with a particular tool to see it happen. At that moment in time, there was an MEF in the mind of the person teaching, and because of that, the method itself could easily be, and likely was checked all along the way to ensure that it was acting in accordance with the purpose for which it had been selected.

As decades and centuries passed on, however, and as generation after generation of educator did mostly what had been modeled for them, there slowly grew a gap between the principle means and the method ends, that ultimately became a great gulf. The practical methods in this chapter are shared, whether they be new or old, in close proximity to how they connect to how people learn, and a big part of the practical power of this chapter has to do with bringing methods of instruction back into alignment with the learning principle they serve.

Chapter 9

Curriculum and Instructional Systems Design

The golden key to failure is curriculum. The technical reason for this is quite subtle but when viewed through the lens of motivational immediacy, the fundamental problem is stark. Curriculum has come to be about content. Curriculum has come to be about process. Curriculum has come to be about documents and prescriptions. Teaching and training, on the other hand, continue to be, as they really always have been, about *people*. Unfortunately, the right hand is very far from the left on this. There are very few problems in workplace training or any other educational domain that cannot, in fact, be attributed to this basic loss of focus on the human soul at the center.

In keeping with this, and in accordance with the entire rest of the book, this chapter is about curriculum only insofar as it is related to human learning. This discussion on curriculum is predicated on a number of assumptions based on the theoretical and empirical information provided heavily in the first half of this book. I have accused on more than one account of spewing "curricular heresy" and some of the following ideas will be exactly that.

Kraiger and Mattingly (2018) claim that training and learning share an overlap, but differ in that training focuses on "specifically what works" (p. 11). While I don't disagree that there is a connection between the two, Kraiger and Mattingly's statement is a significant understatement. All of the theory and empirical research represented in this book would lean toward that relationship being correlational if not one of cause. What works, in terms of learning transfer, is employee *learning*.

Well over 20 years ago, Smith et al. (1997) pointed out that "few attempts have been made to understand transfer from the perspective of what it means to learn" (p. 91). This may be true in terms of the particular route

DOI: 10.4324/9781003144137-11

that has been taken, empirically speaking, within the academic "silo" of workplace training and its affiliate fields of study, but the larger empirical work on human learning has a great deal to say about training transfer (often referred to as learning transfer in other fields). The "successful encoding, retention, and application of training information are the most crucial for performance by maximizing the likelihood of application of expected behaviors" (Marand & Noe, 2018, p. 85), and encoding, retention, and application, we have seen, are connected to readiness, motivation, and motivational immediacy. Taking all of this together, the following sections provide different ways of thinking about curriculum design and use. These ways of thinking, however, lead directly to different ways of doing curriculum design as well.

MOTIVATIONAL IMMEDIACY IN THE CURRICULUM DESIGN PROCESS

This primary curricular message borne out of motivational immediacy is that curriculum must be about the people who are learning the content, not the content itself. This is not a technical run-down on how to design curriculum, it is a call to bring it into alignment the concepts and goals of motivational immediacy. In order for effective learning to occur, training professionals must facilitate learner engagement, and in order to do so, learning resistance has to be conceptually understood, acknowledged, identified, and addressed as a part of the curriculum for any given class, course, or program. This is a fundamental step toward practicing motivational immediacy.

Means-ends fusion relates here as it does nearly everywhere else – in order to ensure that curriculum is designed with the learner's capacity, incentive, and volition to learn, the ultimate goal must be kept squarely in view while engaging in all of the steps required to reach that goal. One way to do that is to break, temporarily, from the various instructional systems design (ISD) models (e.g., ADDIE) and to return (repeatedly) to one's philosophical base. Curriculum, it is important to remember, is always supposed to be a means, rather than an end. The best way to keep it from drifting back towards "ends" status, as is quite natural for professionals everywhere while engaged in their own professional practice, is to remain focused on the task at hand only and always in relationship to the whole. The following theoretical alignment pyramid (TAP) is intended to be helpful in that effort.

The TAP is, first and foremost, a guide to assist *practitioners* in analyzing the drive (conscious or unconscious) behind their practices. While some

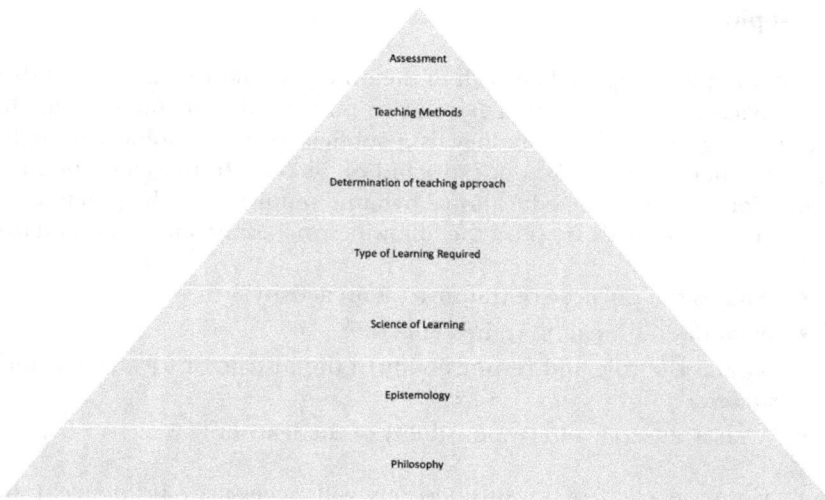

Figure 9.1 *Theoretical alignment.*

claim to be philosophers and others claim to have a strong dislike of philosophy, everyone actually *has* a philosophy, and it drives everything that one does. The point here is to ensure that one is: (a) completely aware of what that underlying meaning structure is and (b) following that structure (or changing it) as much as possible for the purpose of practicing in a way that is *internally consistent.* A pyramid is chosen here, as a figurative notion, to emphasize that each construct is based upon the foundation of the one below it and, in a very necessary way, requires that one proceed through these constructs and the meaning they each have, in a specifically relational way. However, the point is to ensure alignment, and like all complex systems-based devices, doing so may also be an iterative and recursive process. That is, one may move up and down the pyramid at various times in an effort to modify something above or below, in order to return it to alignment.

The bottom line is that all practitioners should begin analysis for ANY instructional decision at the bottom of the pyramid and work upwards. It is not uncommon for someone to adopt a new teaching method, or even worse, take a teaching methods class that begins on the sixth level of the pyramid without taking any notice or accounting of the five levels below it, upon which, the given methods were by necessity birthed, and in accordance with they will either be successful or fail.

The following paragraphs provide a brief explanation of the categories of the TAP. These paragraphs begin with the bottom category – Philosophy – and work upward through the pyramid as you read down the page.

Philosophy

The philosophy category, like each of the others, would require a great deal more space than is permitted here. The reader will also notice that the second category up, Epistemology, is a subfield of philosophical thought, which has here been broken out to stand on its own. In this case, the most foundational level on the educational pyramid requires that the practitioner consider the most basic views on the following (including but not limited to):

- What is the purpose of training (as an activity)?
- What does it mean to train someone?
- What is the role and responsibility of the instructor for the learner's success?
- What is the role and responsibility of the learner?

One's views on each of these questions will necessarily influence (and certainly should) any and all beliefs and decisions above it.

Epistemology

Epistemology usually, in its broadest sense, is the study of knowledge and truth. What it refers to here, most specifically, is questions of what truth is, how we evaluate and discriminate between conflicting truth claims, and, most specifically, what knowledge is and what its relationship to truth is. It is very important to note that even among those who agree on many questions of ultimate reality, words like knowledge can be defined differently, and how they are defined has a very significant and direct relationship to all other questions of educational practice. Every practitioner must be aware explicitly of how they define these terms, and should make sure that any dialogue with others about the topics, follows only after terms are defined. In truth, most significant educational issues, practically speaking, are disconnect at this fundamental level of the pyramid, even though those arguing about them might never dip below the top one or two levels at the tip of the pyramid.

This entire paragraph may seem out of place here and unimportant with regards to workplace training, but the opening discussion about the difference, overlap, and relationship between learning and training bring it into focus. Another pair is training versus education. And, of course, I have added a number of concepts to the list, such as effectual learning, acquisition, acceptance, resistance, motivational immediacy, and others. Taking the time to figure out what is meant by these terms, how they are related to one another, and what they mean for practice is vital. Additionally, ensuring that everyone at the planning table is aware of how the terms are being used is vital to program planning and curriculum building.

Science of Learning

The science of learning and, in the present context, the science of training, refers to the body of scholarly and academic knowledge of human learning and workplace training. The scientific study of human learning requires both the natural and social sciences because the phenomenon of human learning always occurs physiologically in the natural body while being inextricably situated in a social context (Illeris, 2011, 2017).

Type of Learning Required

The type of learning required refers to a highly specified learning context and the determination of which type of learning is required for that particular context. This is a simple notion. An example is a situation in which an instructor is charged with teaching a group of police recruits how to use their firearms. Knowledge factors for that situation may require physical skills (muscle memory) and also conceptual skills (physics). These two aspects both relate to *how* one uses a firearm. To ensure that officers understand *when* they should use the firearm (would anyone doubt that *when* is as important as how?), there may also need to be conceptual skills and problem-solving skills related to rapid situational assessment and decision making. So, the subject matter here might be quite different and therefore have demands quite distinct from those needed to teach someone about reading technical diagrams, operating machinery, or other technical activities that may require less reliance on executive processing in the brain.

Determination of Teaching Approach

The first important aspect at this level is to understand that a teaching approach is different than a teaching method. Teaching *methods* are highly specific techniques that enable a more broadly engineered and purposeful approach. A teaching *approach* is a broadly cast set of general guiding principles for teaching for which there are usually a number of different possible (some better than others) methods. For instance, teaching for transformation, an approach having to do with using content to develop critical thinking skills, is a general and broad set of principles for an educational approach, whereas there are volumes written about the specific techniques and methods that can be used in a classroom to bring about these transformations. Within transformational learning, for instance, one can use purely collaborative learning situations or one can use a more structured "guided discussions" format.

In the pyramid, *determination of approach* refers to how one determines to approach teaching in the broadest sense. How one sees the lower levels of the pyramid, again, directly influences and directs the instructional approach one chooses to use.

Teaching Methods

Once one has identified and chosen a specific instructional approach, then specific decisions need to be made regarding the moment-by-moment, highly specified, teaching methods to be used in a classroom. Will the teacher lecture, lead discussions, both? Will the learners sit in rows facing the front, in a circle, in pods? Will the learners read materials then discuss them in class, take copious notes in class, use digital materials? All of these are questions that pertain to specific instructional methods.

Assessment

Once all of these other decisions have been made, decisions need to be made regarding how the students should be assessed. This of course, depends on all of the layers below in the pyramid, connected most strongly (in the logical sense) to the type of learning required. For instance, if one is learning leadership skills, conceptual understanding and demonstrated skills might be assessed in a certain way. Conversely, if one is learning how to operate a piece of machinery, assessment might be completely different.

This section has contained only a very brief overview of each of these levels. A great deal more could be said about any one of them, however, the most important thing to remember (and the point of describing them here at all) is that any training considerations and related discussions and/or training, including (especially, perhaps) instructional methods, must begin at the most foundational level of the pyramid. This is important for two reasons. First, whether one cares to admit it or not, each level is, at least implicitly, based on the lower level, and second, because one should strive for theoretical alignment. That is, if one holds beliefs to begin with, one should act in alignment with them and strive to remain internally consistent. Only in this way will one take solely purposeful actions within educational settings. The fact that assessment is at the very top and to be determined last rather than first, is often a point of conflict for basic curricular practice and therefore, it is important to address it further.

CURRICULUM AND INSTRUCTIONAL SYSTEMS DESIGN AND AFFECT

Many of the most prominent and frequently used instructional design models do, in fact, acknowledge the importance of learner characteristics as well as other contextual factors. This can be seen at least as early as 1949 in Tyler's statement that, to have a thorough understanding of possibilities and difficulties involved in drawing interpretations about educational objectives, [one should] jot down data about groups of students with whom you are familiar, formulating a comprehensive set of data about their needs and interests (p. 15).

The Instructional Development Institute Model (Wittich & Schuller, 1973) has, as a second step, *analyzing setting*, which includes learner characteristics. The Air Force Instructional Design Model, developed in 1975, uses the term *system requirements* to refer to learners, instructors, and other environmental and contextual factors (Dick et al., 2009). Smith and Ragan (1993), in their model, include an analysis step, which involves an examination of the learning environment, the learners, and the learning task. Kemp et al. (1994) recommend that learner characteristics be taken into account, and the Dick and Carey Model (Dick et al., 2009) provides that designers should analyze learners and contexts. Willis's R2D2 Model (Willis, 1995) has gone a little further. Its constructivist basis resulted in a model that not only acknowledged learner and contextual factors but suggested that these factors must be continually assessed throughout the entire design process. Verduin (1980) and Cennamo and Kalk (2005) more directly and thoroughly than most others, also expressed the need to take the *affective domain* into account.

Given that the literature does seem to include the importance of the affective, why does practice not generally reflect this? A number of different factors may have given rise to this inadequacy, and unintended consequences have resulted. It is here that it is necessary to return to the foundational premises of motivational immediacy and the learner dynamics that make it necessary – engagement and resistance.

In a practical sense, learning is not about merely *acquiring* content, it is about truly *accepting* content. Training then is not about getting people to know *how* to do (understand) something but about getting people to *agree* that it is actually a good thing to do (understand), and then to do (apply) it, on a prolonged basis. The first part of that statement is the fundamental pathway to the training transfer mentioned in the second part. This is simply said, but to embrace this idea requires a significant paradigm shift for the educator and curriculum designer.

There are at least three specific factors that lead to the theory-practice gap in workplace curriculum design processes. Chief among them is the fallacy of viewing the learner's motivation and engagement as something distinct from the learner's learning. Additionally, the mass production of education via a highly fragmented real-world ISD practice is problematic. Finally, the tendency for assessment to drive the process by which actual learning objectives are chosen in the first place creates a dynamic in which priorities become badly misaligned.

ALL SETUP FOR THEORY-PRACTICE FAILURE

It has been previously noted that the nature of the problem addressed in this chapter is that of a theory-practice gap. While academic writing generally requires support using academic sources, the very nature of pointing out a theory-practice gap requires that one use information gleaned from years of practical experience in real-world settings. This experience is not easily cited (if citing is possible at all) and so often is left out of scholarship. Perhaps this is one of the reasons that theory-practice gaps exist in the first place. That discussion is outside the scope of this chapter, but it is important to note that the points made in this section are a confluence of the academic scholarship in curriculum and ISD, and decades of experience in working with institutional and organizational learning environments to address learning resistance. Those experiences have provided a great deal of certainty and conviction about the actual practice of curriculum design, as it plays out in the real world.

FALSE DISTINCTIONS BETWEEN MOTIVATION AND LEARNING

In practical terms, it is fundamentally problematic to view motivation as a phenomenon distinct from human learning. Perhaps more candidly than anyone, Danish Educational Psychologist Knud Illeris has stressed the inadequacy of separating out aspects of a process as distinct objects. He further pointed out the importance of avoiding the tendencies of educational academic fields to use, as a stepping off point, one single aspect of human learning when trying to explain human learning as a whole (2002, 2003, 2011, 2017). In keeping with this he identified three overlapping and dialectic dimensions of human learning, the *Cognitive*, the *Social,* and the *Emotional* (2002). He later changed this terminology (2017) to *content, incentive,* and *environment,* but his original terminology has been retained here because it requires less exposition. He writes that, "...all learning involves these three dimensions, which must always be considered if an understanding or analysis of a learning situation is to be adequate" (2007, p. 25). This view is entirely consistent with notions such as Vygotsky's (1978) *dialectical development* and Bandura's (1977) *triadic reciprocation,* both foundational frameworks in educational scholarship.

Likewise, on the curriculum end of things, it should not escape notice that Illeris's educational triad very closely resembles Tyler's (1949) claim that *subject matter, student,* and *society* must all be taken into account in the development of curriculum.

Speaking to motivation, specifically, Illeris claims that the connections between learning and motivation "...can only be separated analytically, as the motivation or drive (for or against or of any other kind) will always be an integrated part of both the learning process and the learning product..." (2003, p. 26). He further writes that:

> Even when two persons apparently have learnt the same, they have not if there is a difference of any importance in their motivation. They may be able to immediately answer the same questions correctly and the like. But if learning is driven by an intrinsic motivation, it is more resistant to oblivion, and the learning results may be applied in a broader scope of situations and to a bigger extent be involved in new learning, than if the motivation has been extrinsic. (p. 26)

I am all-in with the idea of not teaching for "oblivion." This sort of dichotomizing, referred to in this section, is not entirely uncommon in academics, and Illeris has indicated that it is connected in many ways, to the evolution of psychological science. "In my opinion, it is one of the most severe mistakes of psychological research that – in order to be "really scientific" – it has been inclined to split apart mental constructs which operate in an integrated way" (p. 25).

Motivational theory itself, when taken together, seems to point toward a holistic view of learning. For instance, *Approach* and *Avoidance* motivation discussed thoroughly in Chapter 3 (Lewin, 2013/1935; Elliot, 2006) provides a framework by which all human learners are motivated in every learning situation, albeit they may be motivated *not* to learn rather than to learn.

The question must be asked then, what contribution does this tendency to separate motivation from learning make to curriculum design practices? The answer to that question is a simple one. By coming to see the two as distinct (practically, not analytically), practitioners are enabled to: (a) focus more on one aspect than on the other, (b) to split responsibility for each of the two allegedly distinct constructs between various persons or divisions within the educational setting as is so commonly done in large-scale curriculum design, and (c) conveniently set aside affective elements when measurement is problematic. The latter two of these form the intersection of this problem with the other two addressed in the following paragraphs.

Curriculum designers and teachers alike cannot afford to view motivation as someone else's problem, or even as their own problem to be handled as a separate event. For instance, in the workplace, there is a common assertion that the punitive steps in place for failing to follow the policies and the procedures sufficiently serves to motivate students to learn what is taught and to do what is learned.

CURRICULUM IN A BOX

The mass production of learning experiences required by very large organizations, government institutions (e.g., military; federal, state, and local governments) and now, at an alarming rate in educational institutions that are more and more often constricted by accreditation and certification standards, also places a burden on the efficacy and integrity of the curricular process. To be clear, this is not to say that those who are involved in this process have any choice in the matter, nor is it to say that this type of practice cannot be done well, or in the least done more, rather than less well.

The advent of online education and increasingly user-friendly online platforms has given rise to this dynamic in higher education, which had previously avoided this sort of factory orientation. If your institution does not pressure you to utilize your online platforms in very specific ways – at least to a much greater degree than would be the case with your physical classroom – then ask around with your peers and you will find those who are subjected to many rules in place to serve an effort of standardization across online courses. Online course structures are not, strictly speaking, curriculums, but they are hopelessly tangled up with them in these domains.

It is possible to think of certain benefits that are derived from such standardization, but the practice does have the potential to lead toward certain flawed outcomes. The first step in mitigating these flaws is to become deeply aware of their existence and their nature. Being truly positive in a meaningful, healthy, and functional way does not mean that one ignores the negative – pretends happily that it doesn't exist – but that one sees the negative, looks it fully in its face, and sees positive opportunities within it.

This chapter, in part, is an effort toward that end. The reason the mass production of curriculum presents the potential for significant problems in the learning process, is that the very effort of capturing any given content and setting it up in a way in which any given teacher, in some cases, even teachers and instructors without any subject matter knowledge (yes, this happens in higher education also), can present it for any given students, requires that one adopt a view of knowledge (and therefore also of learning, and also teaching) similar to what Freire (1996) called "banking education." That is, that knowledge is some static thing that can be packaged and transmitted directly to the brain of the learner via some form of direct instruction.

Additionally, the practice of designing curriculum for very large groups of learners to be taught by a large group (over time) of somewhat generic instructors (those either pressed into service, lacking subject matter knowledge, or lacking a passion for teaching that subject), largely negates the entire principle of analyzing learner characteristics or learning context, or in the very least renders it more theoretical than actual. The natural division of labor that often occurs in this process requires the curriculum designer to produce a product that a different set of teachers may be teaching, and to assume it will equally suit the various educators and students who will be exposed to it. This plan may not dictate disaster, but it is inherently flawed because it facilitates, and often forces a more reified division of labor that coincides with the problem of separating motivation from learning as a whole, to potentially produce a dynamic in which one group of individuals is responsible for designing the curriculum, another set of individuals is responsible for the teaching, and yet another distinct category of individuals (or institutional/organizational structures, such as reward and punitive measures) is responsible for motivating the learners.

The final result can be a cold, clinical collection of information which is, admittedly, very nicely organized and packaged, being fed with varying levels of skill and acumen, to a group of learners who are presumed to be pre-motivated (global motivation) by some long-term endgame (diploma, degree), or some feat of organizational engineering (i.e., policies, rules, punishments, and rewards). Something as integrated and holistic as human learning could have difficulty in this type of structure.

DISINCLINATION TO TEACH WHAT CANNOT BE MEASURED

This is perhaps the most significant and far-reaching problem in curriculum and ISD, both because it has severe outcomes and because it is so firmly rooted in the curriculum process itself. Posner and Rudnitsky (2006) provide a very clear evidentiary statement by saying that, "Evidence is defined as an outward sign; therefore, by definition, evidence of learning must be observable" (p. 199). They go on to say that evaluators should, "look for this evidence in observable student behaviors or observable products of student work" (p. 199).

By invoking this "by definition" sort of statement, Posner and Rudnitsky seem to be making a much stronger argument than they really are. In saying that the very definition of evidence leads one to a forgone conclusion about how learning should be measured, a number of things have gotten confused.

First, there is a clear logical distinction between acknowledging that human learning can be measured, and knowing how to practically, effectively, and accurately be able to measure certain forms of it. The need for measurement does not speak with any clarity to the efficacy of measurement.

> A student of Thorndike, William McCall, is credited with the well-known and often quoted "whatever exists at all, exists in some amount and can be measured" (in Pulliam and Van Patten, 2003, p. 71). This statement is similar to many others like it that make a great deal more sense in theory than in practice. The history of science portrays a nearly endless line of existing phenomena that were first suspected, then verified by a newfound ability to measure them. Very little effort is made to explain away their presence during the time prior to their successful measure. The logic of the way we have applied the statement is problematic also. It is a non sequitur in that it doesn't follow that because something must exist in a quantitative amount, that one would, at any point, have the capacity or skill necessary to measure it. It is a statement about ultimate reality, an ontological proposition, not a practical application. (Taylor, 2020, p. 101).

Second, an acknowledgement that learning may ultimately result in some sort of overt behavior, is not the same thing as saying that such measurable behavior will come in any close proximity to the learning situation. For instance, a learner may come to see that a particular behavior, like texting while driving company vehicles, is dangerous, and may determine not to do it any longer. But it may be that the learner only texted while driving infrequently, and under certain extreme circumstances that might not exist again for weeks or perhaps even months in the future. This is the difficulty with training transfer in the first place, and why it has become such a topic of discussion and study.

Failing to recognize the learning-behavior gap, removes the situation from the bounds of time, which is a luxury not offered to the real-world educational situation. That is, to buy-in to the statement is to make a sort of educational short-term fallacy. If certain types of learning might not show up in the form of behavior, until long after the moment of learning, or only manifest themselves accurately under certain special circumstances (like what is done when nobody is looking or will ever know), then short-term efforts to measure or assess that learning are a waste of time at best, and terribly misleading at worst. For these reasons, Posner and Rudnitsky's statement is not all that powerful when applied to arguments for widespread behavioristic objectives in curriculum.

This particular problem has been mitigated by the inclusion of verbal or written answers as behavior, but this has not translated at all well to the real world, and often might work against its own purpose.

Third, an acknowledgement of the need to measure something does not speak one way or the other to how much focus measurement should have in our curriculum, or to what extent measurement should end up being the driving force for determining what learning is, how we should teach, and, most importantly, what we select to teach at all.

The argument I am making is not about whether or not evidence-based methods are a good idea, but whether or not they are being done well. Likewise, I will at times challenge the obsession with measurement, but stop far short of suggesting that we should not measure at all.

Along the lines of the authors above, but more specifically, Dick et al. (2009) are quick to emphatically point out that, "…test items must correspond one to one with the performance objectives" (p. 132). This, of course, refers to criterion-referenced tests (CRTs). CRT's embody a behavioristic approach to learning in that they expressly measure the ability to "perform specific competencies" (Seels & Glasgow, 1998, p. 83).

In their list of steps for developing outcomes and assessments, Cennamo and Kalk (2005) finish up with "develop[ing] assessments for *each* outcome and subskill" (emphasis added) (p. 40). Verduin (1980) says this in a more general way by referring to the "key" as "specify[ing] clear, concise goals for learning and then specify[ing] some *measures* to see if the new behaviors are present after the learning experiences have taken place" (emphasis added) (p. 133).

It must be stressed that the problem here is not with the idea of measurement, in and of itself. Rather the problem arises, in practice, when the requirement for learning objectives to be behaviorally assessed creates a situation in which the assessment itself begins to determine what actually makes it onto the objective list to begin with. Posner and Rudnitsky (2006), a few pages after their strong statement on the necessity of learning evidence being observable student behavior, appear to walk-back, or at least temper their earlier statement by saying, in respect to affective elements of learning, "It may not always be reasonable to expect a person who has learned an affect to supply behavioral evidence of that effect on demand" (p. 203).

Dick et al. (2009), when referring to the affective aspects of learning write that, "usually there is no direct way to measure a person's attitudes" (p. 135). Seels and Glasgow write those affective objectives are "measured by criterion items that are often voluntary and indirect" (p. 94). The debate regarding the emphasis on behavior objectives is not a new development (for a brief but informative overview, see Ornstein & Behar, 1995), but continues to be largely unresolved and, in my experience, almost completely divorced from actual practice.

For such a widespread problem, the nature of it is quite simple. The curriculum design process, by a preponderance of the literature, promotes the creation of well-defined learning objectives, the clear connection of objectives to specific assessment measures, and the evidence of curricular and instructional effectiveness via that observable behavior of students. This chain of expectations, when coupled with the extreme difficulty and impracticable nature of evaluating affective aspects of learning, creates a situation in which no matter what lip service is paid to addressing the affective elements in curriculum design, the practice of curriculum design will quietly step around the affective. In essence, the mantra, perhaps not spoken quite so plainly, is to "only teach what you can assess." This, on the face of it, seems so common sense that it passes (and is reified in practice) without much notice.

It is, however, in the face of real-world practice and what is known about human learning and motivation and most particularly, learner resistance, a misstep of staggering proportion. Taking into account the holistic nature of human learning, the pervasive presence and power of learning resistance, and the ultimate goal of education to bring about long-term change, the mantra should instead be *"teach what you must; evaluate what you can."*

This measurement factor, taking into account the tendency that separating motivation from learning has toward subsequently separating responsibilities for each, along with the tendency that the mass production of curriculum has on further establishing concrete divisions of labor, combine to produce something of a "perfect storm" for the overall process, which can often (though certainly not always) result in a series of *dis*abling (rather than enabling) and termin*ated* (rather than terminal) objectives.

IMPLICATIONS FOR CURRICULUM DESIGN AND USE

Accepting, as a point of departure, that engaged learning is the only acceptable kind of learning in the workplace, and that engaged learning requires that learner resistance be acknowledged and addressed, certain concrete changes need to be made in the way curriculum is designed and implemented. The following four rules for curriculum design are purposefully stated as colloquialisms, but are grounded in the three problems addressed so far in this chapter.

FOUR HERETICAL RULES FOR CURRICULUM

Rule # 1: The Curriculum Is a Means to an End, Not the End – If Any Part of It Gets in the Way of the Ends, Drop It Like a Bad Habit

The delivery of the content, that is, the actual teaching/training element, also cannot be divorced from the curriculum design process. Once one comes to accept that the actual content of the curriculum, presumably the most static of the parts, must be engineered with the learner's perceptions in mind, it is an easy and logical step to accept that the actual teaching of the material also cannot be a distinct and independent piece of the curriculum design process.

Based on the affective nature of learning and learning resistance, as a real-world dynamic, what the content is and how it is designed, cannot be effectively divorced from how it is taught. The fragmented nature of the overall curriculum and ISD process, further exacerbated by the systemic features of everyday, contemporary working life, result in a gulf between the design of the curriculum, and the actual facilitation involved in having the students learn the material. The proposed solution is to take teaching seriously and see it as more than the idle transmission of prepackaged content to a group of passive learners who are presupposed to be naturally engaged.

Simply put, prepackaged materials, to include lesson plans, no matter how well done, cannot be assumed to be effective as stand-alone components in an ISD process. Not in theory; not in practice.

Rule # 2: The Curriculum Is Not the Boss, You Are – to Paraphrase Kegan (1994) Have Your [Curriculum], Don't Be Had by It (p. 34)

I am going to go even further out on a heretical limb here and call out a few more long accepted practices. Keep in mind I am trying to point out that we do things without thinking about them, not that any one particular thing is always wrong. I will introduce two terms here and like all terms I use in this book, I am using them to assist in the discussion of them, not to insist in the use of them. The two terms are curricular implements and curricular artifacts.

Implements are devices that we use to help us as teachers to foster more learner engagement and learning. Using the term this way, I am referring to all of the things that one might assume to be the goals of all of the curricular practices we write about and adopt in practice. We make curriculum decisions so that our learners learn. An example of a curricular implement would be a learning objective. A learning objective is used so that the learner (and teacher) is/are aware of the task before them and are able to keep focus on the activities that will serve that objective.

Artifacts, on the other hand, are practices or outputs that have arisen for a number of processual or structural reasons over the years, as curriculum development has continued to be further professionalized. It is curricular artifacts that are of interest here because they are the very things we do (or things that happen because of what we do) to help, but which don't.

An example of an artifact is the notion of changing the first "action" word for each learning objective so that they are not all the same. I am not saying, of course, that this is flat out wrong, but I would like to point out that it has nothing to do with learning. It has, rather, to do with wanting our printed document to look good from a professional curriculum standpoint. There is nothing wrong with making it look good so long as it is not done at the cost of making it work well, and I am not sure anyone is questioning the minutia to that extent when writing curriculum. Keeping pen caps on pens might provide a practical purpose but turning all of the caps the same direction to line up with the tiny print on the pen is, well, I will let you decide what that is. If every single objective would be best served by the same action word, use the same action word. Have your action words, don't be had by them.

Making sure we have one assessment item for each learning objective is also a nice bit of squaring away that can actually impede learning. Teach what you must; what needs to be taught. Assess what you can; what we are good enough, at this present time, to measure. If you have a great number of learning objectives out there without assessment buddies, so be it. I told you this would make some people angry. Personally, I would be happy for a discussion at all on this, even an angry one. Nothing should be safe from scrutiny, including a "taken for granted beliefs" or "frames of reference" (Mezirow, 2000, pp. 18–19).

Rule # 3: Curriculum Is by Nature Reductionist – Learning and Teaching by Nature Are Not. Human Learning as a Holistic Phenomenon

First, curriculum designers must recognize that the actual content cannot be divorced from the individual learner's perception of it. That is to say that learning is situated (Lave & Wenger, 1991). Therefore, when designing curriculum, content development must occur at all times with regard for the learner's perception of it and potential resistance toward it.

Admittedly, this constructivist view of learning does not entirely mesh with much of the behaviorist curriculum and ISD models extant in the literature. There have, in recent years, been curriculum and ISD models derived from constructivist orientations (R2D2 Model) but it may be that the long history of more mechanistic models has rendered any change in practice nominal. Contributing to this was the curricular design shift in the late 1960's and early 1970's. Atkin (1971) rather strongly identified this by saying, "make no mistake; ["behaviorist objectives people"] have replaced the academicians and the general curriculum theorists..." (p. 369).

To make a significant difference in mitigating learning resistance, content must be engineered and couched in terms that are specific to the perception and situated nature of the learners to which it is to be presented.

For instance, basic human learning theory might be said to have somewhat of a fixed set of content (at any given time, at least). However, that content will be received very differently by those wishing badly to be school teachers and those who have been school teachers for 20 years but hoping for a pay raise. The context changes the content. Some reading this right now are, perhaps, a bit frustrated, thinking that all of this is a bit of common sense that is already well established in curriculum design. Well, the problem is, really, that it is not common practice. Because the most significant contextual issues are emotive (read Chapters 1–4), and emotive learning objectives are fun to talk about but difficult if not impossible to measure, so the rules of curriculum development forbid them from being included.

Curriculum designers should not be permitted to engage in their craft without a comprehensive education in the philosophy and social, physiological, and psychological sciences of human learning. One's philosophy of education is the foundation of every other decision made in curriculum design whether or not that philosophy is explicit. While there are those who admit to enjoying philosophy and those who claim to eschew it, everyone possesses "one" and to possess it without fully exploring it and identifying it is, to return again to Kegan (1994), to be *had* by one's beliefs rather than to *have* them.

In much the same way, one's understanding of the social, physical, and psychological sciences always drives all the higher-level decisions, which include all aspects of the standard curricular and ISD models. Whether explicit or not; whether accurate or not; our understanding of these realities dictate all of our moves in this arena. As such, curriculum designers should be required to have a comprehensive understanding of all of these disciplines as they relate to human learning.

Again, while this may seem to be rather intuitive, it is very often not the case in real-world practice. Since so many curricular and ISD models are based on behaviorist or neo-behaviorist frameworks, or at least in practice still bear out the effects of those frameworks, a solid understanding of human cognition and the effects of social learning could serve to balance the inherent weaknesses of the accurate but limited explanatory power of behaviorist learning models.

Of special significance, as noted in this chapter, is the need for designers to be thoroughly educated in the area of learning resistance, and more broadly, affective aspects of human learning. Rather than be the peripheral footnote they so often are (at least in practice) they need to be seen as the *driving force* of all learning. It needs to be understood that motivation and learning are inseparable and that to learn something, at least the type of learning that seems to be desired, is more than knowing something; it is accepting something. By extension, therefore, teaching is more than getting someone to know something; it is getting someone to accept something.

This can sound crass when put this way, but it is important to speak frankly about it because it is the crux of a very important matter. The idea of the curriculum designer and teacher having an agenda is just a basic truth that does not conflict with even the views of social justice-oriented critical pedagogy, since at the heart of critical pedagogy is a desire for the learner to think critically, and, as an example, "....it is important that the ground be properly prepared by teachers' building the best case they can as to why critical thinking is important" (Brookfield, 2012, p. 81). Even in these cases, a teacher is trying to express not only the content of the course (critical thinking) but that the content has merit and should be embraced to some degree.

Rule # 4: Measure What You Can – Teach What You Must

Of all the claims made in this chapter, it is likely that none will be received with quite so much discomfort, and perhaps outrage, then the proposition here that assessment should not be driving the curricular process. The reader should be warned, in fact, that the suggestions made here might well approach heresy (as the author was recently told), and even back as far as the very early 1970's those questioning the behavioristically driven obsession with measurement were not kindly received. Atkin (1971) wrote that those "who have a few doubts about the effects of the tide [behavioral objectives] had better be prepared to be considered uninitiated and naïve, if not slightly addlepated and antiquarian" (p. 369).

When taking the literature as a whole, a somewhat simple pattern emerges. First, objectives should be set for the course. Second, learners' learning should be assessed to ensure that objectives are being met. Third, objectives should have a type of one-to-one correlation with assessment items or modules.

This leads to what is possibly an unintended consequence. When taking these precepts together, one arrives with a naturally emerging principle that if there is an item that does not appear on the assessment, then it should not appear in the curriculum. This is usually stated the other way around, but the implication is bidirectional, to the great misfortune of educational endeavors. It is unfortunate because not every objective is easily measurable, and, to go further, it could be that, in a practical sense, some objectives might not be measurable at all. Atkin (1971) pointed out that it is a "primary flaw" to assume "that those attributes which we can measure are the elements which we consider most important" (p. 374). He goes on to say, "the behavioral analyst seems to assume that for an objective to be worthwhile, we must have methods of observing progress" (p. 374). So, what works in the theoretical world might have some serious flaws in the real world. This is borne out in the literature regarding affective aspects which are at best difficult to assess (Dick et al., 2009), and at worst, lacking tangible evidence (Posner & Rudnitsky, 2006).

The end result of this is that a fundamental aspect of learning (the affective domain) is given lip service in the most well-known models, but very seldom really given any purchase in the facilitation of learning content. This might work if it were not for what a clear understanding of human learning at large, and learning resistance specifically, mandates learning that brings about change is learning that includes comprehension and acceptance. Acceptance is a product of the affective domain and as such is as important as any other aspect of the entire curriculum and ISD process. Most importantly, it is a vital part of the process that is almost precluded in the practice of curriculum design and implementation because of the need to be able to assess everything that is taught. By teaching what *must* be taught and assessing what *can* be assessed, this problem can be eliminated. Atkin so aptly pointed this out by saying, "worthwhile goals come first, not our progress toward assessing progress on those goals" (1971, p. 374).

In closing this section, it is probably useful to note that this need to assess every objective, which has led to nonassessable objectives being omitted, most likely arose from an understandable but misguided attempt to bring the rules of physical science to bear on a science that is, in fact, physical *and* social, and psychological. While the merit of scientific principles is, to many, undeniable, it does not necessarily follow that those principles can be applied to all aspects of human life with equal effect. All of the variables that need to be controlled to make curriculum and ISD, and teaching and learning, a completely scientific endeavor, simply cannot be controlled in the non-laboratory setting in which practice always is situated. Curriculum models must move away from the highly reductionist frameworks upon which they are built. Since suggestions such as those made here are rejected often on the grounds that they herald a shift away from scientific education (a valid concern), it is perhaps a suitable conclusion to this section to include a quote from a more scientific perspective. "All that is counted does not count, and all that counts cannot be counted" (Einstein, 1879–1955, quoted in Tokuhama-Espinosa, 2011, p. 75; also cited in Patton, 2008, p. 420).

CONCLUSION

In order for effective learning to occur, teachers must facilitate learner engagement, and in order to do so, learning resistance has to be conceptually understood, acknowledged, identified, and addressed as a part of the curriculum for any given class, course, or program. To do this effectively, one must take a critical look at the theory-practice gap that exists in curriculum design practices.

The three factors discussed in the latter part of this chapter all come together to form a complex of dynamics, the confluence of which results in a lack of learner engagement in the classroom. First, motivation must be seen as an integrated and inextricable part of human learning, and the resulting confluence creates a dynamic in which all learning is both a matter of understanding content and accepting content. The acceptance part of this process is where the intersection of learning resistance, facilitation, and curriculum and ISD design exists. Effective practice demands that curriculum experts be experts of human learning, course design, and teaching and facilitation whether or not these experts will be engaging in all of these activities themselves. Learning philosophy and the physical, social, and psychological sciences of human learning are the absolute foundation, whether explicit or not, of all other curricular aspects and processes, and as such, must be studied, conceptually understood, and explicitly enumerated by all those who purport to be experts in curricular development.

Second, practitioners must acknowledge certain weaknesses inherent in the mass production of curriculum. Despite the necessity to approach curriculum design in this manner under certain conditions, the process must be seen as an integrated whole, learning must be seen as something more than the reception of static information, and the entire ISD process must be carried out with learner engagement as a primary concern.

Lastly, the difficulty in assessing affective aspects of human learning should not result in their omission, intended or unintended, in any aspects of the curriculum design process, especially in the teaching process. To make this so, there must be a willingness on the part of designers to include and even to emphasize affective objectives that may not appear in the assessment items. The messiness required here reflects the messiness of real life as opposed to the neatly ordered machinations of scientific study.

This may be the most difficult to embrace, of all the changes suggested here, but is, nonetheless, the most important if curriculum practices are to be used to facilitate prolonged and meaningful human learning in organizations and institutions. Teach what must be taught, measure what can be measured. As measurement methods are improved over the years, the gap may slowly close, but in the meantime, assessment cannot and must not determine what is actually taught

Chapter 10

Measuring Effectual Learning

Training departments are being asked to operate as "profit centers" and being asked to "provide documentation of the value added as a result of their services" (Kraiger & Jung, 1997, p. 113). Despite the discussion in Chapter 9 about the severely negative effects of allowing measurement constraints to drive training practices, there remains a clear need to, as best we are able, to measure the relative effectiveness of our training programs, and of employee knowledge and skills in the workplace.

The question is not whether or measurement is important, or whether it should be attempted, but to what extent it can be done well and to what extent it is limited in precision and accuracy. Kraiger and Mattingly (2018) have done a nice job pointing out some naturally existing boundaries to present measurement practice, and their comments are particularly relevant when discussing ideas such as effectual learning (acquisition and acceptance) and motivational immediacy, because these concepts are predicated on the importance of emotive and affective dimensions.

> While behavioral change is a pillar of modern training models (e.g., Kraiger et al., 1993), an overreliance on observable behavior is deleterious for several reasons. First, adhering to behavioral instructional objectives sometimes creates disconnects between the stated learning outcomes and what is the true goal of instruction. For example, the Sunday school teacher who states that "given a list of the 10 commandments, the student will correctly identify the 7th one" has created a measurable, behavioral objective, but what he or she really wants is for her charges to know that stealing is morally wrong. Second, the goal for many training programs is for trainees to do (or know) the right thing at the right time whether or not they can behaviorally reproduce skills immediately after training (e.g., preflight instruction on an airliner). Third, and most importantly for present purposes, a focus on behavioral reproduction as a training criterion ignores many important

DOI: 10.4324/9781003144137-12

mental events that we know are necessary for learning (of any form) to occur"
(pp. 12–13).

LIMITED ABILITY TO MEASURE EFFECTUAL LEARNING

It is important to know that a training program is working, and current behaviorally-based assessments are quite good at indicating a particular kind of effectiveness, they do little to inform how well training programs are resulting in *effectual learning*. Engaging in motivational immediacy, and all of the related levels that are required to do it well from the curriculum design process all the way through to the jobsite, is difficult work, consumes time, and since time is often money, can be seen as a financial burden.

The theory, concepts, and empirical work represented in the preceding chapters come together to make a strong case that in the long-run, training programs that result in effectual learning will always be less costly than those that do not. This is because cheaper programs that do not result in training transfer cost the company both wasted money and prolonged inefficiency in production and services.

The continued obsession with measurement in training (and now in higher education as well) gives rise to one of the most troubling difficulties faced by those hoping to invoke paradigm change in training programs – the requirement that any persuasive argument be validated through the medium of measurable outcomes. Many times over the years, while speaking at a workplace training workshops, warm acceptance has hitched against the single question asked from the back of the room – "how can we measure this and demonstrate that it is a valid educational approach?"

My effort to find a way to measure this more complex type of learning reflects my deep belief that it is important to approach learning with both an acquisition and an acceptance duality and to impress on instructors of all types the need to engage and foster motivation in the learner on a moment by moment basis. I realized some time ago that unless I can find a way forward to measure this type of learning, I would never have any powerful way to promote this type of teaching.

When digging into this topic, there is a fundamental truth about measurement that should be noted – not being able to measure something perfectly is not the same thing as not being able to measure something at all. This seems at first glance, to be dangerously near common sense, but it is easy to forget, especially when one is zoomed in so closely to the subject, as both academics and practitioners are. It is important to note because once setting out on a quest to measure something and to do it well, it is very easy to set the bar high for the measurement itself.

My point here is not, of course, to question efforts toward producing quality work. Instead, what I am pointing out, as I have throughout the book, is that one should never permit the means to trip up the ends or, even worse, to actually inadvertently *become* the ends. The question of concern has to do with the point of the effort to begin with. The vital question to ask is "Why are we doing this in the first place?" Also, "is the way we are presently doing this still clearly supporting the primary purpose for why we are doing this?" If not, the focus is lost.

In other areas of life, this makes a great deal of sense without a great deal of discussion. When someone is trying to set up a training room with standard 8 foot tables, it may be completely sufficient to pace of the length of the room, rounding one's shoe size up or down to one foot. This is particularly true if there will be a significant margin of space in the front and back, or sides of the room. Seldom does anyone go to great lengths to "bust out a tape" and measure the room, unless a tape measure happened to be sitting around.

Conversely, it would be difficult to find someone who thinks simply pacing off a distance is sufficient for the purpose pouring the footers for a house. *The purpose of the measurement dictates how precise it must be.* So too, does the purpose of training efforts dictate just how precise a measurement has to be in order to serve its purpose and provide the necessary answer. When a measurement that may be the equivalent of "pacing off a distance" is sufficient to answer the question at hand, but extensive conversations, arguments, and instructional method-shifts occur, this is an indication that measurement has become about measurement, just like curriculum has become about curriculum, and training has become about content.

If the overarching purpose of the entire training enterprise is to foster some sort of employee learning for the extended purpose of long-term training transfer, then training, curriculum, and measurement are all, in the end, about *people*. This particular line of argument about how precise measurement needs to be is extremely important here because in the case of adopting motivational immediacy practices, the measurement only needs to be precise enough to show improvement beyond that of practices as they are. This will not be difficult so long as – and this is key – the training professional remains focused on what, exactly, the other measures were measuring to begin with. After all, a good measure that measures an unimportant thing is not nearly as valuable as a poor measure that provides an index for something vital.

It may seem odd to be dedicating this much space to rationalizing what may be a significantly faulty form of measurement, but it is necessary to do so because the measurement dynamic has gotten so far out of hand, with regards to philosophical, and even scientific clarity. I said at the beginning of the book – we are measuring the wrong sorts of things. It is for this reason that so many books or articles need to be written about training transfer to begin with. Returning to a worn theme now, effectual learning is not merely about making sure that someone knows how to do something, but about facilitating a situation where they feel as though they *should* do it. And, going even beyond this, to a place where they will do it.

In this case, it is not enough to remember that the point of measurement is to justify the instructional strategy. That, it would seem, would be given. The better question is WHY are we trying to measure the effects of the instructional strategy in order to justify the instructional strategy? I realize that assessment and evaluation types have many reasons they think measurement is important, but in this particular case, the most specific reason one would be measuring this sort of "effectual learning" in the context that I have presented it here is to justify the resources required to utilize it.

In order to make this sort of assessment, however, one must know two things – what the cost is and what the benefit is. Further, since this type of instructional approach is always assessed relative to other competing approaches, there needs to be a way to render some sort of standardized index against which to compare two or more approaches. There may doubtless be many ways to do this, but the remainder of this chapter outlines one particular suggestion.

THEORY OF PLANNED BEHAVIOR AND THE MEASUREMENT OF EFFECTUAL LEARNING

In the late 1970s, Fishbein and Ajzen introduced his Theory of Reasoned Behavior (Ajzen & Fishbein, 1980; Fishbein & Ajzen, 1975), which Azjen (1985, 1991) later developed into the theory of planned behavior (TPB). The TPB has been shown to have predictive value for human behavior over and beyond a mere indication from an individual of intent. TPB uses inventory scales to measure variables such as the intentions, perceived behavioral control, subjective norms, and normative beliefs of an individual. These variables, taken together, provide a powerful tool to predict future behavior.

Simply put, someone's verbal indication that they will take a certain action in the future is not effectively predictive of whether they will actually do it. Ajzen's theory added several other factors, such as attitudes toward the behavior, perceived ability to take the action, and subjective norms, and using those together, was able to achieve a greatly increased predictability for the future action (see Figure 10.1).

$$\frac{Acquisition\ (1-5) + Acceptance(1-5)}{Work\ Hours\ (5-1) + Fiscal\ Costs(5-1)} = Learning\ Efficiency\ Index$$

Figure 10.1 *Effectual learning and learning efficiency index formula.*

The TPB has been used in a number of different practical ways to predict specific ranges of behavior. For example, it has been used in a predictive way in relation to sleep deprived driving (Jiang et al., 2017), walking behavior (Darker, 2008), Anorexia Nervosa (Dawson et al., 2015), entrepreneurial intentions (Mendez et al., 2015; Setiaji, 2019), nursing care (Vincentet al., 2015), and recycling behaviors (Passafaro et al., 2019). Buhmann & Brønn (2018) used it to examine and test predictive power in the context of communication. They conducted a study with communication professionals and used TPB to predict measurement and evaluation efforts and in light of the results wrote that "This is encouraging news for educators as it underscores the high relevance and strong potential impact of courses, seminars, and workshops that build knowledge on models, research methods, and applications.. . (p. 387)" and also, more broadly speaking that "These findings highlight especially the potential of education.. . (p. 388)."

One drawback of using the TPB in educational settings is that there would frequently be a strong incentive to be deceptive when completing it. In the case of the truck drivers, there would be very good reasons for a driver to avoid indicating that he was not going to be obeying the law or following required regulations. This sort of response bias would render the results invalid, defeating the purpose. However, when the person completing the inventory is permitted to do so anonymously, without any identifiers, physical or digital, being collected and connected, much of this bias could be avoided.

Administering the TPB inventory anonymously would make it impracticable to use it to assess the learner in any constructive way, but it could be very valuable in assessing the teaching and learning situation itself. Finding out after a course is finished, which 8 out of 10 participants did not buy-in to the content and will not be using it at any point in the future, would be immensely important for the educator.

If the TPB provides a way to measure the level of learner acceptance of content, and the acquisition of the content may be measured in the conventional ways, it would possible to measure what I have been referring to as effectual learning (acquisition of content + acceptance of content). Taking some standardized form of these two measurements and combining then could provide a concrete, quantifiable coefficient or index for effectual learning.

LEARNING EFFICIENCY INDEX

Although it would be very useful to have some form of objective read on effectual learning, being able to measure the *relative* efficiency of a given learning situation would be more powerful. In order to do this, one would need to have an index of effectual learning (benefit) that can be divided into an index of the overall outlay of the educational effort (cost). This sort of formula would allow for a scalable index that could be used for educational initiatives ranging from very small, one-time episodes, to large-scale, multiple year initiatives.

The Formula

The formula shown in Figure 10.1 shows an example of learning efficiency index. The numerator contains two numbers, the *acceptance coefficient* and the *acquisition coefficient*. In the first example, each a range of 1–5, with 5 being the highest level of each possible in the range. In the example, an acquisition score of 4 and an acceptance score of 2 would render an *effectual learning coefficient* of 6.

The denominator of the formula indicates two types of educational outlays – *direct financial cost* and *person-hour costs*. In most if not all cases, there is also a direct financial cost for the person-hours and a decision has to be made whether to add the direct financial cost of the person-hours to the direct financial side, but the person-hour cost in this formula represents the relative magnitude of hours required for the educational initiative and, in a sense, the labor opportunity cost, rather than fiscal cost, of those hours. The ranges here are the same as for the numerator above but are reversed, ranging from 5 to 1, indicating highest to lowest cost in the respective areas.

The combined score of the numerator (effectual learning) could range from 2 to 10, and the denominator (combined cost) from 10 to 2. The combined *learning efficiency ratio* score then could range from 0.2 to 5.0, with the higher number indicating a greater degree of efficiency.

Figure 10.2 contains three examples of effectual learning and efficiency calculations to lend clarity. I will expand on a few of them here. In the first

$$\frac{Acquisition\ (5) + Acceptance(1)}{Work\ Hours\ (4) + Fiscal\ Costs(3)} = \frac{6}{7} = .857$$

$$\frac{Acquisition\ (5) + Acceptance(1)}{Work\ Hours\ (4) + Fiscal\ Costs(3)} = \frac{10}{2} = 5.0$$

$$\frac{Acquisition\ (5) + Acceptance(1)}{Work\ Hours\ (4) + Fiscal\ Costs(3)} = \frac{2}{10} = 0.2$$

Figure 10.2 Three examples of the learning efficiency index.

example, the denominator consists of a 4 for person-hour costs, and a 3 for financial costs, for a total of 7. Taking the numerator (effectual learning) from above (6) and putting it over the denominator from the same example (7) the ration would be 6/7 or .857, indicating a relatively low efficiency, since the scale ranges from .2 to 5.0, with 5 being the most efficient.

In the second example in Figure 10.2, you have the highest level of effectual learning (10) over the lowest level of work hour and financial cost (2), which results in a Learning Efficiency Index of "5" which is the highest potential score. Example three shows the exact opposite, with the lowest possible effectual learning score (2) over the highest possible cost score (10), which results in a learning efficiency index of ".2" which is the lowest possible score.

Keep in mind that the level from 1 to 5 indicated for the work-intensive score is a relative score, not a raw score, and can be easily applied to an extremely wide range of training programs. For instance, if one engages in semester-long graduate courses and the number of dedicated hours is in the hundreds, the range of 1–5 can be applied to it as well as to a one-time 45-minute in-service course that requires 3–4 hours of preparation. In both cases, a choice of 1 would indicate a low level of work *relative to that particular project size*, and as such is a standardized score. Purely abstract examples are limited so in the final section of this chapter, a more concrete example will be provided, one with a high learning efficiency coefficient and the other with a low one.

$$\frac{Acquisition\ (1-5)+Acceptance(1-5)}{Work\ Hours\ (5-1)+Fiscal\ Costs(5-1)} = Learning\ Efficiency\ Index$$

*Range of .2–5 (Higher indicates a higher degree of learning efficiency)

$$\frac{Acquisition(5)+Acceptance\ (1)}{Work\ Hours(4)+Fiscal\ Costs\ (3)} = \frac{6}{7} = .857$$

$$\frac{Acquisition(5)+Acceptance\ (1)}{Work\ Hours(4)+Fiscal\ Costs\ (3)} = \frac{10}{2} = 5.0$$

$$\frac{Acquisition(5)+Acceptance\ (1)}{Work\ Hours(4)+Fiscal\ Costs\ (3)} = \frac{2}{10} = 0.2$$

THE CASE OF THE SOMEWHAT EFFICIENT LMS TRAINING

Consider a mandated in-service training program for the organizations Logistics Tracking System (LTS). The organization had recently switched LTS and the scheduled training was part of the transitional process to migrate to the new system. Employees were sent an email telling them that they were required to complete online LTS training by a certain date. The informational email also laid out some basic information. The online training consisted of about 15 different modules that ranged in length from 5 to 12 minutes. Employees could complete this training from any location so long as they had internet access. The training was entirely automated but also interactive. It consisted of brilliantly produced videos and required technical exercises which required the employees to work in the LTS and demonstrate certain selective functions that were being taught in the lesson.

Behind the Scenes

There were employees who closely watched the videos, completed all of the exercises, and went beyond that, spending time outside of the training messing around with the stuff they had learned. But time was tight. So, most employees simply put the thing on autopilot and did other things, while the videos were playing. The IT personnel involved in producing the training were on to this trick and had worked to mitigate it ahead of time. They had built in a pause every few minutes so if a participant walked away for more than a few minutes it would wait for them to return. Going even further than this, occasional questions were asked in little pop-up boxes and missing too much just prior to it could be a problem. All of this required that employees not wander too far or "check out" too much.

Using the Formula

The Learning Efficiency Formula was computed for the training as a whole. The administrators and personnel from the training department that made it a requirement and developed it, assigned a Work Hour Cost of 4 (out of 5) because the production hours required for the videos, tests, and other technical aspects was very high. The Fiscal costs were set at 3 because although the cost was high, it was cheaper than it would have been to pay all of the employees to be out of service for an entire day in a single location. That provided a total cost of 7.

Taking the data from the tests that were embedded in the online training, a high score of 5 was assigned to the acquisition side of things. This was due in part to the fact that employees had to answer all questions correctly in order to move forward. But when an anonymous survey was administered to all employees across the organization, using the TPB and measuring whether or not employees were intending to utilize all of the content that was transmitted to them, it was found that the majority of employees indicated that they had no intention of using the great majority of the features that were covered because first, they did not have the time to do so, and secondly (a related issue), they reported that they had learned all of the content in a way that was entirely unconnected to their own questions, interests, needs, and work production habits and would not be able to remember how to do any of it. Many also were honest enough to indicate that they didn't actually watch most of it. This is important, of course, because many might not be willing to report this even anonymously because it might end up costing them days in face-to-face training that they would be happy to avoid. These results led the administrators to assign an acceptance value of 1.

Plugging in the numbers to the formula ended up with the following numbers: 6/7 = .86; Learning Efficiency Index Coefficient (range of 0.2–5.0). This is not an impressive value. See Figure 10.3.

$$\frac{Acquisition\ (5) + Acceptance(1)}{Work\ Hours\ (4) + Fiscal\ Costs(3)} = \frac{6}{7} = .86$$

Figure 10.3 *Efficiency index formula Example # 1.*

*Range of .2–5 (Higher indicates a higher degree of learning efficiency)

THE CASE OF THE MORE EFFICIENT LMS TRAINING

Consider the same basic training program for the organization's LTS. Rather than being online, the training is scheduled for a full 8-hour day with lunch provided. The decision was made to offer lunch, adding to the fiscal costs, because of the location of the training facility and the limited time for a lunch break based on the amount of content deemed necessary to cover.

The training consisted of having nearly 75 employees gather in a large room and, using laptops, follows the instructions of the facilitator in the front. There was much grumbling about the required day of training, and when the employees arrived to the training it was fair to assume that they were not excited, as a whole, nor were they engaged with the experience.

The facilitator at the front surprised everyone by having everyone get into groups of 3–5 and to discuss the following:

- What types of things do you like to do in the LTS?
- What types of things do you often have trouble with?

- What types of things would you do if you could do them easily?
- What are some questions you have always had but never gone to the trouble of asking about?

After about 20 minutes of talking in groups (each group was told to select a "scribe" and spokesperson to report out), the facilitator called everyone back to order and asked for one of the groups to shout out one of the questions. Someone from a group on the left side of the room spoke up and said, "one of the questions that came up in our group is about why we need to go to the trouble of selecting "no" or "n/a" for all of the fields where there is not something specific to enter. It takes time and is a complete waste. Why can't it be set up so that we only need to add something if there is something to add? Why not just set "no" or "n/a" as a default?"

The facilitator said, "great! Let's talk about that. First, how many of you had a question that was related to that one?" about seven other hands went up around the room. "Okay," she said, "let's talk about this for a bit." Then, she let the entire group in a discussion about the pros and cons of such a move and why it may have been set up the way it is. Somehwere along the line, someone pointed out that if there was a default of "no" or "n/a" and someone forgot to make an entry, it would be impossible to know because "no" is an answer itself (albiet the wrong one in that case). If it is left blank, then at least it is obvious that someone didn't complete the fields.

Someone else pointed out that although that made sense, it also didn't because if everyone just got frustrated and left them blank anyway, it became an assumption that the answer was "no." Otherwise, it was pointed out, a "yes" would have been entered. In the commonly accepted practice, no news was, essentially, good news.

This discussion had several effects. First, it provided very good information to the instructor, which could be used to improve both the system and the cultural practices surrounding it. Second, it allowed the employees to think through the effects of their decisions on others, to see the other side of things, and to hear at least some of their fellow-workers provide reasons to do it the way it is supposed to be done. The net effect of all of this was a general attitude shift toward having to check the box, and a feeling of having been able to give their opinions and be heard.

After this, the facilitator continued to work around the room and answer questions. However, she did have a master list of learning objectives and referred to it constantly so that she could connect every one of the objectives to the questions that were being asked. For the few objectives that remained at the end (the ones she couldn't figure out how to connect with participant questions), she addressed by having everyone get together in groups again and work on discussing some carefully constructed questions that would develop at least a temporary need-to-know among participants.

Behind the Scenes

Many of the employees who went into the situation with the normal skeptical attitude toward a full day of training. Attitudes were not optimal overall and expectations were low. This is not because the employees at this organization are particularly grumpy or cynical people, just that they are responsible for quite a lot of work and generally struggle, like many of us, just to keep up and survive, never mind excelling.

But as the day wore on, attitudes improved because the facilitator was answering their specific, personally-relevant questions. Even though many of them would not have gone if it were not required, there was also an attitude of making the best of it and trying to find the answers to some of the questions (or gripes) they had had for years. At the very end, the participants were required to demonstrate the ability to navigate the LTS system and to use its basic functions. Groups were put into teams and had a competition for accurate procedurally-correct LTS entry completions. The process was, of course, largely subjective, but all participants in the end, voted for one of the two teams because of a particularly dynamic and interesting feature they had employed within the LTS, and the process overall, was festive in nature.

Using the Formula

The Learning Efficiency Formula was computed for the training as a whole. The administrators and personnel from the organization that required the training and developed it assigned a Work Hour Cost of 5 (out of 5) because while the preparation time was much less, all of the employees from the entire organization had to be assembled. The Fiscal costs were set at 4 because although the technical cost was lower than the online model, it was costly to provide lunch and travel costs for some of the remote, off-site employees. That provided a total cost of 9.

Given that everyone was demonstrating their ability in the classroom immediately after being shown how to do it, a high score of 5 was assigned to the acquisition side of the house. This was due, similarly to the online model, in part to the fact that employees had peer assistance and were required to conduct the functions correctly before leaving. But when the anonymous survey was administered to all employees across the organization, using the TPB and measuring whether or not employees were intending to utilize all of the content that was transmitted to them, it was found that the majority of employees indicated that they absolutely intended on using the great majority of the features that were covered because they knew how to do things that were specifically relevant to them and how they used the system, and because they were able to interact with others in real-time, about those personally-relevant questions (and answers). Simply put, they understood more clearly what the system was set up the way it was, but in relation to their own work (not some historical lesson for the sake of passing on inert knowledge). These results led the administrators to assign an acceptance value of 5.

Plugging in the numbers to the formula ended up with the following numbers: $10/9 = 1.11$; Learning Efficiency Index Coefficient (range of 0.2–5.0). See Figure 10.4.

$$\frac{Acquisition\ (5) + Acceptance(5)}{Work\ Hours\ (5) + Fiscal\ Costs(4)} = \frac{10}{9} = 1.11$$

Figure 10.4 *Efficiency index formula Example # 2.*

*Range of .2–5 (Higher indicates a higher degree of learning efficiency)

DISCUSSION OF THE TWO EXAMPLES

The first thing I should probably say here is that my point is not at all to try to make some sort of a case that face-to-face training is, in all cases, superior. Something worth noticing here is that, in the case of the above examples, a training program that cost more in both work hour and fiscal costs, was actually be *more* efficient than one costing less in both ways. The exact opposite could be true also, but that is the point, really – it is a ratio of the two that determines the learning efficiency situation. Costs could, at times, close off options for certain types of programs, and when that is the case, there is no point complaining about how much better it would be otherwise. But it is important to understand the moving parts that go into this sort of analysis and to understand that it is the effectual learning (acquire and accept) part of the learning side (numerator) that makes a great deal of difference in the efficiency coefficient. And, given that the point of the entire enterprise is some form of learning, and, by extension, training transfer, that ought to be sufficient.

The question that needs to be carefully considered is this: "is a $5,000 course that produces very little employee change more or less cost-efficient, than a $7,000 course that results in a significant amount of employee change?" This is not a new question, but what changes the nature of it quite a bit is shifting our conception of "employee change" away from paper tests or the performance of skills properly while being watched, and toward one where employees make internalized, long-term decisions to buy-in to those answers and skills being applied in the workplace.

Remember, the whole reason for this discussion in the first place is that administrators tend to like the idea of helping people learn better, but are in need of some sort of evidence that the extra effort is worth it, or, for more moderate but still important expectations, simply to merit a change in the way business is being done. Everyone tends to like evidence and the training enterprise is no exception. To summarize this, the value of this formula, or perhaps a better one similar to it, is that it can establish to some extent that it is worth the effort to teach differently, because everyone learns better. It is not to justify, per se, the cheapest way to go about it.

The proposed formula here is not the final destination in this particular route of thought, but it is an example of a way forward in the face of the measurement problem. There are probably many potential pitfalls to what I have suggested but from my perspective, an inherent weakness of the formula is the *acquisition coefficient*, simply because of the inherent problem with knowledge assessment itself. In the example above, both types of LTS training resulted in a "5.0" of acquisition simply because in both cases, success was required for each answer in order to pass/complete the course. The example was constructed the example this way because it seemed more real-world for this sort of thing. This could be a problem because simply getting a multiple-choice answer correct on a quiz doesn't mean the individual has deeply integrated that knowledge in a lasting or applicable way. This sort of problem exists outside of the specific issue that is being addressed in this chapter and so, of course, it also exists inside it. Using assessments that require more accurate acquisition might tighten up the calculations.

This approach bears some rigorous testing for sure, but on the other hand, when nothing like it is being done at all, the measurement bar is, at least initially, necessarily lower. That is, it is an area ripe for testing and I intend to do so in the near future. The problem it would address is significant enough that I felt it important to include the concept here, prior to its empirical testing. If this idea spurs a much better one that will be beneficial to all of us.

Chapter 11

Motivational Immediacy, Ethical Dilemmas, and Facilitator as Mediator

Ethical dilemmas are a part of life and all good people experience them. Working the training world brings its own set along with it, and practicing motivational immediacy concepts can increase tensions all around. Mitchell (1988) considered it unfortunate that ". . . staff development means personality displacement" (p. 58), and this sort of claim could be made about so many of the dynamics involved at the intersection of education and profit. Indeed, it is troubling when the kinder moments in the general history of workplace and vocational learning are those moments when employers finally began to think of their employees as assets that were worth investing in. The following chapter begins by addressing some basic and inherent ethical concerns having to do with learning resistance mitigation (LRM) in general, and then moves forward to address a few significant ethical dilemmas that instructors striving for motivational immediacy often find themselves exposed to along the way.

If there were easy solutions to sticky ethical situations, they wouldn't be referred to dilemmas in the first place. There are not foolproof ways to avoid such conflicts for the conscientious person, but there are ways to position oneself that can be very helpful in finding a path forward for ethical practice.

LEARNING RESISTANCE MITIGATION (LRM) APPROACHES

It is vital to discuss the ethical implications and entanglements surrounding any attempt to motivate learners to learn in more efficient ways. At first glance, it does not seem like there are any ethical gymnastics involved in trying to motivate students to learn, but that is an illusion, if a comfortable one at times.

DOI: 10.4324/9781003144137-13

For one thing, fostering motivation is, in its essence, an emotional manipulation. It is true that in educational circles, attempts to motivate learners have been considered acceptable, desirable, and in many ways, expected. The clarity of this situation is marred when one casts doubt about the goodness of the learning that one is motivated to undertake. For instance, we might agree that it is wrong to motivate people to learn "wrong" things, however much we disagree about just what "wrong things" might be. But it seems dangerous to provide carte blanch to any and all efforts to motivate others to learn without careful discussions about where those boundaries are, particularly when this moral freedom is extended to the business world, where for-profit motivations cloud the sky. Should we be accepting of training practices that are employed to enlarge the profit margin of a given organization at the expense of worker safety? Are we to assume, with confidence that this *never* happens? So it may be that there is not a great deal of energy surrounding ethical discussions regarding the practice of learner motivation, but it also seems reasonable not avoid the conversation entirely. Due diligence is in order.

Secondly, at least one inhibiting force in learning is the student's resistance to learning (Frye et al., 2017; Illeris, 2017; Taylor & Lounsbury, 2016), which, as defined in this book, is the opposite of learner engagement (see Chapter 2). Since motivation to learn is, in effect, motivation to engage with the learning situation, to declare student motivation above reproach is to declare LRM also above reproach. LRM is about overcoming, through one avenue of action or another, the learner's resistance to learning. Resistance is a personal thing; it is an extension of individual agency and decision-making, and to declare attempts to overcome it universally okay seems irresponsible.

The basic underpinning of any effort to motivate a learner is to deal with that learner's resistance to learning in a given situation by either facilitating the removal of it or safe passage around it. But when we speak of using any sort of device or practice to quell an individual's internal resistance to learning, we are, in effect, speaking of manipulating them to do something that they were, at least initially, opposed to doing.

The following pages will stop short of providing deep discussions of each of the many available ethical theories and a run-through of a formal analysis of each. For one thing, this would accomplish little because not everyone subscribes to the same basis for making ethical decisions and long runs of analysis of each becomes more of an academic discussion than a practical one. Also, the point of this chapter is not to resolve all potential ethical sticking points, but to clarify some basic premises that will likely resolve a number of misunderstandings that feed many of the ethical objections that might be raised.

LEARNING RESISTANCE APPROACHES ARE NOT DEFICIT-BASED

One of the most frequent objections I have heard over the years has to do with the perception that focusing on learning resistance is a "negative" approach; that it doesn't focus on the strengths of the learner. Given this, I will start by saying that choosing to examine teaching and learning from a learner resistance perspective is simply not based on a "deficit model." However, it is a reasonable assertion, at least on the surface, and it makes sense to address it.

It would seem that the rise of positive psychology (Seligman, 1998) and its general practice of avoiding deficit models brought with it a tendency, for better at times and perhaps worse at others, of avoiding negative terms across the board and considering them out of vogue. While there is not much, at least in the overt sense, in the literature decrying the use of the word resistance, it has been voiced often enough over the years that it bears mention here.

Constructs such as love of learning (McFarlane, 2003), learner resilience (Carr & Claxton, 2002; Quirk et al., 2012), and learner engagement (Marks, 2000) have been addressed as more positive terms that indirectly provide understanding of learning resistance even if the term resistance was avoided in the work.

Approaching the topic from this direction has been beneficial in many ways, but to be clear, the point of view being expressed here is that the general approach of avoiding negative terms such as rejection and resistance might be advantageous in many cases, but when used exclusively, is not an adequate way to address learning resistance in the classroom.

Imagine for a moment, being stuck on a hot, rainy night on the side of a long, dark, and lonely highway in the middle of the night, with a flat tire. Your phone is not working because water spilled on it from a leaking plastic bottle (true story. . .), so you are stuck sitting there, with no protective road-shoulder to work on, your vehicle being rocked violently every time a large truck blasts by at a high speed. There is the dilemma of whether to try to flag someone down for help (and hope that works out okay), or to sit and hope that the person expecting you home is awake and will miss you rather than asleep and oblivious (true story, but I was the one sleeping).

Take a minute and think of this experience. Try to embrace the emotions you would be feeling at that time – perhaps anger, despair, anxiety, disgust, or some combination of all of those. Now imagine a positive ending. Imagine that while you are sitting there in the extreme heat and pouring rain, with a badly flat tire, and imagine that after hours of trying to get help from someone (who wasn't going to commit a violent act upon you), someone finally slows down and pulls in behind you. A friendly looking person gets out and you feel a little relief at this point. Then, the person comes up and tries to peddle some fuel additive that will bring out the strengths of your particular vehicle. At this point, there would not be a simple – "no thank you," but a much more strongly-worded admonition to go away and leave you alone (maybe for some of us there would be some shouting at the car as it recedes into the distance – they can't hear us but that's not the point). Everyday life experience would reveal to us that what we generally want when we have a problem is to *have our problem addressed.* What we generally don't want is some sort of a pep talk about how we are a good person, noble king, gentle warrior, or kind person. Even worse, perhaps, is hearing that "we will get through this – we are strong!" Find out what my problem is and then work it. . . or leave me alone.

That brief story may seem grossly story-like and unprofessional in its very messy humanness. But learning takes place, always, on a personal level, not a professional one. The setting may be professional, the content may be professional, but the learning part of things is always grossly story like and unprofessional. Learning is deeply human and deeply messy.

Focusing on the learner's behavior and cognitions in a given case (i.e., resistance) is paramount to legitimizing the experiences and feelings of the learner, while generally approaching from a point of "what is going well" steps widely around the learner's point of view. Furthermore, focusing on the strengths of the learner as the primary means of mitigating resistance presupposes that any random solution is the precise fit for any particular problem (although the positive psychology literature on this is couched in terms of strengths and weaknesses rather than problems and solutions).

If a learner is resisting in a given learning environment because, for instance, the learning environment is too distracting, approaching this problem by addressing all of the positive aspects of human learning (i.e., which one of these things might be improved to facilitate the natural strengths of the learner) might likely be the long way around the problem. Additionally, this places the focus almost entirely on motivational approach goals (Schunk & Zimmerman, 2007), while completely ignoring avoidance goals and the specific reasons a given learner may be resisting in a particular situation.

To use the word resistance is to actually address what the learner is feeling, for good or bad, working the problem from that end, and therefore can be considered a highly learner-centered approach. It is my view that to ignore the learner's reason for resisting the learning is to ignore the learner.

The conception of learning resistance provided in this book is, as I have already pointed out, not about negative behavior, per se. Rather it is about a lack of openness and engagement in the learning process writ large.

In fact, many times the resistance that learners invoke in a given learning situation is well-merited and represents rather sound decision-making. Brookfield (2006) pointed this out while weighing in on the subject some years back (though he was, perhaps, defining resistance in a slightly different way).

In this case, it is the lack of openness that is the problem, not the behavior that indicates its presence. Therefore, there is no a priori assumption that something is "wrong" with the learner to begin with. There may be, in fact, an assumption that something is wrong with the *environment* (Tolman & Kremling, 2017). Looking at learning resistance is about attempting to find out what is going on, from the learner's perspective, and seeing if anything can be done about it. C. Peterson (2006) in his Primer on Positive Psychology explains it this way: "Positive psychologists study positive traits and dispositions – characteristics like kindness, curiosity, and the ability to work on a team – as well as values, interests, talents, and abilities" (p. 8). All of these positive traits are good things for sure, but if one holds more than a very simplistic uni-directional view of learning resistance, one understands that these very positive and good things are the very reasons that learners might not engage in a particular thing.

We are missing the point a bit when we refuse to discuss learning resistance because we think it is good to only talk about good things. I have attempted to make the case throughout this book that it is often because of very good and positive human traits that humans do not engage in a situation – in fact they are actually motivated to not learn. If we, as educators wish for our students to learn, then we must consider all reasons they may be motivated to learn and also all of the reasons they may be motivated to not learn. Both directions of this motivation can arise out of the many positive traits humans possess. Being extremely conscientious about one's career might be the main reason one chooses not to engage in a particular workplace training session.

Beyond this, Peterson also acknowledged that, ".. . positive psychology regards both the good and the bad about life as genuine. . . " (p. 9), but a defining difference is that positive psychology is not based on a "disease model" (p. 5). My treatment of learning resistance in this book is, in accordance with this sentiment, not based on a disease model. In essence, anytime that someone dismisses a discussion and study of learning resistance, they are calling themselves out on their view that learning resistance is always and only bad behavior. I do not see this to be the case, although it certainly can be. In this sense, I would suggest that one may have a more positive or more negative view of learning resistance. My own view is that to lean too far either direction is artificial and will lead to ignoring the needs of the learner in direction or the other.

Going further, specifically because of, rather than despite the direction it approaches from, learning resistance scholarship is highly learner-centered and practical. Learning resistance scholarship starts with the individual learner, asks what that individual learner is doing, asks the individual learner why she or he is doing it, and then sets out to rectify the situation and create a more efficient learning environment.

Trying to improve everything that is going well in a learning experience and choosing to boost the individual strengths of the learners in a given learning situation is not the same thing as attempting to address the learner's actual difficulty in the first place. When a student engages in learning resistance in the training room, there is always a reason. To ignore that reason is to marginalize the learner.

Some of these reasons may be deemed more legitimate by some than others, but it would be difficult to deny the presence of a reason to being with. To mitigate learning resistance is to give voice to the learner and to address the specific reason that the learner is consciously or unconsciously, closing off to the given learning experience. Because of this, it is both learner-centered, as well as practical.

Meeting the learner where they are, connecting with the learner, and helping the learner shift to a place where the material can be critically and openly reflected upon, is an intensely leaner-centered and service-oriented way to give voice back to the learner. But this last statement, powerful though it may be to the humanistic educator, can seem to be in stark contrast with the purpose of workplace training, which is ultimately about the organization, not the individual. Certainly, lots can be said about the good that corporations do for their employees from time to time, but it doesn't change the ultimate purpose of nearly all organizations, which is to increase profit margins, market-share, and sustainability. Service toward individuals inside the company is most often at worst a means to an end, and at best, something nice done along the way to the corporate objectives. That raises the question about how one can be focused expressly on the individual learner, be motivationally immediate, and still serve the needs of the organization at large.

THREE ETHICAL DILEMMAS FOR THE MOTIVATIONALLY IMMEDIATE TRAINING INSTRUCTOR

It is possible to organize the most routinely occurring ethical dilemmas into three significant types within the workplace training environment. The following break-down of these types does draws them out for visibility but does not in every case provide immediate foolproof solutions.

Instructor Values vs. the Supervisor Values

Everyone has different values. Adding to the complexity, and also difficulty, everyone has many ways through which the implement and practice those values. Whether you are an instructor with a training director above you in the hierarchy, or a training director with the division manager in the larger office upstairs, their support can make your job so much better, or so terrible worse.

Disagreements can arise over a million small things, like how training rooms should be arranged; whether PowerPoint should be used, and if so, how many slides and who gets to design them; what content, specifically, should be included, and what, if any can (or maybe even should) be skipped. Sometimes the disagreements are centered on more significant issues, like whether certain training courses should be dropped from the program; whether the instructor should have any freedom to change the ways the content is delivered, depending on the learners in the individual class session, or, perhaps the most difficult, when one of the parties, but not both, feel that a particular sort of content, or a particular teaching method is itself, unethical. These sorts of conflicts and the resultant obstructions can become a real impediment to the training professional who has determined to engage in motivational immediacy in the classroom.

Instructor Values vs. the Content

Training professionals can also regularly have difficulties with the content they have been tasked with teaching. All of these sorts of issues are interwoven in some ways, but problems with content can manifest themselves in at least three ways.

Content vs. Interest

A common problem that is raised when talking with training professional around the country and the world, is that the training content is so uninteresting, and perhaps irrelevant, that the instructor can't stand teaching it, and therefore totally "gets" why the learner doesn't like it much either. Returning to the quote from Frye et al. (2017) from Chapter 1, "own what you teach, know why you teach it, feel deeply about its importance, and then share that honestly and directly with your students" (p. 340).

Content vs. Job

Nearly every training professional has, at one time or another, been stuck with teaching content that seems, professionally-speaking, to be at odds with the realities of the job that the employee learners actually do. That is, sometimes the training that filters down from upper levels within an organization pick up the flavoring of boardroom thinking and become an odd, or even, at times, dangerous fit for the employee engaged at ground level on the job.

These sorts of difficulties are serious, particularly if there perceived concerns for safety. There is no suggestion here, of course, that such badly fitting content elements are forced upon the trainer or the employee learner with malicious or negligent intent. However, large bureaucratic systems can breed these sorts of problems, and the person often left in the awkward spot of trying to find a way to balance professional ethics, company loyalty, personal career sustainability, and a genuine care for the employee learner. Adding to this dynamic is that the training instructor is the exact point of contact between the decisions made far up in the corporate hierarchy, and the learners who are the ultimate subjects of any fallout from those decisions. Because of this, it is often at the last minute and in the middle of a course when these sorts of conflict arise.

Content vs. Learner

Another form of content-oriented dilemmas are those situations in which the particular content in the required training regimen is not a good fit with the particular learners in the classroom. In a qualitative study some years back, a school teacher shared that she was forced to sit through an 8-hour class on how to help her students use ipads in the classroom. This was a meaningful experience for half of the teachers because they were issued ipads for the children in their classrooms, but the teacher I was talking to was in the half who did not have the devices, nor did they have the means to acquire them any time soon. That class was simply a very bad fit for half of the learners in it. Given how busy everyone is in the workplace, how many demands are placed against employees, this sort of a "forced" waste of time can generate quite a bit of frustration and even open hostility in the training room.

Some training professionals are permitted the space to adjust on-the-fly while teaching and so can adjust for this sort of problem. Others, however, are tightly controlled by the rules of their particular training division and must roll forward with predetermined content exactly as it is. These situations bring the instructor quickly into the realm of experiencing an ethical dilemma.

INSTRUCTOR VALUES VS. THE LEARNER

Beyond all of these professional issues that can develop between the training professional and supervisors and training content, learners themselves can often present problems. Personality conflicts can be a very significant problem for the motivationally immediate instructor, because when a teacher is working to be motivationally immediate, learners are given space to express themselves in the classroom as part of the content, and part of the learning process. This can open the proverbial can of worms when there are those in the classroom who may be loud, overly assertive, prideful, and yes, even what most would consider obnoxious.

During these moments, the instructor is forced to make a tough decision. Should one press on and use classroom management strategies to handle the different personalities, or revert back to the comfort of backing off, boxing learners out, and simply talking the content at them. Next slide please. Click.

FACILITATOR AS MEDIATOR: A POSSIBLE WAY FORWARD

One way of working through these difficulties is to see oneself as a negotiator. Seeing the instructional task as one of negotiating can be a very powerful way for a training professional to navigate the many conflicts mentioned above, because it allows the instructor to see teaching as a process by which the learning content must be negotiated with the learner, rather than simply one of transmitting content to the learner. This notion, in fact, is someone aligned with the idea of LRM as they have been expressed all throughout this book.

This view sees the instructor as a negotiator who has a set of considerations to bring before the learner (or perhaps the boss), with the purpose of getting as many through as possible and keeping their essence intact somehow in the process. This view has some power to it that the "sage on the stage" approach lacks, because it assumes that the learner is not going to simply swallow everything spooned their way, and that a good teacher is one who engages in some form of work to win the buy-in of the learner.

However, it does very little to eliminate the ethical dilemmas above because it places the training professional in the place of being an active agent of the organization (by definition, a negotiator is on one side of the conflict), and therefore being forced back into the same relative position the instructor had before adopting the mindset of negotiator in the first place. This may sound odd because it is natural that a paid training professional who is also an employee of the organization, either directly or indirectly through contract would act in the interest of the employer.

My point here is not to suggest that an instructor should be disloyal to the employer – that would simply be to suggest an additional ethical dilemma. What I am suggesting, however, is a *mindset* that will assist in easing some of the tensions and stand-stills caused by the dilemmas listed above.

I am suggesting that seeing the facilitator as mediator (FAM; Taylor, 2010), rather than negotiator, can be a useful way to work through these conflicts, if not eliminate them. Unlike a negotiator, a mediator is someone who is not aligned with one side or the other, but is assigned the task of making the two ends meet. And, unlike an arbiter, or arbitrator, a mediator does not have the ultimate authority to force an agreement. This is more closely aligned with the workplace training scenario than one might, at first, think. The training professional can neither force a supervisor to give-in to the instructional demands, nor can the training professional force an employee learner to learn anything at all in the classroom.

Before going further, it is likely important that I make a further comment about that last line. One might be inclined to argue that a learner can, indeed, be forced to learn something. This happens all the time in training contexts, where employees are forced to pass a test or perform a certain skill, at a certain level, before a required certification can be issued. This is true, but it is not exactly what I am talking about above. I am speaking of effectual learning, acquisition and acceptance, and therefore long-term, consistent training transfer. An instructor may be able to force a learner to learn something by rote, but an instructor cannot force someone to buy-in to doing something, to make a personal, internalized decision to apply it for all time, and then to do so even when no one is watching.

A full read of Taylor (2010) will fill out the entire picture and the literature it is rooted in, but a brief explanation is provided here because adopting this type of thinking can assist the training professional in working in the space between the management and employee learners, between the content and the learner, between the learner and the learner, and even between the instructor and the instructor, all without being disloyal to either party.

The FAM concept is unique in at least three ways (Taylor, 2010). First, it focuses on the training professional's need to negotiate it two different directions, with two different parties, both of which are more powerful than the trainer – upper management and the learners. Second, FAM addresses learning resistance and engagement, and it is these dynamics that cause the learner to be in the ultimate power position in the training context. The third is that FAM relies on very fluid, "boots on the ground" real time negotiation with learners during training sessions.

The negotiator "model" would have the training instructor, negotiating with the learners on behalf of the supervisors, which means that the positional space between what is supposed to be taught, and what learners are willing to buy-in to, is divided between the instructor and the learner. But, when the learners have a legitimate reason to not like the training content, and, given the way training content is determined sometimes, this will happen. It is entirely possible for the instructor to have a problem with the content that they are required to teach. In other words, they think it is not that great either. Who decides what is in curriculum is one of the more significant issues in curriculum design (Walker & Soltis, 2009), and it is often the case that someone very far removed from the job site ends up deciding the best way to do something on the job site.

When the instructor or training directly ends up disagreeing with the employer (i.e., training content), then there is positional space that must be navigated in the other direction between the training professional and the member of management. It is this tension, from two different directions, that can create an ethical tension field. Clearly the instructor doesn't want to just abandon the training content and be subversive, but to teach others to do something that either doesn't work, or creates a safety risk, doesn't seem right either.

In these cases, the training professional can set aside the negotiator mindset and adapt that of a mediator. This seems like a subtle shift that would not have substantial impact, but it has significant impact.

First, as a mediator, the training professional can approach the member of the management who made the initial training determination, and, instead of doing so as the idealistic opponent they can do so as the concerned mediator who is professionally aware that although the employee learners may pass a test, effectual learning is very unlikely to occur. In this sense, the mediator professional, is simply sharing the reasons (and concern) that particular aspects of the training content will very likely be acquired (known) but not accepted (bought-in to). Given this, professional instructor being asked to train employees a certain way, would be on reasonable grounds to talk through these issues with the supervisor, to find out what suggestions the supervisor may have for what should be done about this (this is where the concept of effectual learning is very useful because it allows for rote memory with no transfer).

Certainly the supervisor may then just say "get it done," but the chances of having a meaningful discourse about it are greatly improved when it is not the instructor against the boss, but the instructor sharing the mindset of the learners with the boss, and also using professional concepts such as effectual learning (acquisition and acceptance) as the objective in order for training transfer to occur. Saying "I don't like this" is different from saying "the employees are not going to buy this for these reasons. . . "

On the other end of the mediation, as the instructor is in the classroom with the employee learners, there are traditionally two choices. First, the instructor can just talk the slide, share the content that they don't professionally agree with. This is problematic for a number of reasons, chief among them that it can be ethically challenging to do so, and that it is highly unlikely that the learners are actually going to end up with effectual learning, which means that there will not be training transfer. Second, the instructor can just be subversive and either skip the content or trash talk the content. I have heard so many times over the years (as both an instructor and a trainee) "Look, I don't want to be here and you don't either. You don't agree with this stuff and I don't either. Let's just get this done and go home." This, of course, has the exact same two problems as the first option – it has ethical implications and the learners are not going to have effectual learning.

The FAM option would have the training instructor – acting as a mediator between the upper management person who decided to include the controversial bit of content, and the employee learner who is simply not going to buy-it – talking with the employee learners about the content, why the management has decided it is necessary (which the instructor would now know), and under what circumstances the learners think it could work. Likely, the employee learners would point out all of the reasons it is a problem, but this a good thing, given what we know about motivational immediacy. Only at this point is the instructor really drawing out the learner, finding out what they are about (what they think and feel), and having meaningful conversations about how to follow the mandates in an effective way that is safe.

This likely sounds far too simple and optimistic, but it is not when one considers that effectual learning is not taking place much of the time anyway. That is, they were not going to do what your training them to do anyway. It won't get worse if you talk through all of the reasons with them, allow them to "ventilate" (Mitchell, 1988, p. 45). Just about all of the considerable theory and research provided in this volume would speak to the fact that allowing learners to dialogue, be heard and understood as well as being told and tested, will definitively increase the probability that the learners will both acquire and accept the content that you are teaching.

FAM then allows the training professional to mediate between the boss and the employee learner, with the interests of both ultimately in mind, and the instructor's own professional knowledge and ethics being brought to bear in a reasonable way. Added to this, motivational immediacy concepts would suggest that this dynamic will have the greatest likelihood of having the learner experience effectual learning. FAM brings about a subtle shift, but can have significant impact in the workplace training context. It will not, of course, solve all problems or resolve all ethical dilemmas. What it does do is allow the training professional to act as a training professional who is actually trying to close the gap as best as possible between the employer's required training content and the employee learner's willingness to engage and experience effectual learning (i.e., training transfer).

Chapter 12

Learning as Connection

Learning is about connection. If there is anything else that can be drawn from the principles in this book, it is that learning is about knowing people more than about knowing content. Learning is intensely personal and therefore it is an unavoidable truth that teaching is intensely personal as well. I wrote in the first chapter that the principles are of more worth than the practical tips in this book, and I will reiterate this in the final chapter. Appropriate methods change like the wind, with each group of learners, each subject area, and particularly, each social and cultural era. Principles, however, remain valid in their essence for near eternity and constitute what I often call the "underneath" of the things we do. And so, learning is about connection and teaching is too. There are at least six different ways that teaching is about connection, and they are used in this final chapter to tie off all of the loose ends and provide unified message for what has been quite a large number of ideas shared throughout the chapters of this book.

CONNECTION: TEACHER TO LEARNER

Fostering motivation in the learner is about knowing the learner. It is about *listening* first and talking second. It is about knowing where the learner is so that you can reach them and lead them to where you want them to be. This, perhaps, can be done even in physical distance via technology, but it absolutely cannot be done with interpersonal and relational distance.

I often refer to my own teaching philosophy as a "feet under the table" approach, by which I mean, in a mostly metaphorical way, that if a teacher is going to influence a learner, then the teacher simply must have feet under the table with the learner. That is, teaching an individual human

DOI: 10.4324/9781003144137-14

being is about fellowshipping with an individual human being. This notion no doubt creates a bit of discomfort for the more technical and clinical instructors out there, but that reflects a content-related way of being, not a teaching-learning way of being.

It may be that the greatest distinction between knowing how to do something and knowing how to teach someone else how to do something is that the former is impersonal while the latter is deeply and uncomfortably personal. Those who cannot countenance a shift from impersonal to personal may always be good at doing stuff but will seldom be great at teaching stuff. Simply put – in order to be motivationally immediate, foster effectual learning, and facilitate long-term training transfer, you must form a connection with the learner.

The popular notion of subject-matter-experts (SME) in the workplace, and particularly in the instructional systems design (ISD) sector, has likely contributed to a harmful distinction between knowledge and teaching. If an instructor truly realizes that teaching is about connecting with people and helping them learn something the instructor knows, then the instructor will be forced to realize that the learner's existing knowledge, thinking, feeling, personal culture, history, and world view are all vital factors in any learning actually taking place. These learner personal factors together make up what could be considered a subject matter expertise as well, though not in the traditional sense of the word. What this means for the instructor, in a practical sense, is that teaching is always about considering both the instructor and the learner as an SME, and therefore seeing the instructional task of one in which the instructor works with the learner to facilitate a connection between those two different areas of expertise.

CONNECTION: OLD KNOWLEDGE TO NEW KNOWLEDGE

A human learner can only ever learn something new by integrating it in some way with something that has already been experienced and learned before (Illeris, 2017; Piaget, 1951; Vygotsky, 1978). This reality, referred to, among other things, as constructivism, requires that the instructor be aware of what the learner already knows, thinks, feels, and believes about the specific learning content, the broader training context, and all other related conceptual pieces (Vosniadou, 2013). It is for this particular type of connection, that the connection between teacher and learner is required. It is the learning ends for which that interpersonal means must be applied.

As an instructor, one must find ways to connect the new learning content in a way that is harmonious with the life world of the individual. One might achieve teaching something by rote, of course, but this sort of knowledge has very limited applicability in the long-term (Ward, 1988). To facilitate an accurate and long-term application of learned content, one must ensure that the new information sits well with the old. Otherwise, a conflict arises between the new and the old, and in that case, the new information is always at a disadvantage (Salaman & Butler, 1990). It is an age-old truism that well-defended, entrenched positions have the advantage, and the literature on learning resistance makes it very clear that a learner's starting place is quite often exactly that – well-defended and entrenched.

CONNECTION: SHORT-TERM MEMORY
TO LONG-TERM MEMORY

There are many different theories that provide a variety of ways to understand the way human memory works. These explanations are increasingly accurate but often at the expense of being increasingly complex and difficult to grasp. Accuracy is important, particularly when trying to understand something as important as human memory, but there is utility in understanding the dynamics involved through more metaphoric models, such as the dated (emerging initially in the 1960's) and somewhat faulty information processing theory that hangs on with rugged determination (e.g., McCrudden & McNamara, 2017) for the very reason that it provides somewhat accurate teaching guidance, even if it falls short as a full neurological explanation. What nearly all models of human memory have in common, however, is the understanding that all new information must make it through a series of processes before it becomes embedded in long-term memory in a way that can be readily retrieved and utilized. All information going in does not necessarily become embedded in this way. The implication of this fact is that the instructor must face another type of connection task – facilitating a connection between the learner's short-term memory and the learner's long-term memory. This is accomplished first and foremost through evoking the learners' selective attention (McCrudden & McNamara, 2017), and this facilitation of selective attention can be said to be the essence of what I have referred to as *motivational immediacy* in this book.

CONNECTION: LEARNER TO LEARNER

Connecting learners to one another is a vital part of ensuring that learners are able to adopt the relevant conceptual framework, make cognitive sense of the content in ways that will transfer into workplace practice outside the classroom, and remain personally engaged in the learning Anderson, 2000; Wenger, 1991). It is impossible for instructors who have multiple learners, to be able to provide the interpersonal didactic that is required to make meaning, and nearly all effective methods of teaching require some sort of mechanism for have learners collaborate, share personal interpretations, and form accurate, long-term transferable knowledge. As cultural anthropologist Rosen (2006) wrote, "the other is a detour to the self" (p. 53).

CONNECTION: PRINCIPLE TO APPLICATION

Those who only learn applications for some sort of rote memorization are very likely to apply the wrong thing at the wrong time, for the wrong purposes. A key principle in this book is that training transfer is, in the end, all about motivational immediacy at the *beginning*. Much of what was covered in the preceding chapters provides a framework for understanding the necessity of fostering deep, conceptual understanding of training content, but it has been very clear that the ultimate purpose of such conceptual clarity is practical efficacy. Knowing conceptual principles is essential for having durable practices, but in order for the one to flow from the other, the instructor must work to connect those two aspects in every learning moment, throughout every instructional activity. There must be a fusion between the principle and the application and this principle-application fusion (PAF), leads directly to the final form of connection – means to ends.

CONNECTION: MEANS TO ENDS (MOTIVATIONAL IMMEDIACY)

Providing a connection for the learner between the desired (and often exciting) ends and the required (and often tedious) means is the fundamental point of this entire book. Motivational immediacy is both a noun and a verb. It is a thing that one needs to ensure is present, but it is also a thing that one needs to be sure to *be*. One of the primary disadvantages of the training course in typical workplaces is that it is by its very nature far removed from the situation in which it needs to be applied. It is noteworthy that the very term we use to refer to as being of vital necessity is referred to training transfer and refers to the ability (or, I would argue, willingness) to apply at a later date. The very fact that we have found it necessary to focus on training transfer at all is the very sign that we do not have means-ends-fusion (MEF). We rely on some sort of global motivation to carry the day in a given situation at a precise moment in time. Learning is about making connections between the means and the ends, and therefore, teaching and instructing must be about facilitating a connection between the means and the ends. We must be motivationally immediate.

BRINGING IT ALL TOGETHER

We have come to the end of what may have been a long and winding journey. I have tried in the pages of this book to share solid information, empirical support, and theoretical soundness, with the purpose of promoting a conceptual shift in the way teaching is seen. In that sense, this is most clearly a teaching book, though I hope it can be useful in other ways as well. What you have read is an attempt at connecting theory to practice and to travel all the way through the ideas to a point where the reader can see some practical way forward.

Having said that, I want to make sure I am clear that the power here, such as there is, lies in the concepts, not the specific applications I have laid out as exemplars. To be clear, I am not saying that theory is more important than practice – I think either one is at a loss without the other. What I am trying to say is that my practical ideas are fraught with all of the weaknesses of practice everywhere: situations limit transferability; lifeworld limits scope; and the strength of practical applications – their narrow nature – is their weakness as well.

The few remaining pages provide a brief summary of the key points I have worked to make over the course of the past 12 chapters.

MOTIVATION IS NOT A UNIDIRECTIONAL DYNAMIC

Learners do not enter a learning situation in a motivational stasis. When we speak of learners needing to be motivated or when we make plans to motivate learners, we are implicitly making the assumption that the learner is either at worst, sitting in a state of motivational neutrality, or at best, motivated to learn. This is a false and damaging assumption that goes against nearly 100 years of research and scholarship. If motivational neutrality exists, it is a vague sort of thing and certainly more hypothetical than practical. Learners are motivated to learn in your classrooms, or they are motivated to *not* learn in your classrooms.

What makes this mistake so damaging is that it allows and even promotes a misunderstanding of the teaching task. Trying to push a stalled car in neutral on a flat surface is a different task than trying to stop one as it is rolling down a hill toward you. The difference in these two tasks is quite remarkable in that on the one hand, there is a probability of difficulty, while on the other there is the probability of getting run over. Learners are not simply unmotivated to learn; they are quite often very motivated to avoid it. Missing this reality will reduce the effectiveness of any teacher.

FOCUSING ON LEARNER RESISTANCE IS POSITIVE AND LEARNER-CENTERED

Studying and thinking about learning resistance is a positive and strongly learner-centered approach to teaching. It always surprises me that this needs to be discussed at all. How can those involved in higher education so strongly speak for the alleged espoused value of teaching for the other; changing lives; and empowering students, while at the same time speaking ill of the teacher having an authentic, openness to the "closeness" of the learner? Horton said it well – "It is very important that you understand the difference between your perceptions of people's problems and their perceptions of them. You shouldn't be trying to discover your perception of their perception. You must find a way to determine what their perception is" (1998, pp. 70–71).

BOTH ACQUISITION AND ACCEPTANCE ARE VITAL

Effectual learning, that is, learning that is effective, efficient, and has a long-term impact, requires both *acquisition* and *acceptance* of content on the part of the learner. Any teaching that stops at the end of an acquisition status will have a limited and stunted potential.

For many years I have interviewed teachers and trainers, sometimes formally but often times casually, about the nature of the physical or intellectual behaviors they are seeking to influence in their respective teaching domains. A common thread that has been woven through nearly all of them is the notion that almost always, when something is not being done in a particular way, it is *will* that lies at the bottom of it, not knowledge. I certainly would not deny that there are situations in which not knowing how to do something lies at the bottom of failing to do it, but this type of dynamic is heavily outweighed by situations in which the individual (myself included) knows how to do something a particular way but quite simply doesn't feel like doing it that way.

An easy example of this for those involved in higher education is faculty committees. At this point, I have had the opportunity to chair quite a large number of committees, and if I were to add up all the times that a given task wasn't done on time, or done properly (or both), including my own tasks, and sort them into the categories of "didn't know to/how to" and "didn't want to/wasn't able to" nine of every ten would be in the latter category. Making sure everyone knows *when* the deadline is simply not the most pressing issue.

Strictly epistemological arguments aside, the everyday practical nature of education would indicate that the learner's acceptance of content is absolutely vital for the learner's living of the content. Affect, emotion, and feeling are not simple add-ons for meaningful knowledge; they are inseparable parts of it (Illeris, 2017). Any teacher, who wants to make an impact in the life of the learner and/or in society at large, absolutely must teach for both acquisition and acceptance, what I have here referred to as effectual learning.

IMMEDIATE MOTIVATION MUST NOT BE OVERLOOKED

Global motivation refers to the long-term goals that drive learners to engage in an educational activity. Examples of this may be getting a job, becoming an officer in the military, getting a promotion, or even earning a college degree. These are worthy goals and dive a learner to register and enroll, but they stop far short of fostering engagement in a given moment of a given course. Kruglanski et al. (2018) have referred to this a lack of "means-ends fusion" that results in something being extrinsically motivated when it could be more powerfully intrinsically motivated.

Immediate Motivation refers to the in-the-moment motivation to engage in a specific learning situation for the sake of learning in that moment. This requires the teacher to foster MEF with each bit of content during the course. While Global Motivation is important, highly effective teaching (teaching that facilitates effectual learning) requires a constant focus on Immediate Motivation. The highly effective teacher must be motivationally immediate; must practice motivational immediacy.

It would be bad enough if an exclusive focus on global motivation costs us only the missed opportunities to connect with a learner's most ardent passion. However, it is much worse than that. The exclusive focus on the learner's global motivation actually causes us to set up systems and structures that effectively work to diminish the learner's immediate motivation.

When the training professional focuses on the global motivation of the learner – say, the final certification of the employee to be a unit leader, then the trainer sets up a system that emphasizes the long-term goal to the natural detriment of the short-term goal. Indeed, this concept first caught my attention after hearing for what seemed like the thousandth time, a statement like, "my learners are already highly motivated because they are proud to be. . . " "Proud to be" or "hoping to earn" do not naturally lend themselves to an effort to engage in a particularly boring lecture or discussion in a particular training course on a particular day and time during a lengthy workplace training course series.

RESISTANCE MITIGATION IS A PART OF GOOD CURRICULUM DESIGN PROCESSES

Curriculum design and use should include learning resistance mitigation if it is to be used to foster engagement rather than stifle it. In my view, nothing has wrought such injury to effectual curriculum as the present-day mandate to be able to measure every objective of the curriculum. To say it strongly, although well-intended, this bit of nonsense has sucked much of the soul out of the learning that issues from it. Certainly, measurement is important, where possible, but that is a very different thing than trying to say or implicitly act as though an objective can't be a good one (or sMart) unless it can be measured. Measure what you can, teach what you must. SMART objectives often aren't.

The real effect of enforcing measurable outcomes in the curriculum is that other than a very vague sort of lip service, most, if not all authentic affective objectives are removed. In Chapter 9, I cited a great many texts on curriculum design and nearly all of them indicate that the feelings of the learner must be taken into account, but the actual practice of curriculum design (and ISD) does not bear this out. The continued heavy reliance on the cognitive emphasis of Bloom's (1956) taxonomy lends credibility to this claim. If it is to facilitate true learner engagement, and by extension, effectual learning, the curriculum must embrace and be heavily laced with emotional "feel" words rather than the presently orthodox act words. Somewhere along the way, designing a tightly-written, highly organized curriculum (means) has overcome the effort to provide a roadmap for authentic, meaningful learning (ends).

Maritain (1943) wisely pointed out that ".. . The surprising weakness of today. . . proceeds from our attachment to the very perfection of our modern educational means and methods, and our failure to bend them toward the end" (p. 3). I summed all of these sentiments in what I have called the Four Heretical Rules for Curriculum (treated fully in Chapter 7):

- Rule # 1: The Curriculum is a *means* to an end, not the end - if any part of it gets in the way of the ends, drop it like a bad habit.
- Rule # 2: The Curriculum is NOT the boss, you are – to paraphrase Kegan (1994) have your [curriculum], don't be had by it (p. 34).
- Rule # 3: Curriculum is by nature reductionist - learning and teaching by nature are not.
- Rule # 4: Measure what you can – teach what you must.

PRACTICING MOTIVATIONAL IMMEDIACY IS VITAL

Motivational Immediacy, while most tightly-connected to the concept of immediate motivation, transcends that and is really the integrated culmination of all of the points I have worked to make in this book. *Motivational immediacy* can be seen as a *state* of being in a moment-by-moment motivational relationship with the student. Defined as an *action process*, motivational immediacy is the practice of purposefully adopting as a part of one's teaching method, the consistent, pervasive, and habitual attempt to connect with each individual learner and ensure that the learner is motivated in the immediate sense, regardless of whether global motivation is present or not.

TEACHING FOR EFFECTUAL LEARNING

New instructors, and instructors who are not versed in an understanding of human learning, often make the mistake of teaching by method rather than by principle. By principle, I am referring to the "why" behind the "what." When teaching by method, one can easily lose sight of why the method was chosen to begin with, and what principle of learning it is actually serving. It may often be the case the principle behind the method isn't known in the first place. We have all probably adopted methods we have seen without a deep analysis of what purpose they might be serving. The problem with this is that when one is not aware of what purpose a method is meant to serve, one cannot, with any efficiency or accuracy, tell when the method is actually serving it.

Situations render one method suitable for achieving a certain goal (i.e., learner engagement), while the exact opposite method might do so in another context. For instance, using group work can foster engagement in certain sized groups in certain types of courses. In others, however, it can cause resentment and withdrawal. Only when the instructor is fully aware in the moment, that the use of group work has been adopted for the purpose of increasing engagement, can that teacher see that it is failing for some reason to achieve its purpose and therefore abandon it and do something different – no matter what the lesson plan has in print.

Methods are tightly bound to highly specific contextual factors, but principles largely transcend such boundaries. Because of this, I have chosen to focus this book on principles that transcend rather than on methods that are constrained. The use of concrete practical examples was meant to support the underlying principle rather than to promote the sample method itself. The five principles I put forward can support many different sorts of approaches and specific classroom methods, but it is the principles that must remain the driving force.

ON BECOMING

Teaching of any sort is a humbling experience. I hope that the concepts I have shared in this book will help you be even better at what you do in the classroom or online, but I am certain that if you have taken the time to read this, that you are already above average as an instructor and trainer. We work hard and have little time. As I have traveled around the past 25 years and had the privilege of hanging out with so many different types of teachers in so many different domains, I have seen one common theme they all seem to have.

These teachers of human beings all have an ethic that puts the other first that seeks to help others come to know more and develop more fully as individuals. There is an undeterred focus on helping others learn, succeed. I have spent considerable time in the past 12 chapters sharing some strong views, and sharing them, at times, strongly. I have done that with the same passion that I teach with. I have written it for the other, and I know you are reading it for the other. Thank you for the effort you make so tirelessly to improve the lives of others around you, the social structures we all benefit from, and the world we all live in.

It is difficult to try new things, and especially difficult to see things in completely new ways. I have no doubt that these ideas can be improved upon and I hope you will do just that. If you take anything away from this book, I hope that it will be to have developed a different, more full perspective of learning and teaching, from the *learner's* point of view. In the course of reading this, thinking about it, and trying out some of your own applications, I hope that you may *become* something different rather than simply knowing something different. That is an ambitious goal, for sure, and as I mentioned earlier in the book, although I am not sure I am THAT good, I have certainly given it my best shot. I am passionate about what I have written. I believe it to be true, and I hope that I have provided a clear and supported case for it.

Finally, I believe that starting with the learner works. I believe that being motivationally immediate will help us help others, and helping others has a way of helping the organization as well. If you are still reading this book, you will know that it is not just another workplace training book. For better or worse, there was not a chapter (or even a paragraph) on organizational bottom-lines, although there is a strong case that fostering significant, authentic, and highly transferable learning in employee-learners is good for bottom lines. There was not a chapter on legal issues in the workplace, although it may be intuitive that being sensitive to the lifeworld of the learner and fostering meaningful learning might mitigate some legal issues that often arise in the absence of those things. There were not chapters on staffing, management, or technology either, although, again, connecting with the learner where they are and walking the journey with them will help fewer people do more, poor management become better, and utilize all of the rapidly evolving technology to better help learners have effectual learning.

This book is fully and shamelessly about helping the learner learn. In this regard, it is not for the expert welder, it is for the expert welder who yearns to be an expert teacher of welding. It is not for those who love content, procedures, or skills. It is for those who love people, and want to help them learn the things that they need to be safe, successful, and satisfied in their employment. Only when employees learn for real, will they work for real. Only when they know deeply will they apply widely. Only when they agree that the content should be learned, will they demonstrate that the content can be transferred.

I have met excellent instructors from all over the world and despite the incredible variety of personalities, domains, and methods, they all have one thing in common. The best instructors share stories over coffee or lunch about the dumpsters they have dug in to find some training prop or another, about the tool or technology they purchased on their own to help a learner grasp a concept, and about the time they have taken, away from their personal life, friends, and family, to go back and find the one learner who was left behind.

This book is dedicated to these great people and the dumpster-diving that they might occasionally be caught engaged in. These types of instructors will do much the same with this book – root around and see what can be used to make the world better for one of the learners who depend on them. Motivational immediacy is, in the end, what all good instructors are breaking through with in their very best moments. Hopefully the ideas shared here will provoke a renewed passion for those who are weary, a spark for those who may be interested in training, and fresh innovation for those who are already knocking it out of the park.

References

Abowitz, K. (2000). A pragmatist revisioning of resistance theory. *American Educational Research Journal, 37*(4), 877–907.

Ajzen, I. (1985). From intentions to actions: A theory of planned behavior. In J. Kuhl, & J. Beckmann (Eds.), *Action control: From cognition to behavior* (pp. 11–39). Springer-Verlag.

Ajzen, I. (1991). The theory of planned behavior. *Organizational Behavior and Human Decision Processes, 50*(2), 179–211.

Ajzen, I., & Fishbein, M. (1980). *Understanding attitudes and predicting social behavior.* Prentice-Hall.

Alatis, J. (1974, January 2–5). *The urge to communicate vs. resistance to learning English as a second language.* [Paper presentation]. Seventh Annual Conference of the International Association of Teachers of English as a Foreign Language (IATEFL), London, England.

Althusser, L. (1969). *For marx.* Vintage Books.

Anderson, J. F. (1979). Teacher immediacy as a predictor of teaching effectiveness. *Communication Yearbook, 3,* 543–559.

Antonelli, M., Kempe, J., & Sidberry, G. (2000). And now for something completely different. . . theatrical techniques for library instruction. *Research Strategies, 17*(2/3), 177–185. https://doi.org/10.1016/S0734-3310(00)00045-8

Applebaum, B. (2016). "Listening silence" and its discursive effects. *Educational Theory, 66*(3), 389–404. https://doi.org/10.1111/edth.12172

Argyris, C., & Schon, D. A. (1996). *Organizational learning II: Theory, method and practice reading.* Reading, MA: Addison-Wesley.

Arnstine, D. (1967). *Philosophy of education: Learning and schooling.* Harper & Row.

Asiyai, R. (2014). Students' perception of the condition of their classroom physical learning environment and its impact on their learning and motivation. *College Student Journal, 48*(4), 716–725.

Atkin, M. J. (1971). Behavioral objectives in curriculum design: A cautionary note. In M. B. Kapfer (Ed.), *Behavioral objectives in curriculum development: Selected readings and bibliography* (pp. 368–382). Educational Technology Publications.

Atherton, J. (1999). Resistance to learning: A discussion based on participants in in-service professional training programmes. *Journal of Vocational Education and Training, 51*(1), 77–90.

Baker, E. W., & Hill, S. (2017). Investigating student resistance and student perceptions of course quality and instructor performance in a flipped information systems classroom. *Information Systems Educational Journal, 15*(6), 17–26.

Baldwin-Evans, K. (2006). Key steps to implementing a successful blended learning strategy. *Industrial & Commercial Training, 38,* 156–163.

Baldwin, T., & Ford, K. (1998). Transfer of training: A review and directions for future research. *Personal Psychology, 41*(1), 63–105. Doi:10.111/j.1744-6570.1988.tb00632.

Bandura, A. (1986). *Social foundations of thought and action: A social cognitive theory.* Prentice-Hall.

Bandura, A. (1977). *Social learning theory.* Prentice-Hall.

Bannerman, L. (2006). *Networking in 90 minutes.* Management Books 2000 Ltd.

Bargh. (1997). The automaticity of everyday life. In R. Wyer (Ed.), *The automaticity of everyday life: Advances in Social Cognition, LEA* (Vol. 10, pp. 1–61). Mahwah, NJ.: Lawrance Erlbaum Associates, Inc.

Bass, M., Nijstad, B. A., Koen, J., Boot, N. C., & DeDreu, C. K. W. (2019). Vulnerability to psychopathology and creativity: The role of approach-avoidance motivation and novelty seeking. *Psychology of Aesthetics, Creativity, and the Arts.* https://doi.org/10.1037/aca0000223

Baumann, K., & Sidebottom, J. (2018). *The effects of non-verbal and verbal teacher immediacy on motivation* [Poster presentation]. University Presentation Showcase Event, Eastern Kentucky University, Richmond, KY, United States. https://encompass.eku.edu/swps/2018/undergraduate/6/

Bell, B. S., & Kozlowski, S. W. J. (2008). Active learning: Effects of core training design elements on self-regulatory processes, learning, and adaptability. *Journal of Applied Psychology, 93,* 296–316.

Bell, S., Morrow, M., & Tastsogloul, E. (1999). Teaching in environments of resistance: Toward a critical, feminist, and anti-racist pedagogy. In Rose, & Mayberry (Eds.), *Meeting the challenge* (pp. 23–46). Routledge.

Berglund, M. M. U. (2014). Learning turning points—in life with long-term illness—Visualized with the help of the life-world philosophy. *International Journal of Qualitative Studies on Health and Well-Being, 9*(0), 1–10. http://dx.doi.org.spot.lib.auburn.edu/10.3402/qhw.v9

Bernstein, B. (1977). *Class, codes, and control: Towards a theory of educational transmission* (Vol. 3, 2nd ed.). Routledge & Kegan Paul.

Bialowas, A., & Steimel, S. (2019). Less is more: Use of video to address the problem of teacher immediacy and presence in online courses. *International Journal of Teaching & Learning in Higher Education, 31*(2), 354–364.

Bloom, B. S. (1956). *Taxonomy of educational objectives, handbook 1: The cognitive domain.* David McKay Co. Inc.

Boldt, G. (2006). Resistance, loss, and love in learning to read: A psychoanalytic inquiry. *Research in the Teaching of English, 40*(3), 272–309.

Bourdieu, P. (1977). *Outline of a theory of practice.* Cambridge University Press.

Bowles, S., & Gintis, H. (1976). *Schooling in capitalist America.* Basic Books.

Bowlby, J. (1969). *Attachment.* Basic Books.

Boyer, E. L. (1990). *Scholarship reconsidered: Priorities of the professoriate.* Carnegie Foundation for the Advancement of Teaching.

Brady, T. C. (1975). *A study in the application of the C. A. Curran Counseling-Learning Model to adults.* [Unpublished doctoral dissertation]. Walden University.

Brockett, R. G. (2015). *Teaching adults: A practical guide for new teachers.* Jossey-Bass.

Brockett, R. G., & Hiemstra, R. (2004). *Toward ethical practice.* Krieger.

Brockett, R. G. (1997). Humanism as an instructional paradigm. In A. J. Romiszowski (Ed.), *Instructional development paradigms* (Vol. 3). Englewood Cliffs, NJ: Educational Technology Publications.

Brookfield, S. D. (2005). *The power of critical theory: Liberating adult learning and teaching.* Jossey-Bass.

Brookfield, S. D. (2006). *The skillful teacher: On technique, trust, and responsiveness in the classroom* (2nd ed.). Jossey-Bass.

Brookfield, S. D. (2012). *Developing critical thinkers.* Jossey-Bass.

Brophy, J. (2004). *Motivating students to learn* (2nd ed.). Lawrence Erlbaum Associates, Inc.

Brown, K. G. (Ed.) (2018). *The Cambridge handbook of workplace training and employee development.* New York: Cambridge University Press.

Bryne, J. V. (1998). Outreach, engagement, and the changing culture of the university. *Journal of Higher Education Outreach and Engagement, 3*(2), 3–8.

Buhmann, A., & Brønn, P. S. (2018). Applying Ajzen's theory of planned behavior to predict practitioners' intentions to measure and evaluate communication outcomes. *Corporate Communications: An International Journal, 23*(3), 377–391. https://doi.org/10.1108/CCIJ-11-2017-0107

Burke, M. A., & Banks, K. H. (2012). Sociology by any other name: Teaching the sociological perspective in campus diversity programs. *Teaching Sociology, 40*(1), 21–33. https://journals.sagepub.com/doi/abs/10.1177/0092055X11418686

Burke, L. A., & Hutchins, H. M. (2008). A study of best practices in training transfer and proposed model of transfer. *Human Resource Development Quarterly, 19*(2), 107–128.

Burroughs, N. F. (2007). A reinvestigation of the relationship of teacher nonverbal immediacy and student compliance-resistance with learning. *Communication Education, 56*(4), 453–475. https://doi.org/10.1080/03634520701530896

Burroughs, N. F., Kearney, P., & Plax, T. G. (1989). Compliance-resistance in the college classroom. *Communication Education, 38*(3), 214–229. https://doi.org/10.1080/03634528909378758

Cabranes-Grant, L. (2018). Kierkegaard, Wagner and the quest for operatic immediacy. *The Wagner Journal, 12*(1), 4–18.

Canagarajah, A. S. (1993). Critical ethnography of a Sri Lankan classroom: Ambiguities in opposition to reproduction through ESOL. *TESOL Quarterly, 22*(2), 601–626.

Cannon-Bowers, J. A., Salas, E. S., Tannenbaum, S. I., & Matheiu, J. E. (1995). Toward theoretically based principles of training effectiveness: A model and initial empirical investigation. *Military Psychology, 7*(3), 141–164.

Caplin, M. D. (1969). Resistance to learning. *Peabody Journal of Education, 47*(1), 36–39.

Carr, M., & Claxton, G. (2002). Tracking the development of learning dispositions. *Assessment in Education: Principles, Policy and Practice, 9(1),* 9–37.

Cennamo, K., & Kalk, D. (2005). *Real world instructional design.* Thomson Wadsworth.

Chi, M. T. H. (1992). Conceptual change within and across ontological categories: Examples from learning and discovery in science. In R. Giere (Ed.), *Cognitive models of science: Minnesota Studies of in the philosophy of science* (pp. 129–186). University of Minnesota Press.

Chi, M. T. H. (2013). Two kinds and four sub-types of misconceived knowledge, ways to change it, and the learning outcomes. In S. Vosniadou (Ed.), *The handbook of research of conceptual change* (2nd ed., pp. 49–70). Routledge. https://doi.org/10.4324/9780203154472.ch3

Chi, M. T. H., Slotta, J. D., & de Leeuw, N. (1994). From things to processes: A theory of conceptual change for learning science concepts. *Learning and Instruction, 4*(1), 27–43. https://doi.org/10.1016/0959-4752(94)90017-5

Clarke, N. (2004). HRD and the challenges of assessing learning in the workplace. *International Journal of Training and Development, 8,* 140–156.

Cloninger, R. (2000). *Theories of personality: Understanding persons* (3rd ed.). Prentice Hall.

Cohen, J. (2018). Overcoming SMEs' resistance to learning through a metaphor/storyline approach: A qualitative assessment of a novel marketing intervention. *Middle East Journal of Business, 13*(1), 17–31.

Collins, J. (2001). *Good to great: Why some companies make the leap and others don't.* Harper Business.

Colquitt, J. A., LePine, J. A., & Noe, R. A. (2000). Toward an integrative theory of training motivation: a meta-analytic path analysis of 20 years of research. *Journal of Applied Psychology, 85*(5), 678–707.

Cook, P. (Ed.). (2015). *A systems view of community engagement: Exploration for simple rules of interaction to explain community resistance in landfill siting situations. Proceedings of the 58th Annual Meeting of the ISSS—2014.* http://journals.isss.org/index.php/proceedings58th/article/view/2323/786

Corno, L. (1977). Teacher autonomy and instructional systems. In L. Rubin (Ed.), *Curriculum handbook: Administration and theory* (pp. 234–247). Allyn and Bacon, Inc.

Corwin, G. (1921). Minor studies from the psychological laboratory of Cornell University. *American Journal of Psychology, 32,* 563–570.

Cowles, S. L. (2001, March 14–17). *Educating for identity & resistance: Situated learning among the older Mennonites* [Paper presentation]. 45th Annual Meeting of the Comparative and International Education Society. Washington DC, United States.

Craig, R. L. (Ed.) (1996). *The ASTD training and development handbook: A guide to human resource development* (4th ed.). McGraw-Hill.

Craik, F. I. M., and Lockart, R. S. (1972). Levels of processing: A framework for memory research. *Journal of Verbal Learning and Verbal Behavior,* 11, 671–684.

Csikszentmihalyi, M. (1990). *Flow: The psychology of optimal experience.* Harper & Row Publishers.

Cutcher, L. (2009). Resisting change from within and without the organization. *Journal of Organizational Change Management, 22*(3), 275–289. https://doi.org/10.1108/09534810910951069

Damasio, A. (2003). *Looking for Spinoza: Joy, sorrow, and the feeling brain.* Houghton-Mifflin Harcourt.

Damasio, A. (2012). *Self comes to mind.* Random House.

Darker, C. D. D. (2008). *Applying the theory of planned behaviour to walking: Development and evaluation of measures and an intervention.* [Doctorates Thesis, University of Birmingham]. UB Campus Repository, UBIRA E Theses. https://etheses.bham.ac.uk/id/eprint/1433/

Daulay, S. H. (2018). Ice breaker: A strategy to enhance students' ability in speaking of Islamic junior high school at Sawit Seberang, Langkat regency. *Indonesian Journal of English Teaching, 7*(1), 359–365.

Dawson, L., Mullan, B., & Sainsbury, K. (2015). Using the theory of planned behaviour to measure motivation for recovery in anorexia nervosa. *Appetite, 84,* 309–315. https://doi.org/10.1016/j.appet.2014.10.028

Dale, M. and Bell, J. (1999) Informal Learning in the Workplace. Research Brief No. 134, Department for Education and Employment, London.

Dembo, M. H., & Seli, H. P. (2004). Student's resistance to change in learning strategies courses. *Journal of Developmental Education, 27*(3), 2–11.

Dick, W., Carey, L., & Carey, J. (2009). *The systematic design of instruction* (7th ed.). Merrill/Pearson. https://doi.org/10.1007/s11031-006-9028-7

Dijk, D. V., Seger-Guttmann, T., & Heller, D. (2013). Life-threatening event reduces subjective will-being through activating avoidance motivation: A longitudinal study. *Emotion, 13*(2), 216–225.

DiSessa, A. A. (1983). Phenomenology and the evolution of intuition. In D. Genter, & A. Stevens (Eds.) pp. 15–33. *Mental models*. Lawrence Erlbaum.

DiSessa, A. A. (1993). Toward an epistemology of physics. *Cognition and Instruction, 10*, 105–225.

Doeringer, P. B. (Ed.) (1981). *Workplace perspectives on education and training* (Vol.1). Martinus Nijhoff Publishing.

Eder, A. B., Elliot, A. J., & Harmon-Jones, E. (2013). Approach and avoidance motivation: Issues and advances. *Emotion Review, 5*(3), 227–229.

Elliot, A. J. (1999). Approach and avoidance motivation and achievement goals. *Educational Psychologist, 34*(3), 169–189.

Elliot, A. J. (2006). The hierarchical model of approach-avoidance motivation. *Motivation and Emotion, 30*, 111–116. https://doi.org/10.1007/s11031-006-9028-7

Elliot, A. J. (2008). *Handbook of approach and avoidance motivation*. LLC: Taylor & Francis Group.

Elliot, A. J., & Church, M. (1997). A hierarchical model of approach and avoidance achievement motivation. *Journal of Personality and Social Psychology, 77*(1), 218–232.

Elliot, A. J., & Covington, M. V. (2001). Approach and avoidance motivation. *Educational Psychology Review, 13*(2), 73–92.

Elliot, A. J., Eder, A. B., & Harmon-Jones, E. (2013). Approach-avoidance motivation and emotion: Convergence and divergence. *Emotion Review, 5*(3), 308–311. https://doi.org/10.1177/1754073913477517

Elliot, A. J., & Harackiewicz, J. M. (1996). Approach and avoidance achievement goals and intrinsic motivation: A mediational analysis. *Journal of Personality and Social Psychology, 70*, 461–475.

Elliot, A. J., & Thrash, T. M. (2002). Approach-avoidance motivation in personality: Approach and avoidance temperaments and goals. *Journal of Personality and Social Psychology, 82*(5), 804–818. https://doi.org/10.1037/0022-3514.82.5.804

Empathy. (2003). In *Merriam-Webster's collegiate dictionary* (11th ed.).

Estepp, C. M., Stripling, C. T., Conner, N. W., Giorgi, A., & Roberts, G. T. (2013). An examination of the learning activities, cognitive level of instruction, and teacher immediacy behaviors of successful instructors in a college of agriculture. *Journal of Agricultural Education, 54*(2), 15–28.

Eysenck, H. (1967). *The biological basis of personality*. Charles Thomas.

Ferris, D. L., Johnson, R. E., Rosen, C. C., Djurdjevic, E., Chang, C. H., & Tan, J. A. (2012). When is success not satisfying? Integrating regulatory focus and approach/avoidance motivation theories to explain the relation between core self-evaluation and job satisfaction. *Journal of Applied Psychology, 98*(2), 342–353. https://doi.org/10.1037/a0029776

Field, J. C., & Olafson, L. J. (1999). Understanding resistance in students at risk. *Canadian Journal of Education, 24*(1), 70–75.

Fishbein, M., & Ajzen, I. (1975). *Belief, attitude, intention, and behavior.* Addison-Wesley.

Ford, J. K., Smith, E. M., Weissbein, D. A., Gully, S. M., & Salas, E. (1998). Relationships of goal orientation, metacognitive activity, and practice strategies with learning outcomes and transfer. *Journal of Applied Psychology, 83*(2), 218–233.

Foucault, M. (2001). *Michel Foucault: Fearless speech.* Semiotext(e).

Fredricks, J. A., Blumenfeld, P. C., & Paris, A. H. (2004). School engagement: Potential of the concept, state of the evidence. *Review of Educational Research, 74*(1), 59–109.

Freire, P. (1996). *Pedagogy of the oppressed* (2nd ed.). Penguin.

Freud, S. (1915). Repression. In J. Stratchey (Ed.) *Standard edition of complete psychological works of Sigmund Freud* (Vol. 14). Hogarth.

Frye, S., Taylor, J., & Stafford, A. (2017). The first fifteen minutes: Learning engagement, learning resistance, and the impact of initial teacher-student contact. In C. X. Wang (Ed.), *Theory and practice of adult and higher education* (p. 342). Information Age Publishing Inc.

Gable, G., Sedera, D., & Chan, T. (2003). Enterprise systems success: A measurement model. *ICIS 2003 Proceedings,* 48.

Gagne, R. M. (1965). *The conditions of learning.* Holt, Rinehart & Winston.

Gagne, R. M. (1968). Contributions of learning to human development. *Psychological Review, 75*(3), 177–191.

Garber, S. H. (2002, April 1–5). *"Hearing their voices": Perceptions of high-school students who evidence resistance to schooling* [Paper presentation]. Annual Meeting of the American Educational Research Association, New Orleans, LA, United States.

Ghodisan, D., Bjork, R., & Benjamin, A. (1997). Evaluating training during training: Obstacles and opportunities. In M. Quiniones & A. Ehrenstein (Eds.) *Training for a rapidly changing workplace: Applications of psychological research.* American Psychological Association.

Giddens, A. (1984). Elements of the theory of structuration. In A. Giddens (Ed.), *The constitution of society.* Policy Press.

Gino, F., & Schweitzer, M. (2008). Blinded by anger or feeling the love: How emotions influence advice taking. *Journal of Applied Psychology, 93*(5), 1165–1173.

Giroux, H. A. (2001). *Theory and resistance in education.* Bergin & Garvey.

Giroux, H. A. (1983). *Theory and resistance in education: A pedagogy for the opposition.* South Bergin & Garvey Publishers, Inc.

Goisman, R. M. (1988). Resistances to learning behavior therapy. *American Journal of Psychotherapy, 32*(1), 67–75.

Gold, J. (2005). Anxiety, conflict, and the resistance in learning an integrative perspective on psychotherapy. *Journal of Psychotherapy Integration, 15*(4), 374–383. https://doi.org/10.1037/1053-0479.15.4.374

Goodboy, A. K., & Bolkan, S. (2009). College teacher misbehaviors: Direct and indirect effects on student communication behavior and traditional learning outcomes. *Western Journal of Communication, 73*(2), 204–219. https://doi.org/10.1080/10570310902856089

Grossman, R., & Salas, E. (2011). The transfer of training: What really matters. *International Journal of Training and Development, 15*(2), 103–120.

Habermas, J. (2003). *The future of human nature.* Polity.

Harre, R., & Langenhove, L. V. (1999a). Introducing positioning theory. In R. Harre, & L. V. Langenhove (Eds.), *Positioning theory* (pp. 14–31). Blackwell.

Harre, R., & Langenhove, L. V. (1999b). The dynamics of social episodes. In R. Harre, & L. V. Langenhove (Eds.), *Positioning theory* (pp. 1–13). Blackwell.

Heider, F. (1958). *The psychology of interpersonal relations.* New York: Wiley.

Henson, J., & Gilles, C. (2003). Al's story: Overcoming beliefs that inhibit learning. *Language Arts, 80*(4), 259–267.

Hiemstra, R., & Brockett, R. G. (1994a). *Overcoming resistance to self-direction in adult learning.* In R. Hiemstra, & R. Brocket (Eds.), *Overcoming resistance to self-direction in adult learning* (pp. 89–92). (New Directions for Adult and Continuing Education, no.64 1994.). Jossey-Bass.

Hiemstra, R., & Brockett, R. G. (1994b). Resistance to self-direction in learning can be overcome. In R. Hiemstra and R. Brocket (Eds.), *Overcoming resistance to self-direction in adult learning* (pp. 89–92). (New Directions for Adult and Continuing Education, no.64 1994.) Jossey-Bass. https://doi.org/10.1002/ace.36719946413

Holly, L., & Rainbird, H. (2000). Workplace learning and the limits to evaluation. In H. Rainbird (Ed.), *Training in the workplace: Critical perspectives on learning at work* (pp. 2640282). New York: St. Marten's Press Inc.

Holton, E. F. III, Bates, R. A., & Ruona, W. E. (2000). Development of a generalized learning transfer system inventory. *Human Resource Development Quarterly, 11*(4), 333–360. Doi:10.1002/1532-1096(200024)11:4<333::AID-HRDQ2>3.0.CO;2-P

Horton, M., Kohl, J., & Kohl, H. (1998). *The long haul: An autobiography.* Teachers College Press.

Hull, C. (1943). *Principles of behavior.* Appleton-Century-Crofts.

Hultman, K. (1995). Training 101: Scaling the wall of resistance. *Training & Development, 49*(10), 15–18.

Hughes, J. (2005). Bringing emotion to work: Emotional intelligence, employee resistance and the reinvention of character. *Work, Employment and Society, 19*(3), 603–625. doi:10.1177/0950017005055675

Husserl, E. (1970/1954). *The crisis of European sciences and transcendental phenomenology.* Northwestern University Press.

Huang, Q. (2016). Learners' perceptions of blended learning and the roles and interaction of f2f and online learning. *ORTESOL Journal, 33*, 14–33.

Huang, Q. (2019). Comparing teacher's roles of f2f learning and online learning in a blended English course. *Computer Assisted Language Learning, 32*(3), 190–209. https://doi.org/10.1080/09588221.2018.1540434

Hutchins, H. M., & Burke, L. A. (2007). Identifying trainers' knowledge of training transfer research findings–closing the gap between research and practice. *International Journal of Training and Development, 11*(4), 236–264.

Illeris, K. (2002). *The three dimensions of learning: Contemporary learning theory in the tension field between the cognitive, emotional and the social.* Krieger Publishing Company.

Illeris, K. (2003). Workplace learning and learning theory. *Journal of Workplace Learning, 15*(4), 167–178. https://doi.org/10.1108/13665620310474615

Illeris, K. (2007). *How we learn: Learning and non-learning in school and beyond.* Routledge.

Illeris, K. (2011). *The fundamentals of workplace learning: Understanding how people learn in working life.* Routledge.

Illeris, K. (2017). *How we learn: Learning and non-learning in school and beyond* (2nd ed.). Routledge.

Immordino-Yang, M. H. (2011). Implications of affective and social neuroscience for educational theory. *Educational Philosophy and Theory, 43*(1), 98–103.

Jahn, C. (2011). Changing behaviors. *RDH, 31*(12), 66–67.

James, W. (1890). *The principles of psychology* (Vol. 1). Henry Holt.

Janas, M., & Boudreaux, M. (1997). Beyond resistance: A functional approach to building a shared agenda. *Reading and Writing Quarterly: Overcoming Learning Difficulties, 13*(2), 193–198. https://doi.org/10.1080/1057356970130207

Jarvensivu, A., & Koski, P. (2012). Combating learning. *Journal of Workplace Learning*, *24*(1), 5–18. https://doi.org/10.1108/13665621211191078

Jarvis, P. (1992). *Paradoxes of learning: On becoming an individual in society*. Jossey-Bass.

Jensen, A. R. (1969). *Understanding readiness: An occasional paper*. ERIC Clearinghouse on Early Childhood Education.

Jiang, K., Ling, F., Feng, Z., Wang, K., & Shao, C. (2017). Why do drivers continue driving while fatigued? An application of the theory of planned behaviour. *Transportation Research: Part A: Policy and Practice*, *98*, 141–149. https://doi.org/10.1016/j.tra.2017.02.003

Jing, H. (2006). Learning resistance in metacognition training? An exploration of mismatches between learner and teacher agendas. *Language Teaching Research*, *10*(1), 95–117.

Jung, C. (1921). Psychological types. In *Collected Works of C. G. Jung* (Vol. 6). Princeton, NJ.: Princeton University Press 1971.

Kearney, P., Plax, T. G., & Wednt-Wasco, N. J. (1985). Teacher immediacy for effective learning in divergent classrooms. *Communication Quarterly*, *33*(1), 61–74.

Kegan, R. (1994). *In over our heads. The mental demands of modern life*. Harvard University Press.

Kelly, S., Rice, C., Wyatt, B., Ducking, J., & Denton, Z. (2015). Teacher immediacy and decreased student quantitative reasoning anxiety: The mediating effect of perception. *Communication Education*, *64*(2), 171–186. https://doi.org/10.1080/03634523.2015.1014383

Kemp, J. E., Morrison, G. R., & Ross, S. M. (1994). *Designing effective instruction*. Merrill.

Kidd, J. R. (1959). *How adults learn: Tapping the great learning potential . . . a synthesis of theory and experience exploring new knowledge for best teaching results*. Association Press.

Knowles, M. (1980). *The modern practice of adult education: From pedagogy to andragogy* (2nd ed.). Cambridge Books.

Kotinsky, R. (1933). *Adult education and the social scene*. D. Appleton-Century Company Inc.

Kraiger, K., & Jung, K. M. (1997). Linking training objectives to evaluation. In M. A. Quinones, & A. Ehrenstein (Eds.), *Training for a rapidly changing workplace: Applications of psychological research*. American Psychological Association.

Kraiger, K., & Mattingly, V. P. (2018). Cognitive and neural foundations of learning. In K. G. Brown (Ed.), *The Cambridge handbook of workplace training and employee development* (pp. 11–37). Cambridge University Press.

Kruglanski, A. W., Fishback, A., Woolley, K., Belanger, J. J., Chernikova, M., Molinario, E., & Pierro, A. (2018). A structural model of intrinsic motivation: On the psychology of means-ends fusion. *Psychological Review*, *125*(2), 165–182. https://doi.org/10.1037/rev0000095

Kuh, G. D. (2003). What we're learning about student engagement from NSSE. *Change*, *35*(2), 24–32.

Kwitonda, J. C. (2017). Foundational aspects of classroom relations: Associations between teachers' immediacy behaviors, classroom democracy, class identification and learning. *Learning Environments Research*, *20*, 383–401. https://doi.org/10.1007/s10984-017-9231-3

Kunst, M. S. (1959). Learning disabilities: Their dynamics. *Social Worker*, *4*(1), 95–101.

Lave, J., & Wenger, E. (1991). *Situated learning: Legitimate peripheral participation*. University of Cambridge Press.

Layte, R. (2017). Why do working-class kids do worse in school? An empirical test of two theories of educational disadvantage. *European Sociological Review, 33*(4), 489–503. https://doi.org/10.1093/esr/jcx054

Lecky, P. (1945). *Self-consistency; A theory of personality.* Island Press.

LeFebvre, L., & Allen, M. (2014). Teacher immediacy and student learning: An examination of lecture/laboratory and self-contained course sections. *Journal of the Scholarship of Teaching and Learning, 14*(2), 29–45.

Leggett, N. C., Thomas, N. A., & Nicholls, M. E. R. (2016). End of the line: Line bisection, an unreliable measure of approach and avoidance. *Cognition and Emotion, 30*(6), 1164–1179. https://doi.org/10.1080/02699931.2015.1053842

Lewin, K. (2013). *A dynamic theory of personality – Selected papers.* Read Books, Ltd. (Original work published in 1935).

Lewis, C. S. (1996/1944). *The abolition of man.* Simon & Schuster.

Lim, D. H., & Johnson, S. D. (2002). Trainee perceptions of factors that influence learning transfer. *International Journal of Training and Development, 6*(1), 36–48. Doi:10.1111/1468-2419.00148

Linnenbrink-Garcia, L., & Patall, E. A. (2016). Motivation. In L. Corno, & E. M. Andermen (Eds.), *Handbook of educational psychology* (pp. 91–103). Routledge.

Little, G. D., & Sanders, S. L. (1990). *Resistance to learning? Student reaction to communicative language teaching.* ERIC.

Lizano-DiMare, M., & Bruciati, A. P. (2016). Faculty development initiative for converting F2F courses into online courses. In *E-Learn: World Conference on E-Learning in Corporate, Government, Healthcare, and Higher Education* [Conference paper]. November 14, 2016, Washington D.C. https://www.learntechlib.org/p/174081/

Long, H. B. (1994). Resources related to overcoming resistance to self-direction in learning. In R. Hiemstra, & R. Brocket (Eds.), *Overcoming resistance to self-direction in adult learning* (pp. 13–21). (New Directions for Adult and Continuing Education, no. 64.). Jossey-Bass.

Machin, A. M., & Fogarty, G. J. (2004). Assessing the antecedents of transfer intentions in a training context. *International Journal of Training and Development, 8*(3), 222–236. Doin:10.111/j.1360-3736.2004.00210.x

Maier, S. F., & Seligman, M. E. (1976). Learned helplessness: Theory and evidence. *Journal of Experimental Psychology: General, 105*(1), 3–46.

Marand, A. D., & Noe, R. A. (2018). Facilitating the development of expertise: An individual to organizational perspective. In K. G. Brown (Ed.), *The Cambridge handbook of workplace training and employee development* (pp. 38–74). New York: Cambridge University Press.

Maritain, J. (1943). *Education at the crossroads.* Yale University Press.

Marks, H. M. (2000). Student engagement in instructional activity: Patterns in the elementary, middle, and high school years. *American Educational Research Journal, 37*(1), 153–184.

Marques, B. P., Carvalho, P., Escudeiro, P., Barata, A., Silva, A., & Queiros, S. (2017). *Post graduations in technologies and computing applied to education: From F2F classes to multimedia online open courses.* ERIC.

Maslow, A. (1954). *Motivation and personality.* New York: Harper & Row.

Mayer, R. E. (2008). Applying the science of learning:Evidence-based principles for the design of multimedia instruction. *American Psychologist, 63*(8), 760–769.

McCrudden, M. T., & McNamara, D. S. (2017). *Cognition in education.* Routledge.

McFarland, D. (2001). Student resistance: How the formal and informal organization of classrooms facilitate everyday forms of student defiance. *American Journal of Sociology, 107*(3), 612–678.

McFarland, D. A. (2004). Resistance as social drama: A study of change-oriented encounters. *American Journal of Sociology, 109*(6), 1249–1318.

McFarlane, T. A. (2003). *Defining and measuring the love of learning.* [Unpublished doctoral dissertation]. University of Colorado at Denver.

McLaren, M. R., & Arnold, J. (2016). Transforming pedagogies: Encouraging pre-service teachers to engage the power of the arts in their approach to teaching and learning. *Australian Journal of Teacher Education, 41*(5), 21–35.

McLaughlin, M. L., Cody, M. J., & Robey, C. S. (1980). Situational influences on the selection of strategies to resist compliance-gaining attempts. *Human Communication Research, 7*(1), 14–36.

McNamee, K., Atwood, K., Noddings, N., & Taylor, P. C. (2002). Power. In J. Wallace, & W. Louden (Eds.), *Dilemmas of science teaching* (pp. 98–111). Routledge.

Mehrabian, A. (1969). Some referents and measures of nonverbal behavior. *Behavioral Research Methods and Instruments, 1,* 213–217.

Mehrabian, A. (1971). *Silent messages.* Wadsworth.

Mehrabian, A. (1981). *Silent messages: Implicit communication of emotions and attitudes* (2nd ed.). Wadsworth Publishing Company, Inc.

MÈndez, S. R., LÈon, J. A. M., & LiÒ·n, F. (2015). *Validating a theory of planned behavior questionnaire to measure entrepreneurial intentions.*

Merriam, S. B., & Bierma, L. L. (2014). *Adult learning: Linking theory and practice.* Jossey-Bass.

Merriam-Webster. (2018, October 24). *Effectual.* Merriam-Webster.com. https://www.merriam-webster.com/dictionary/effectual

Mezirow, J. (2000). *Learning as transformation: Critical perspectives on a theory in progress.* Jossey Bass.

Miller, N. (1944). Experimental studies of conflict. *Personality and the Behavioral Disorders, 1,* 431–465.

Mitchell, G. (1988). *The trainer's handbook: The AMA guide to effective training* (3rd ed.). AMACON American Management Association.

Moore, H. A. (2007). Student resistance in sociology classrooms: Tools for learning and teaching. *Sociological Viewpoints, 23,* 29–44.

Moscovici, H. (2003). The way I see it: Resisting teacher control or canceling the effect of science immersion. *Journal of Research in Science Teaching, 40*(1), 98–100.

Murphy, C. A., & Stewart, J. C. (2015). The impact of online or F2F lecture choice on student achievement and engagement in a large lecture-based science course: Closing the gap. *Online Learning, 19*(3), 91–110.

Murray, H. (1938). *Explorations in personality.* Oxford University Press.

Nijman, D. J. J., Nijhog, W. J., Wognum, A. A., & Veldkamp, b. P. (2006). Exploring differential effects of supervisor support on transfer of training. *Journal of European Industrial Training,* 30(7), 529–549. Doi:10.1108/03090590610704394

Nikitin, J., & Freund, A. M. (2015). What you want to avoid is what you see: Social avoidance motivation affects the interpretation of emotional faces. *Motivation and Emotion, 39(3),* 384–391. https://doi.org/10.1007/s11031-014-9459-5

Numeroff, L. J. (2000). *If you give a pig a pancake.* Harper Collins Publishers.

Ochoa, G. L., & Pineda, D. (2008). Deconstructing power, privilege, and silence in the classroom. *Radical History Review,* 45–61. https://doi.org/10.1215/01636545-2008-012

Odiorne, G. S., & Rummler, G. A. (1988). *Training and development: A guide for professionals.* Commerce Clearing House, Inc.

Ogbu, J. (1991). Cultural diversity and school experience. In C. E. Walsh (Ed.), *Literacy as praxis: Culture, language, and pedagogy* (pp. 25–50). Ablex.

Ornstein, A., & Behar, L. (Eds.). (1995). *Contemporary issues in curriculum.* Allyn and Bacon.

Osgood, C., Suci, G., & Tannenbaum, P. (1957). *The measurement of meaning.* University of Illinois Press.

Passafaro, P., Livi, S., & Kosic, A. (2019). Local norms and the theory of planned behavior: Understanding the effects of spatial proximity on recycling intentions and self-reported behavior. *Frontiers in Psychology, 10.* https://doi.org/10.3389/fpsyg.2019

Pascal, B. (1958). *Pensees* (W. F. Trotter, Trans.). Dutton. (Original work published 1670).

Patton, M. Q. (2008). *Utilization-focused evaluation.* Sage Publications.

Paulus, T., Evans, K., Halic, O., Lester, J., & Taylor, J., (2009). *Knowledge and learning claims in blog conversations: A discourse analysis in social psychology (DASP) perspective* [Conference proceedings]. Computer-Supported Collaborative Learning Practices, International Society of Learning Sciences. June 9th, Rhodes, Greece.

Pavlov, I. (1927). *Conditioned reflexes: An investigation into the psychological activity of the cortex* (G. Anrep. trans. ed.). Dover, New York.

Pearce, E., Launay, J., & Dunbar, R. I. M. (2015). The ice-breaker effect: Singing mediates fast social bonding. *Royal Society Open Science, 2*(10), 150–221. https://doi.org/10.1098/rsos.150221

Perry, N. E., Turner, J. C., & Meyer, D. K. (2007). Classrooms as contexts for motivating learning. In P. A. Alexander, & P. H. Winne (Eds.), *Handbook of educational psychology* (2nd ed., pp. 327–347). Lawrence Erlbaum Associates.

Peters, J., & Armstrong, J. (1998). Collaborative learning: People laboring together to construct knowledge. In I. Saltiel, A. Sgroi, & R. Brockett (Eds.), *The power and potential of collaborative learning partnerships. New directions for adult and Continuing education* (pp.75–85). San Francisco: Jossey-Bass.

Peterson, B. G. (1971). Mediation in the classroom. *Personnel and Guidance Journal, 49*(7), 558–561.

Peterson, C. (2006). *A primer in positive psychology.* Oxford University Press.

Pham, N. T. P., Segers, M. S. R., & Gijselaers, W. H. (2012). Effects of work environment on transfer of learning: Empirical evidence from Master of Business Administration programs in Vietnam. *International Journal of Training and Development, 17*(1), 1–19.

Piaget, J. (1951). *Play, dreams and imitation in childhood.* Norton.

Plax, T. G., Kearney, P., McCroskey, J. C., & Richmond, V. P. (1986). Power in the classroom VI: Verbal control strategies, nonverbal immediacy and affective learning. *Communication Education, 35*(1), 43–55.

Posner, G., & Rudnitsky, A. (2006). *Course design: A guide to curriculum development for teachers* (7th ed.). Pearson.

Posner, G. J., Strike, K. A., Hewson, P. W., & Gertzog, W. A. (1982). Accommodation of a scientific conception: Toward a theory of conceptual change. *Science Education, 66,* 211–227.

Pulliam, J. D., & Van Patten, J. J. (2003). *History of education in America.* Merrill Prentice Hall.

Quigley, B. A. (1997). *Rethinking literacy education: The critical need for practice-based change.* Jossey-Bass.

Quinones, M. Á., & Ehrenstein, A. (Eds.). (1997). *Training for a rapidly changing workplace: Applications of psychological research.* American Psychological Association.

Quirk, M., Thornbery, E., Power, M., & Samuel, E. (2012). Resilience in learning: A report on action research in a West Midlands primary school. *Psychology of Education Review, 36*(2), 46–53.

Rabak, L., & Cleveland-Innes, M. (2006). Acceptance and resistance to corporate e-learning: A case from the retail sector. *Journal of Distance Education, 21*(2), 115–134.

Rainbird, H. (Ed.) (2000). *Training in the workplace: Critical perspectives on learning at work.* New York: St. Martin's Press.

Raney, D. (2003). Whose authority? Learning and active resistance. *College Teaching, 51*(3), 86–91.

Rank, O. (1945). *Will therapy and truth in reality.* Knopf.

Reeve, J. (2015). *Understanding motivation and emotion.* John Wiley & Son.

Renninger, K. A., Yanyon, R., & Kern, H. M. (2018). Motivation, engagement, and interest: "In the end, it came down to you and how you think of the problem." In F. Fischer, C. Hmelo-Silver, S. R. Goldman, & P. Reimann (Eds.), *International handbook of the learning sciences.* Routledge.

Reyes, M. E. (Ed.). (2002). *Proceedings of the Annual Meeting of the National Association of African American Studies, the National Association of Hispanic and Latino Studies, the National Association of Native American Studies, and the International Association of Asian Studies.* https://eric.ed.gov/?id=ED477416

Richey, R. C. (1992). *Designing instructin for the adult learning: Systematic training theory and practice.* Taylor and Francis.

Rogers, A., & Illeris, K. (2003). How do adults learn? *Adults Learning, 15*(3), 24–27.

Rosen, L. (2006). *Law as culture.* Princeton University Press.

Roskes, M., Elliot, A. J., Nijstad, B. A., & DeDreu, C. K. W. (2013). Time pressure undermines performance more under avoidance than approach motivation. *Personality and Social Psychology Bulletin, 39*(6), 803–813.

Saks, A. M., & Gruman, J. A. (2018). Implications of positive organizational behavior and psychological capital for learning and training effectiveness. In K. G. Brown (Ed.), *The Cambridge handbook of workplace training and employee development* (pp. 441–470). Cambridge University Press.

Salaman, G., & Butler, J. (1990). Why managers won't learn. *Management Education and Development, 21,* 183–191.

Salas, E., Tannenbaum, S. I., Kraiger, K., & Smith-Jentsch, K. A. (2012). The science of training and development in organizations: What matters in practice. *Psychological Science in the Public Interest, 13*(2), 74–101.

Sandlin, J. A. (2011). Popular culture, cultural resistance, and anti-consumption activism. In S. B. Merriam, & A. P. Grace (Eds.), *The Jossey-Bass reader on contemporary issues in adult education* (pp. 401–412). Jossey-Bass.

Sawin, D. A., & Scerbo, M. W. (1995). Effects of instruction type and boredom proneness in vigilance: Implications for boredom and workload. *Human Factors, 37,* 752–765. https://doi.org/10.1518/001872095778995616

Schraw, G., & Lehman, S. (2001). Situational interest: A review of the literature and directions for future research. *Educational Psychology Review, 13*(1), 23–52.

Schraw, G., Flowerday, T., & Lehman, S. (2001). Increasing situational interest in the classroom. *Educational Psychology Review, 13*(3), 211–224.

Schunk, D. (1995). Self-efficacy and education and instruction. In J. D. Maddux (Ed.), *Self-efficacy, adaptation, and adjustment: Theory, research, and application* (pp. 281–303). Springer. https://doi.org/10.1007/978-1-4419-6868-5

Schunk, D. E., & Zimmerman, B. J. (2007). Competence and control beliefs: Distinguishing the means and ends. In P. A. Alexander, & P. H. Winne (Eds.), *Handbook of educational psychology* (2nd ed., pp. 349–367). Lawrence Erlbaum Associates.

Seels, B., & Glasgow, Z. (1998). *Making instructional design decisions* (2nd ed.). Merrill.

Seiler, G., Tobin, K., & Sokolic, J. (2001). Design, technology, and science: Sites for learning, resistance, and social reproduction in urban schools. *Journal of Research in Science Teaching, 38*(7), 746–767.

Seiler, G., Tobin, K., & Sokolic, J. (2003). Reply: Reconstituting resistance in urban science education. *Journal of Research in Science Teaching, 40*(1), 101–103.

Seligman, M. E. P. (1998). Positive social science. *APA Monitor Online, 29*(4), 181–182.

Senge, P, & Lannon-Kim, C. (1991). Recapturing the spirit of learning through a systems approach. *School Administrator, 48*(9), 9–13.

Setiaji, K. (2019). A measure of entrepreneurial behavior of university students: A theory of planned behavior approach. *Dinamika Pendidikan, 13*(2), 143–56. https://doi.org/10.15294/dp.v13i2.18327

Shakespeare, W. (1936). Timon of Athens. In George L. Kittredge (Ed.), *The Kittredge-Players Edition of the Complete Works of William Shakespeare.* Grolier. (Original work published in 1623).

Shaw, S. M., Caldwell, L. L., & Kleiber, D. A. (1996). Boredom, stress, and social control in daily activities of adolescents. *Journal of Leisure Research, 28*(4), 274–292.

Skinner, B. F. (1938). *The behavior of organisms: An experimental analysis.* Englewood Cliffs, NJ.: Prentice-Hall.

Smith, I. (2005). Continuing professional development and workplace learning 13. *Library Management, 26*(8/9), 519–522. https://doi.org/10.1108/01435120510631800

Smith, E. M., Ford, J. K., & Kozlowski, S. W. J. (1997). Building adaptive expertise: Implications for training design strategies. In M. A. Quinones, & A. Ehrenstien (Eds.), *Training for a rapidly changing workplace* (pp. 89–118). American Psychological Association.

Smith, P. L., & Ragan, T. J. (1993). *Instructional design.* Macmillan.

Snowman, J., McCown, R., & Biehler, R. (2012). *Psychology applied to teaching.* Wadsworth Cengage.

Sun, A. (1995). Development and factor analyses of the student resistance to schooling inventory. *Educational and Psychological Measurement, 55*(5), 841–849.

Sympathy (1966). *In Webster's new world dictionary of the American language.* The World Publishing Company.

Taylor, J. E. (2010). *Resistance to learning in mandatory training contexts: A psychometric approach to measuring resistance and related factors.* [Unpublished doctoral dissertation]. University of Tennessee.

Taylor, J. E. (2014). Starting with the learner: Designing learner engagement into the curriculum. In V. C. X. Wang & V. C. Bryan (Eds.), *Andragogical and pedagogical methods for curriculum and program development* (pp. 55–80). IGI Global. https://doi.org/10.4018/978-1-4666-5872-1.ch004

Taylor, J. E., & McKissack, J. (2014). Zones of intervention: Teaching and learning at all times and at all places. *International Journal of Vocational Education and Technology, 5*(3), 21–33.

Taylor, J. E. (2017). Following the drum: Motivation to engage and resist. In V. C. X. Wang (Ed.), *Handbook of research on program development and assessment methodologies in K-20 education* (pp. 244–274). IGI Global. https://doi.org/10.4018/978-1-5225-3132-6.ch012

Taylor, J. E. (2020). The emperor's weavers: S.M.A.R.T. Objectives and the ethical hazard of doing bad philosophy. In V. C. X. Wang (Ed.), *Handbook of research on ethical challenges in higher education leadership and administration* (pp. 92–111). IGI Global.

Taylor, J. E., & Frye, S. (2020). "Disillusioned by experience" using conceptual framework theories to understand and mitigate learning resistance in teacher in-service training. *International Journal of Adult Vocational Education and Technology, 11(2)*, 24–39. https://doi.org/10.4018/IJAET.2020040103

Taylor, J. E. (2022). *Motivational immediacy: Fostering engagement in adult learners.* Sterling, VA: Stylus.

Taylor, J., & Lounsbury, J. W. (2016). Measuring learning resistance to workplace training. *International Journal of Adult Vocational Education and Technology, 7(1)*, 25–38.

Thorndike, E. L. (1911). *Animal intelligence.* Macmillan.

Thorndike, E. L. (1913). *Educational psychology(Vol 2). The psychology of learning.* Teachers College Press.

Tokuhama-Espinosa, T. (2011). *Mind, brain, and education science: A comprehensive brain-based teaching.* W. W. Norton Company.

Tolman, E. (1925). Behaviorism and purpose. *J. Philosophy, 22*, 35–41.

Tolman, A. O., & Kremling, J. (Eds.). (2017). *Why students resist learning: A practical model for understanding and helping.* Stylus.

Tolman, A. O., Sechler, A., & Smart, S. (2016). Defining and understanding student resistance. In A. O. Tolman, & J. Kremling (Eds.), *Why students resist learning: A practical model for understanding and helping students* (pp. 1–14). Stylus.

Torrance, P. (1949). The phenomenon of resistance in learning. *Journal of Abnormal and Social Psychology, 45(4)*, 592–597.

Tracey, J. B., Tannenbaubm, S. I., & Kavenaugh, M. J. (1995). Applying trained skills on the job: The importance of the work environment. *The Journal of Applied Psychology, 80(2)*, 239–252. Doi:10.1037/0021-9010.80.2.239

Tyler, R. W. (1949). *Basic principles of curriculum and instruction.* University of Chicago Press.

Verduin, J. R. (1980). *Curriculum building for adult learning.* Southern Illinois University Press.

Vijayan, V., & Joshith, V. P. (2017). edTPA: An evidence-based assessment of teacher effectiveness in the context of online and face-to-face (F2F) teacher preparation programs in higher education. *My Research Journal, 4(36)*, 6931–6940. https://doi.org/10.21922/srjis.v4i36.10066

Vincent, C., Riley, B. B., & Wilkie, D. J. (2015). Developing items to measure theory of planned behavior constructs for opioid administration for children: Pilot testing. *Pain Management Nursing, 16(6)*, 900–909. https://doi.org/10.1016/j.pmn.2015.07.005

Vosniadou, S. (2013). *International handbook of research and conceptual change* (2nd ed.). Routledge.

Vosniadou, S. (2013). Conceptual change in learning and instruction: The framework theory approach. In S. Vosniadou (Ed.), *International handbook of research on conceptual change* (2nd ed., pp. 11–30). New York: Routledge.

Vygotsky, L. S. (1978). *Mind in society: The development of higher psychological processes.* Harvard University Press.

Walberg, H. (1995). Productive teachers: Assessing the knowledge base. In A. C. Ornstein & L. S. Behar (Eds.), *Contemporary issues in curriculum.* Allyn and Bacon.

Walker, D. F., & Soltis, J. F. (2009). *Curriculum and aims* (Fifth Edition ed.). New York: Teachers College Press.

Ward, G. (1988). *High-risk training : Managing training programs for high-risk occupations*. New York: Nichols Publishing.

Wells, H., Jones, A., & Jones, S. C. (2014). Teaching reluctant students: Using the principles and techniques of motivational interviewing to foster better student-teacher interactions. *Innovations in Education and Teaching International, 51*(2), 175–184. https://doi.org/10.1080/14703297.2013.778066

Wenger, E. (1998). *Communities of practice: learning, meaning, and identity.* Cambridge University Press.

Wenger, E. (2000). *Communities of practice: Learning, meaning, and identity* (1st ed.). Cambridge University Press.

Wexler, L. M. (2006). Learning resistance: Inupiat and the US Bureau of Education, 1885–1906—Deconstructing assimilation strategies and implications for today. *Journal of American Indian Education, 45*(1), 17–34.

White, J., Pinnegar, S., & Esplin, P. (2010). When learning and change collide: Examining student claims to have "learned nothing". *The Journal of General Education, 59*(2), 125–140. https://www-jstor-org.spot.lib.auburn.edu/stable/10.5325/jgeneeduc.59.2.0124

Wilke, D. J., King, E., Ashmore, M., & Stanley, C. (2016). Can clinical skills be taught online? Comparing skill development between online and f2f students using a blinded review. *Journal of Social Work Education, 52*(4), 484–492. https://doi.org/10.1080/10437797.2016.1215276

Willis, J. (1995). A recursive, reflective instructional design model based on constructivist-interpretivist theory. *Educational Technology, 35*(6), 5–23.

Wittich, W., & Schuller, C. (1973). *Instructional technology: Its nature and use* (5th ed.). Harper & Row Publishers, Inc.

Wlodkowski, R. J., & Ginsberg, M. B. (2017). *Enhancing adult motivation to learn: A comprehensive guide for teaching all adults.* Jossey-Bass.

Zajonc, R. B. (1998). Emotion. In D. Gilbert, S. Fiske, & G. Lindzey (Eds.), *The Handbook of Social Psychology* (4th ed., pp. 591–632). New York: McGraw-Hill.

Zhang, Q. (2007). Teacher misbehaviors as learning demotivators in college classrooms: A cross-cultural investigation in China, Germany, Japan, and the United States. *Communication Education, 56*(2), 209–227.

Zuna, N., & McDougall, D. (2004). Using positive behavioral support to manage avoidance of academic tasks. *Teaching Exceptional Children, 37*(1), 18–24. https://doi.org/10.1177/004005990403700102

Index

Note: **Boldface** page references indicate tables. *Italic* references indicate figures.

academic scholarship 144, 145
acceptance: and acquisition 8, 55–56, 57, 61, 64, 80, 159, 180, 188–189; coefficient 163; of content 8, 64, 162, 188, 189; curriculum and instructional systems design (ISD) process 155, 156; learning efficiency index formula 164, 166, 169
achievement motivation 44
acquisition: and acceptance 8, 55–56, 57, 61, 64, 80, 159, 180, 188–189; axis 65; coefficient 163, 170; of content 8, 64, 162, 188; human skill 117; learning efficiency index formula 164, 165, 166, 168, 169; processes 65
adult education 10, 12, 22
affect: curriculum and instructional systems design (ISD) 143–144; and feelings 39, 40; positive-negative affect continuum 42; Spinozian concept of 39
affective domain: and cognitive, affective social (CAS) worksheet 118; curriculum and instructional systems design (ISD) 143–144; *see also* cognitive, affective social (CAS) worksheet
Air Force Instructional Design Model 143

Air Handler room 27
Ajzen, I. 161
Althusser, L. 28
anger 28, 173
anxiety 28, 32, 173
appetitive motivation 43
approach motivation: approach-avoidance motivation 40–47, 49, 106, 145; defined 43; determination of 141–142
Argyris, C. 9
Aristippus 41
Armstrong, J. 60
artifacts, curricular 151–152
assessments 11, 141, 144; behaviorally-based 159; developing 149; knowledge 170; for learning objectives 152, 154–155; measures 150; practices 94; preliminary threat 124; progress 154–155; for training 85, 142–143; types 161
asynchronous learning 121, 135
Atherton, J. 20, 24, 25, 26, 27, 31
Atkin, M. J. 153, 154, 155
attitudes 84, 102–103, 149–150, 161, 167, 168
avoidance motivation: approach-avoidance motivation 40–47, 49, 106, 145; defined 38, 43, 44

axis of learning 67–68; context axis 67–68; individual context 67–68; organizational context 67, 68

Bandura, A. 104, 145
banking education 147
Bass, M. 43
behavior(s): defensive 20, 22; defined 25; objectives 149, 150, 153, 158
Belanger, J. J. 31, 47, 48, 189
beliefs: false 93; learner 85; teacher in-service study 89, 90; and training, measurement practices 8; workplace cultural 85
Bentham, J. 41
Bernstein, B. 28
Bierma, L. L. 6, 17–18
blocking 20, 22
Bloom, B. S. 190
Boot, N. C. 43
Bourdieu, P. 28
Bowlby, J. 41
Bowles, S. 28
box(es): building 96; curriculum in 146–147; defined 94; series of 82; testing 96–97; understanding 94–95
Brady, T. C. 31, 60
Brønn, P. S. 162
Brookfield, S. D. 21–22, 27, 29, 31, 175
Brophy, J. 18
Buhmann, A. 162
Burke, L. A. 16–17
Burroughs, N. F. 21, 31
Butler, J. 117

Cabranes-Grant, L. 51
Canagarajah, A. S. 22
Caplin, M. D. 20, 26, 31
Carey, J. 143, 149
Carey, L. 143, 149
CAS. *see* cognitive, affective social (CAS) worksheet
categorization, defined 81
category mistakes 93
CCT. *see* conceptual change theories (CCT)
Cennamo, K. 143, 149
Chernikova, M. 31, 47, 48, 189
Chi, M. T. H. 81, 83, 92, 93
classroom(s): environmental resistance 27; instructor-centered *vs.* learner-centered 127–129; intervention 68, 69, 70, 71, 74, 76–77; and jobsite 118–119; means-end fusion (MEF) in 128, 129, 130–133, 136; music in 125; teaching methods in 136, 142
classroom(s), facilitating conceptual change in 94–97; building box 96; testing box 96–97; understanding box 94–95
classroom(s), motivational immediacy in: F2F and distance learning 135–136; F2F and online, choice between 121–123; F2F applications 124–135; means-end fusion (MEF) in our teaching principles and teaching methods 136; overview 120
cognition and learning concepts 116–117
cognitions, defined 25
cognitive, affective social (CAS) worksheet 114–119; affective domain 118; class on field 119; cognition 116–117; field on class 118–119; in practice 116; social dimension 117–118
cognitive ability 17
cognitive-psychological resistance 27–28
Collins, J. 56
Colquitt, J. A. 6, 17
communication: expert 106, 107; and professionals, TPB 162; teacher immediacy from 51
communities of practice 64–65
community intervention 68, 69, 70–72, 73, 74–76, 78–79
conceptual change theories (CCT): example in workplace 84–87; facilitating in classroom 94–97; framework theories, resistance, and workplace learning context 83–84; inaccurate *vs.* incommensurate knowledge 92–94; overview 80–83; research from workplace 87–90; utilizing, to mitigate resistance 91–92
conflicts, personality 179
connection, learning as 60; acquisition and acceptance 188–189; curriculum design processes, resistance mitigation 190; immediate motivation 189–190; learner to learner 185–186; learning

resistance, positive and learner-centered approach 188; means to ends 186; motivation, unidirectional dynamic 187; old knowledge to new knowledge 184–185; overview 183; practicing motivational immediacy 191; principle to application 186; short-term memory to long-term memory 185; teacher to learner 183–184; teaching for effectual learning 191–192

CONNECT method 60, 106, 108–114

content: acceptance of 8, 55–56, 57, 64, 162, 188, 189; acquisition of 8, 55–56, 57, 64, 162, 188; curriculum 151, 152–154; instructor values *vs.* 177–178; interest *vs.* 177; job *vs.* 178; learner *vs.* 178; learning 95, 96; training 112–114, 177–178

content-oriented definitions 47

context, training 95

context axis 67–68

cost(s): cost-effective choices 121; direct financial 163; fiscal 163, 164, 165, 166, 168, 169; person-hour 163, 164; technical 168; travel 168; work hour 165, 168, 169

Covey, S. 94

Covington, M. V. 49

Craik, F. I. M. 62

criterion-referenced tests (CRTs) 149

curiosity 175

curriculum and instructional systems design (ISD): affective domain 143–144; assessing progress 154–156; in box 146–147; from constructivist orientations 152–153; content 151, 152–154; curricular implements and curricular artifacts 151–152; designing curriculum 152–154; design process 138–143; design processes, resistance mitigation 190; disinclination to teach 147–150; heretical rules for 151–156, 190; implications for 150–156; motivation and learning 144–146; overview 137–138; reductionist frameworks 152–154; TAP 138–143; theory-practice gaps 144

customer service training class 109, 111–112

Damasio, A. 39, 40

decision making 122–123

DeDreu, C. K. W. 43

defensive behavior 20, 22

deficit models, learning resistance approaches 173–176

Democritus 41

despair 173

Dick, W. 143, 149

digital learning 122

direct financial cost 163

DiSessa, A. A. 81

disgust 173

disinclination to teach 147–150

distance learning 121–122, 123, 135–136

Eder, A. B. 41, 44, 45

education 19; adult 10, 12, 22; banking 147; community 63; continuing 87; objectives 122, 143; philosophy of 153; psychology 10, 20, 129; settings 143, 146, 162; triad 145; *see also* face-to-face (F2F) learning; learners; learning; online learning

effectual learning: abysmally low 122; acquisition and acceptance 8, 188; cognitive, affective social (CAS) worksheet 115, 118; and conceptual change theories (CCT) 80, 91; conceptualization of 52; defined 57, 64; F2F learning 129; and learning efficiency index formula 161, 162–164; position theory 103; principles for fostering 58–60; teaching for 191–192; *see also* learning resistance to efficient and effectual learning

effectual learning measurement: discussion 169–170; learning efficiency index 162–164, 165–166; limited ability 159–161; logistics tracking system (LTS) training 164–169; overview 158–159; and theory of planned behavior (TPB) 161–162

Ehrenstein, A. 16

Elliot, A. J. 41, 44, 45

emotion(s) 53, 74, 93, 116, 118, 145; in cognition 39; defined 39; and feelings 39–40; in learning resistance 39; and motivation 39;

readiness 28; safety 124; and technical skills 102–103; understanding of 43

emotional disruption: learning resistance 28, 30, 31–32; notion of 123

emotional stress 32

empathy 110, 111

employee(s) 10–12; learners and employers 20, 29–30, 66, 92, 127, 171; training program for 27

employers: disloyal to 179, 180; and employee learners 20, 29–30, 66, 92, 127, 171

engaged learners 54–55

engagement, learning. *see* learning engagement

environmental resistance 27

epistemological resistance 29–30

epistemology, category of theoretical alignment pyramid (TAP) 140–141

Esplin, P. 19, 29, 31

ethical dilemmas and facilitator as mediator (FAM): facilitator as mediator (FAM) 179–182; instructor values *vs.* learner 179; learning resistance approaches, deficit-based 173–176; learning resistance mitigation (LRM) approaches 171–172; for motivationally immediate training instructor 176–178; overview 171

ethical hedonism 41

Evans, K. 30

evidence 91, 149, 150, 170; defined 147; evidence-based methods 149; of learning 147–148

extrinsic motivation 47

Eysenck, H. 41

face-to-face (F2F) learning: after class 133–134; applications 124–135; before class 124–126; during class 126–134; and distance learning 135–136; handouts 133; icebreakers 126–127; instructor-centered *vs.* learner-centered classrooms 127–129; learning energy, questions, and means-end fusion (MEF) 127–133; logistics tracking system (LTS) training 166–169; and motivational immediacy 121–123;

music 125; personal conversations 126; PowerPoint 133–134; questions from learners 127–129; unexpected and unwelcomed questions 129–130

facilitator as mediator (FAM) 179–182; *see also* ethical dilemmas and facilitator as mediator (FAM)

false beliefs 93

family problems 27

feelings: defined 39; learn without 39–40; in resistance to learning 39; and technical skills training 102–103

F2F. *see* face-to-face (F2F) learning

field on class, effect of 118–119

fiscal cost 163, 164, 165, 166, 168, 169

Fishback, A. 31, 47, 48, 189

Fishbein, M. 161

flawed mental models 93

Ford, J. K. 12, 137

Foucault, M. 28

framework theories 81–82, 83–85, 87–88

Freire, P. 28, 147

Freud, S. 41

Freund, A. M. 44

Frye, S. 43, 55, 177

Gagne, R. M. 19, 60

Garber, S. H. 27, 31

Gertzog, W. A. 81

Giddens, A. 28

Gijselaers, W. H. 63

Gilles, C. 21

Gino, F. 118

Ginsberg, M. B. 18, 21, 37, 38, 49

Gintis, H. 28

Giroux, H. A. 21, 22, 28, 31

Glasgow, Z. 149–150

global motivation 36, 48–51, 189

Goisman, R. M. 29, 31

Gold, J. 30, 31, 32, 123

Habermas, J. 28

Halic, O. 30

hammer 115, 116, 117

Handbook of Educational Psychology 18

handouts in motivational immediacy discussion 133

Harmon-Jones, E. 41, 44, 45

Harre, R. 103

Heider, F. 41
Henson, J. 21
Hewson, P. W. 81
Horton, M. 28, 101, 188
Hull, C. 41
Hultman, K. 24, 31
Husserl, E. 59
Hutchins, H. M. 16–17
HVAC/Air Handler room 27

icebreakers 126–127
ill-defined problems 97, 132
Illeris, K. 9, 22, 28, 65, 66, 67, 68, 72,
    115, 144–145
immediate motivation 36, 48–51,
    189–190, 191
implements, curricular 151–152
inaccurate knowledge,
    incommensurate *vs.* 92–94
incommensurate knowledge 92–94
individual context 67–68, 69–71,
    74–76
in-service training: defined 87;
    framework theories 84–85, 87–88;
    program, logistics tracking system
    (LTS) training 164–169; school
    teacher 87–90; specific theories
    85–86, 88–89
Instructional Development Institute
    Model 143
instructional methods and lesson plans:
    cognitive, affective social (CAS)
    worksheet 114–119; CONNECT
    method 108–114; overview 101–102;
    position theory 103–108; technical
    skills training and feelings 102–103
instructional strategy, effects of 161
instructional systems design (ISD)
    models 184; *see also* curriculum and
    instructional systems design (ISD)
instructor(s)/trainer(s): ethical
    dilemmas for 176–178; group and
    organizational learning 9, 58–59;
    individual learners 9; instructor-
    centered classrooms 127–129;
    interdisciplinary approach 9–10;
    and learners 108–114, 126
instructor values: content *vs.* 177–178;
    learner *vs.* 179; supervisor *vs.* 177
interaction process 65
interdisciplinary approach, instructors
    and trainers 9–10

interest *vs.* content 177
intervention axis: classroom
    intervention 69; community
    intervention 69
intrinsic motivation 47, 48

James, W. 41
Jarvis, P. 7, 22
Jensen, A. R. 20, 28
Jing, H. 22, 31
job satisfaction 106
jobsite, classroom and 118–119
job *vs.* content 178
Jones, A. 21, 24
Jones, S. C. 21, 24
Jung, C. 41

Kalk, D. 143, 149
Kearney, P. 21, 31
Kegan, R. 151–152, 153
Kemp, J. E. 143
Kern, H. M. 18
Kidd, J. R. 20, 31, 59
kindness 175
knowledge 74, 80–81, 132, 147;
    assessment 170; clinical 79; gaps
    132; of human learning 141;
    inaccurate *vs.* incommensurate
    92–94; long-term transferable 186;
    old knowledge to new knowledge
    184–185; study of 140; and teaching
    184; technical 79, 113
Koen, J. 43
Kohl, H. 101
Kohl, J. 101
Kozlowski, S. W. J. 12, 137
Kraiger, K. 54, 62, 137, 158
Kruglanski, A. W. 31, 47, 48, 189
Kuh, G. D. 18

Langenhove, L. V. 103
Lave, J. 64, 71
law enforcement 92–93
learner-centered approach, learning
    resistance and 9, 188–189
learner-centered classrooms 127–129
learner(s) 10–12; argumentative 8;
    connecting 185–186; content *vs.*
    178; and disengagement, lack of
    means-end fusion (MEF) 47–48;
    engaged 54–55; individual/group 9,
    58–59; and instructors 108–114, 126;

instructor values *vs.* 179; teacher to, connection 60, 183–184; turn-off 20, 28; *see also* learning resistance

learning: abysmally low effectual 122; axis of 67–68; communities of practice 64–65; dimensions of 65–67; distance 121–122, 123; efficiency index 162–164; efficiency ratio 163; evidence of 147–148; and methods 136; moment-by-moment 6–7; and motivation 144–146, 154; objectives 56, 112, 144, 149, 150, 151–152, 153, 154–155, 167; online and F2F 121–123, 135; organizational type of 73; principle of 136, 191; spaces, workplace 63, 65, 66; synchronous/asynchronous 135; teaching-learning continuum 104; transfer 63–64; type of 141; workplace learning context 83–84; zones of 67–72; *see also* connection, learning as; effectual learning

learning efficiency 57–58; formula 161, 163–164, 168–169; logistics tracking system (LTS) training 165–166, 168–169

learning engagement 63, 86, 173, 174; categories 25–30; and conceptual change theories (CCT) 86, 88, 91; continuum 19–20, 23, 38; curriculum and instructional systems design (ISD) process 138, 143, 144, 151, 156; defined 18–19; and effort 61–62; expressions 24–25; FAM concept 180; fostering 63, 91, 103, 104, 106, 108, 120, 122, 126, 133, 134, 189, 190, 191; lack of 174; learning resistance to 19–20; and motivational immediacy 60–61; motivation and engagement 17–19; overview 16–17; and persistent argument from employee learner 8; reduction in 133; resistance to engagement 19–20; rules of 78; *see also* zones of intervention

learning environment 11, 24, 27, 46, 135, 143–144, 174, 176

learning resistance 172; approaches, deficit-based 173–176; categories 25–30; causes of 26, 30, **31**; cognitive-psychological 27–28; defined 17, 20–24, 38;

environmental 27; epistemological 29–30; expressions 24–25; mitigation 91–92, 153, 174–175, 176, 190; and motivation 38; as negative construct 20–22, 23–24; positive and learner-centered approach 9, 188; as positive construct 22; range and intensity of 30–33, *123*; reasons 10; scholarship by domain **21**; situational 25; sociocultural 28–29; treatment of 175; ulterior 25; as a unified negative concept 23–24; utilizing conceptual change frameworks to mitigate 91–92; and workplace learning context 83–84, 86; *see also* learning engagement

learning resistance mitigation (LRM) approaches 171–172

learning resistance to efficient and effectual learning: acquisition and acceptance 55–56, 57, 61; engaged learners 54–55; engagement and effort 61–62; learning efficiency 57–58; overview 53–54; resistance mitigation approach (RMA) as positive approach 61

Leeuw, N. de 81

Leggett, N. C. 42

LePine, J. A. 6, 17

lesson plans, instructional methods and. *see* instructional methods and lesson plans

Lester, J. 30

Lewin, K. 21, 41, 42

Lewis, C. S. 40

lineman's tool 115, 116, 117, 118–119

Linnenbrink-Garcia, L. 18

Lockart, R. S. 62

locutionary acts 104, 105, 107–108

logistics tracking system (LTS) training 164–169; learning efficiency formula 165–166, 168–169

Long, H. B. 20

Looking for Spinoza: Joy, Sorrow, and the Feeling Brain (Damasio) 39

Lounsbury, J. W. 21, 22

Maritain, J. 190

Maslow, A. 41

Mattingly, V. P. 54, 62, 137, 158

Mayer, R. E. 54

McCall, W. 148

McFarland, D. 20–21, 25
means-ends fusion (MEF): in classroom 128, 129, 130–133; connection 186; curriculum design process 138; lack of 47–48, 189; in teaching principles and teaching methods 136
measurement 154–155; challenges 149; disinclination to teach 147–150; human learning 148; learning objectives 149–150, 153, 154–155; outcomes 121, 190; person's attitudes 149; and practices, training beliefs 8; problematic 146; *see also* effectual learning measurement
mediator, facilitator as 179–182
MEF. *see* means-ends fusion (MEF)
Mehrabian, A. 51
mental models 82, 83
mental representations 85–86
Merriam, S. B. 6, 17–18
Merriam-Webster 57
Miller, N. 41
mislearning 7, 16, 20
missing schemas 93
Mitchell, G. 4, 9, 11, 26, 28, 29, 59, 80, 91, 171
Molinario, E. 31, 47, 48, 189
Morrison, G. R. 143
motivation: achievement 44; appetitive 43; defined 18; global 36, 48–51, 189; immediate 36, 48–51, 189–190, 191; intrinsic and extrinsic 47, 48; and learning 144–146, 154; and learning engagement 17–19; and learning resistance 38; moment-by-moment 6–7; not unidirectional–learners 40–47; unidirectional dynamic 187; value-neutral and bidirectional construct 5–6; withdrawal 43; *see also* approach motivation; avoidance motivation
motivational immediacy: in the curriculum design process 138–143; engaging in 60–61; immediacy principle 51; immediate motivation and global motivation 48–51; and lack of means-end fusion (MEF), learner disengagement 47–48; learning without feeling 39–40; motivational theory 37–38; overview 35–36; practicing 51–52, 191; teacher immediacy 51; training

instructor, ethical dilemmas for 176–178; *see also* classroom(s), motivational immediacy in; ethical dilemmas and facilitator as mediator (FAM)
Murray, H. 41
music in classroom 125

Nicholls, M. E. R. 42
Nijstad, B. A. 43
Nikitin, J. 44
Noe, R. A. 6, 17

objective(s): behavioral 149, 150, 153, 158; of curriculum 149, 190; educational 143; form of 162; learning 56, 112, 144, 149, 150, 151–152, 153, 154–155, 167; for training class session 108–109
Odiorne, G. S. 11, 12, 19, 42
online learning: logistics tracking system (LTS) training 165–166, 168; and motivational immediacy 121–123, 135, 146
OPERATE 108
organizational context 67, 68, 70, 71–72, 76–79
outcome(s): in curriculum 190; developing 149; measurement 121, 190

Pascal, B. 60
passion 55, 112, 147
Patall, E. A. 18
Paulus, T. 30
Pavlov, I. 41
perceptions 101; cultural 85; of in-service training 87; learner's 114, 151, 152, 153; on learning resistance 173; negative 81; of people's problems 188; in workplace 84
personality conflicts 179
person-hour costs 163, 164
personological factors 17
Peters, J. 60
Peterson, C. 175
Pham, N. T. P. 63
phenomenological primitives and coordination classes (P-prims) 81
philosophy, category of theoretical alignment pyramid (TAP) 140
Piaget, J. 25

Pierro, A. 31, 47, 48, 189
Pinnegar, S. 19, 29, 31
Plax, T. G. 21, 31
position theory 103–108
positive psychology 175
Posner, G. J. 81, 148, 149
PowerPoint presentation 78, 118, 130, 133–134, 177
P-prims (phenomenological primitives and coordination classes) 81
Prezi slides 130
principle-application fusion (PAF) 186
principle to application 186
psychological hedonism 41

questions, motivational immediacy and: from learners 127–129; and learning energy 130–133; unexpected and unwelcomed 129–130
Quigley, B. A. 21, 26, 28–29, 31
Quinones, M. A. 16

Ragan, T. J. 143
Rainbird, H. 17, 21, 22, 29, 31, 92
Reeve, J. 38, 39
Renninger, K. A. 18
research from workplace 87–90
resistance, learning. see learning resistance
resistance mitigation approach (RMA) 61
Rockefeller, J. D. 56
Rosen, L. 37, 186
Ross, S. M. 143
Rudnitsky, A. 148, 149
rules for curriculum 151–156, 190
Rummler, G. A. 11, 12, 19, 42

Salaman, G. 117
scholarship: academic, in curriculum and instructional systems design (ISD) 144, 145; learning resistance 176
Schon, D. A. 9
school teacher in-service training 87–90
Schweitzer, M. 118
science of learning, category of theoretical alignment pyramid (TAP) 141
Sechler, A. 21
Seels, B. 149–150

Segers, M. S. R. 63
self-efficacy 17, 28
Shakespeare, W. 40
short-term memory to long-term memory 185
signage 75–76
situational resistance, defined 25
Skinner, B. F. 41
Slotta, J. D. 81
Smart, S. 21
Smith, E. M. 12, 137
Smith, P. L. 143
social dimension, cognitive, affective social (CAS) worksheet and 117–118
sociocultural resistance 28–29
specific theories 82, 83, 85–86, 88–90
Spinoza 39
staffing 72
Stafford, A. 43, 55, 177
storyline in position theory 105–108
stress 32, 108
Strike, K. A. 81
subject-matter-experts (SME) in workplace 184
supervisor values, instructor vs. 177
sympathy 110
synchronous distance learning 122

TAP. see theoretical alignment pyramid (TAP)
Taylor, J. E. 21, 22, 23, 30, 43, 55, 64, 177, 180
teacher: immediacy 51, 59; to learner, connection 60, 183–184; and learners 108–114; position 107
teacher in-service training: framework theory 87–88; specific theory 88–90
teaching: approach, determination of 141–142; for effectual learning 191–192; individual/group 9, 58–59; and knowledge 184; methods 136, 142; principles 136; teaching-learning continuum 104
technical cost, logistics tracking system (LTS) training 168
technical skills training 102–103
terrorism 92
theoretical alignment pyramid (TAP) 138–143; assessment 142–143; determination of teaching approach 141–142; epistemology 140–141;

philosophy 140; science of learning 141; teaching methods 142; type of learning required 141
theory of planned behavior (TPB) 161–162
theory of reasoned behavior 161
theory-practice gaps 144
Thomas, N. A. 42
Thorndike, E. L. 41, 148
Tolman, A. O. 21
Tolman, E. 41
trainees 10–12
training: about knowing people 4; beliefs and measurement practices 8; class, customer service 109, 111–112; class session, objectives 108–109; content 112–114; framework theories 81–82, 83–85, 87–88; instructor, ethical dilemmas for 176–178; logistics tracking system (LTS) 164–169; specific theories 82, 83, 85–86, 88–90; wrong sort of thing 7–8; *see also* conceptual change theories (CCT)
training transfer 11, 57, 138, 144, 161; conditions of 16–17; and increased engagement 62, 63–64; lack of 70; learning resistance and engagement 16, 63–64; levels of 67; literature 63–64; long-term 12, 70, 79; perspective, after class 134–135; suboptimal, causes of 16
transformative learning 81
travel costs, logistics tracking system (LTS) training 168
turn-off, learner 20, 28
Tyler, R. W. 19, 143, 145

ulterior resistance, defined 25
understaffing 72

values, instructor *vs.* supervisor 177
Verduin, J. R. 143, 149
Vosniadou, S. 82, 83, 84, 85, 86
Vygotsky, L. S. 28, 145

Walberg, H. 19
Ward, G. 4
Wells, H. 21, 24

Wenger, E. 57, 64, 65, 66, 67, 68, 71, 73
White, J. 19, 29, 31
Willis, J. 143
withdrawal motivation 43
Wlodkowski, R. J. 18, 21, 37, 38, 49
Woolley, K. 31, 47, 48, 189
work hour cost, logistics tracking system (LTS) training 165, 168, 169
workplace: cultural beliefs 85; distance learning in 121–122, 123, 135–136; example in, conceptual change theories (CCT) 84–87; learning context 83–84; learning spaces 63, 65, 66; reducing learning resistance 91–92; research from 87–90; rules for facilitating conceptual change in 94–97; SME in 184; training room 116; zones of intervention in 67–72
worksheet, cognitive, affective social (CAS) 114–119

Yanyon, R. 18

zones of engagement: communities of practice 64–65; four zones of intervention 67–72; four zones of motivation 74–79; practical implications for the zones 72–73; three dimensions of learning 65–67; training transfer 63–64
zones of intervention 67–72; axis of learning 67–68; classroom intervention-individual context 69–70, 74; classroom intervention-organizational context 71, 76–77; community intervention-individual context 70–71, 74–76; community intervention-organizational context 71–72, 78–79; intervention axis 69; practical implications 72–73
zones of motivation 74–79; classroom intervention-individual context 74; classroom intervention-organizational context 76–77; community intervention-individual context 74–76; community intervention-organizational context 78–79

Printed in the USA
CPSIA information can be obtained
at www.ICGtesting.com
LVHW020631051224
798389LV00023B/454